D1610543

BOOK NUMBER

R12663

940.556 MAS

KENT·INSTITUTE OF·ART·&·DESIGN
LIBRARY

Book No........................ Class No./Mark ....
This book is to be returned on or before the last date
stamped below.

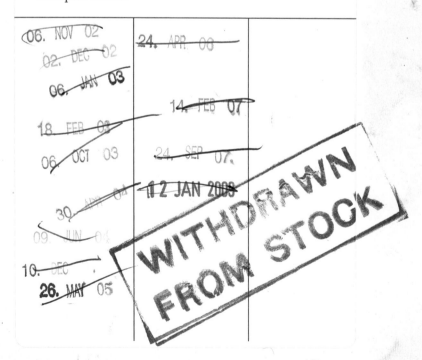

06. NOV 02
02. DEC 02
06. JAN 03
18. FEB 03
06. OCT 03
30. APR 04
09. JUN 04
10. DEC
26. MAY 05

24. APR. 00
14. FEB 07
24. SEP 07.
12 JAN 2008

WITHDRAWN FROM STOCK

The Swinging Sixties

By the same author

Molière (1969)
Sartre (1969)
Saint-Exupéry (1970)
Rabelais (1971)
Camus – A Study (1973)
Wynyard Hall and the Londonderry Family (1974)
Dreams about H.M. The Queen (1974)
The Dukes (1975)
Now Barabbas Was a Rotter:
the Extraordinary Life of Marie Corelli (1978)
The Mistresses of Charles II (1980)
Georgiana, Duchess of Devonshire (1981)
Great Hostesses (1982)
Killing for Company (1985)

Brian Masters

The Swinging Sixties

Constable · London

First published in Great Britain 1985
by Constable and Company Limited
10 Orange Street London WC2H 7EG
Copyright © 1985 by Brian Masters
Set in Linotron Ehrhardt 11pt by
Rowland Phototypesetting Limited
Bury St Edmunds, Suffolk
Printed in Great Britain by
St Edmundsbury Press
Bury St Edmunds, Suffolk

British Library Cataloguing in Publication Data

Masters, Brian
The Swinging Sixties
1. Great Britain – Social conditions – 1945-
I. Title
941.085'6   HN385.5

ISBN 0 09 465280 5

To the memory of
my father
Geoffrey Howard Masters

Contents

Illustrations

The 'Beyond the Fringe' team
(*Raymond Mander and Joe Mitchenson Theatre Collection*)

Judi Dench in *Cabaret*
(*Keystone Press Agency Ltd*)

Mick Jagger driven to prison
(*Keystone Press Agency Ltd*)

Cliff Richard
(*Keystone Press Agency Ltd*)

between pages 160 and 161

The Beatles with Harold Wilson
(*Keystone Press Agency Ltd*)

Crowds outside Boots, Piccadilly
(*Keystone Press Agency Ltd*)

Lord Altrincham
(*Popperfoto*)

The Queen awaiting her coronation
(*Fox Photos Ltd*)

The Royal Family
(*BBC Photographs*)

Lord Russell squatting
(*Popperfoto*)

Mushroom cloud
(*Central Press Photos Ltd*)

'Sit-down' H-bomb protest
(*Keystone Press Agency Ltd*)

Acknowledgements

This book represents a personal view of a period which saw many changes in English social life. It does not pretend to be comprehensive, nor does it hope to satisfy the historian or scholar. With this in mind, I have chosen not to encumber the text with reference notes. Those who wish to explore further will find the material from which I have quoted listed by chapter under the heading SOURCES at the end. It will be apparent to any reader, however, that there have been some books which have been useful throughout, and I should like here to acknowledge my debt to authors and publishers alike. Bernard Levin's *The Pendulum Years* and Christopher Booker's *The Neophiliacs* are rich and kaleidoscopic. Jonathan Aitken's *The Young Meteors* describes some individual success stories, and Andrew Barrow's *Gossip* is fertile in facts not easily accessible elsewhere. My own efforts would have been impoverished without their example.

B.M.

London, 1985

— 1 —

Swinging London?

The man credited with inventing the phrase 'Swinging London' is Melvin Lasky, editor of the severely intellectual monthly magazine *Encounter*, in conversation with Horace Judson of *Time* magazine, who was then preparing a major cover story on the various phenomena which had made London, from about 1963 onwards, the one city in the world where everyone apparently wanted to be. The now-famous article appeared in *Time* on 16 April 1966, giving rise to a torrent of press attention all over the western world which in turn established London as a newly vigorous, youthful, colourful and exciting place, no longer smug or drab but pulsing with bright innovation and sudden talent. As Lasky was an American living in London, his view had a just claim to objectivity; he was not himself part of the 'swinging' population, and could observe what was going on around him with impartial curiosity.

In the article, Melvin Lasky was quoted as saying that: London is the only European metropolis that has managed to maintain a combination of greenness and greyness, vitality and yet a certain gentleness. Paris hasn't got it. Rome is oppressive. Berlin is a special case. All the others are just villages.'

Other people have since tried to articulate what exactly happened, what made London such a dazzlingly attractive place. At a distance of twenty years, it should be possible even for those involved in 'the scene' to look back dispassionately and perceptively. Those who have made the effort fall into two irreconcilable camps. To some, the revolution in social mores was beneficial and constructive; to others, it was a hollow sham, a time of 'relentless frivolity' (in the words of the *New York Times*) for which we are still paying the price.

Jean Shrimpton, top fashion model of the day, said, 'There was energy then, and if you had an idea, however silly, you could get it on the road. People were willing to listen – too much so, but it was better than not listening at all . . . It was a terribly naive period . . . it was like falling in love. You didn't see anything very clearly.' That reminiscence dates from 1981. In 1980, *The Times* had written, 'The Sixties was the decade when England truly emerged from its postwar depression and became a country of joyful and envied achievement.'

In stark contrast, Margaret Thatcher, Prime Minister from 1979, was quoted in the *Daily Mail* in 1982 as follows: 'We are reaping today what was sown in the Sixties . . . fashionable theories and permissive claptrap set the scene for a society in which the old virtues of discipline and restraint were denigrated.' In the first book to look at the period critically (*The Neophiliacs*, 1969), Christopher Booker depicted a godless society intoxicated by a collective dream fantasy based on 'frantic euphoria', 'mass hysteria' and 'hallucination' contributing to a 'gigantic public charade'. Anthony Lejeune in the *Daily Telegraph* thought that there were aspects of British life which, far from exciting the admiration of the world, earned its contempt and derision and offered disturbing symptoms of decadence. For Mrs Thatcher, Mr Booker and Mr Lejeune, the achievements were spurious, the disgrace total. They would all have been quick to agree with Gibbon's dictum, 'How much swifter is the progress of corruption than its cure.'

Something must certainly have been abroad to provoke such strong contrasts in reaction. As usual, there was truth on both sides. It would be idle to deny, for instance, that certain freedoms we now take for granted did not exist in 1960 and were only made inevitable by the prevailing atmosphere of liberal maturity in the years which followed. These must include the freedom of playwrights to write what they want for the stage without submitting their muse to a bureaucratic censor; the freedom of homo-

sexual liberation + (freedom [handwritten marginalia]

sexual men to demonstrate affection in their own homes; the freedom of literate men and women to buy the novels of (inter alios) D. H. Lawrence. Also, London was the focus of much new talent which brought pride to the country. Artists like David Hockney, dress designers like Mary Quant, interior decorators like David Hicks, photographers such as David Bailey, Lord Snowdon, Terence Donovan, writers and performers of popular music, novelists, dramatists, directors, these did not bring anything like derision from the world outside. At the same time, it was clear even then that show rather than substance was the immediate objective. The rise of the advertising agent and the public relations man made the creation of 'image' more important than the disclosure of worth, a new and lamentable emphasis to which even politicians succumbed. Since 1964 there has not been a Prime Minister who has not shamelessly employed advertising to project a manufactured impression of personality, whereby what he has to say takes second place to the way in which he says it. (This kind of organized deceit was, of course, imported from the United States, and cannot be entirely blamed upon the values of 'Swinging London'.)

Possibly the most serious charge one can bring against the London of the period is the most surprising one, namely its insularity. While thousands flocked to the capital to smell the air of excitement, hoping the benefits of the new age might be contagious, those actually 'in the swim' numbered a few hundred only, and the small band of achievers, the swingers' heroes and heroines, were less than fifty individuals. They were all to be found in the same places, eddying around each other in a gavotte of mutual and exclusive congratulation. The rest were mere sightseers, rarely permitted to intrude.

There was nothing especially new in this. Social life in 1790, after all, revolved around a dozen Whig families, in 1930 around a few political hostesses. The exclusive have always enjoyed watching the anguish of the excluded. But it was surprising in the 1960s, when classlessness and relaxation of social divisions were loudly proclaimed. In fact, the new aristocracy of young achievers was as rigidly circumscribed as any of its predecessors. You might find them in the evening at any of half a dozen restaurants. The Trattoria Terrazza in Soho was for those who had the confidence of success and did not mind whether they were seen there or not. Michael Caine was a constant diner. San Lorenzo in Beauchamp Place near Harrods boasted a tree in the middle of the restaurant (it had been created in a garden) and was for tablehoppers; bright young trendies in the latest 'gear' would spend half an hour greeting each other before they sat down to eat, and clearly *did* want to be seen. Film stars and very young nobility mingled here, such as Elizabeth Taylor and Lord Lichfield. The Aretusa in King's Road, Chelsea, had (I thought) filthy food and wealthy customers. Further along the road was Alexander's, where tennis stars always dined during the Wimbledon fortnight (I believe some still do), and further along still was the Casserole, with simple scrubbed tables where the successful liked to show their unpretentiousness. Rudolph Nureyev could frequently be found there. The Pickwick Club off the Charing Cross Road was for actors, and Guys and Dolls coffee-house was for the peripheral characters, who were either on the way towards success, or knew someone who knew someone who was already successful.

After dinner you would find the very rich at the Clermont Club, a gambling casino owned by that very original and very impressive man John Aspinall, whose pioneering work with animals will be remembered and applauded long after his association with glittering or imprudent gamblers has been forgotten. (The son of a peer once won £105,000 in an evening, made to leave with his loot, returned for a last attempt to increase it, and lost £225,000.) Or there was Annabel's in Berkeley Square, owned by Mark Birley and named after his wife Lady Annabel, sister to the Marquess of Londonderry. Annabel's was soon famous on both sides of the Atlantic as the most fashionable discothèque in London, exquisitely furnished and decorated, with a dance-floor on which four people might cavort without bumping into each other. Louder and less expensive disco-

thèques were Tramps in Jermyn Street and Sybilla's, off Piccadilly. Esmeralda's Barn in Knightsbridge, frequented by the
younger élite, was owned by the Kray twins, subsequently notorious as London's premier criminals. The best night-club in town
was Danny La Rue's, near Hanover Square, where England's
first overt 'drag artist', having emerged from pantomime, was
making his name with *risqué* patter, gorgeous clothes and a
straight man half his height called Ronnie Corbett. This, too,
was very small, the stage at arm's length from the front tables, a
discomfort which did not prevent Princess Margaret, among
others, from patronizing the place regularly. If you wandered
into all of these on any evening in, say, 1966, you were almost
certain to encounter at least half the people who constituted
'Swinging London'.

The swingers adopted a new staccato phraseology which made
a fetish of being inarticulate. It was unlikely, on the whole, that
one would hear words like 'cool' and 'square' at Annabel's or
the Clermont Club, although a few aristocrats did affect to use
the language, usually with uncomfortable results. In Chelsea and
at the discos, however, the language rapidly became the lingua
franca of the trendies (itself a trendy word). It was by no
means uncommon for a group which cultivated exclusivity to use
language as a badge, and all jargons, apart from communicating
information from one initiate to another, have the advantage of
conferring status upon the speaker, while casting non-speakers
into the amorphous crowd of plebs beyond. This is harmless
enough. Yet there was an underlying hostility in the jargon of
the Sixties which suggested a more sinister intent.

The language was largely derived from slang used by American
negroes, who had good historical reasons for nursing hostility
after generations of ill-treatment and ritual denial at the hands
of white Americans. In the mouths of the privileged young of
London, this slang sounded like mere decoration. The animosity
to which it tried to give voice was directed not against oppressors,
but against the old (that is, people over thirty), who were con-

temptibly dismissed as unworthy guardians of ridiculous values./
Those guardians, who believed in discipline, restraint, honesty, were the 'squares', people who knew not how to enjoy life, how to realize their potential for self-expression in the glad abandonment of inhibition. They were self-conscious, pompous, conformist and old-fashioned. They were appalled by the Rolling Stones, frightened by marijuana, and bewildered by mini skirts, caftans and beads. The most right-angled of all the Squares, according to the popular prejudice of the young, was the Prime Minister Sir Alec Douglas-Home, the most incongruous national leader for the Sixties that it is possible to imagine./His predecessor Harold Macmillan, on the other hand, though allied to patrician stock, was thought to be 'cool', because in an odd way it was suspected that he did not take himself too seriously. Hence he was the object of affectionate satire, while Douglas-Home had to withstand cruel jibes.

The opposite of a Square was a Swinger, he who was blessed with the knowledge of where he was 'at', who had none of the neuroses of his elders, nor any of their tortured self-doubt./ On the contrary, he was 'together', i.e. not falling apart, not fragmented by curious perceptions of the infinite difficulty of human life. He was in himself a belated rejection of twentieth-century psychological analysis, and proclaimed that life was simply to be lived, not understood. (His counterpart in the United States was intensely, even destructively, analytical, having his personal psychiatrist and developing attention-getting allergies when the psychiatrist's ministrations proved useless. This is why young Americans flocked to London to breathe the air of freedom from introspection.) The modern young man or woman was also 'with-it', up-to-date, enlightened. What was 'it' that the Squares were without? Basically, 'it' was a libertarian creed of self-indulgence, to which believers adhered not from long study of the alternatives, but from childish emotional preference.

Those who were with it habitually got 'carried away' by emotion, enthusiasm, and excitement, and sometimes were 'sent' with the help of pop music and drugs. Indeed, it was the ultimate

accolade bestowed by a generation bereft of critical judgement
to say that a record or a film 'sent' you; if it sent you far enough,
it was 'way out'.

When the young referred to 'the scene', they did not only
mean the places in London where they congregated, but the
entire décor of their lives, what they were doing, what they were
thinking, and above all who was the focus of the moment. The
scene was as much the people who inhabited it as the stage on
which they performed. That they chose a word from theatrical
parlance (they certainly did not have the Lake District in mind),
unwittingly gave weight to the notion that the whole business
was a silly charade, a game enacted by amateurs, who wanted
not so much to 'do their own thing' in peace, but to be seen to
be doing it. They wanted to be observed, and it mattered little
if they were applauded or vilified. They were performers. Their
act, moreover, was meretricious and shallow, with no more body
to it than the jargon they used as dialogue. Later, there were
some who rejected even this 'scene' in favour of one more grim
and private; the 'drop-outs' belong more securely to the decade
which began after the Sixties euphoria had dribbled to a shabby
close.

Self-indulgence presupposed affluence, for a hedonist must
be doomed to frustration in a period of austerity. It is now
platitudinous to point out that the young had money in their
pockets for the first time and that they constituted a brand-new
stratum of the consumer society, but it was nonetheless a crucially
important factor in determining the atmosphere of the 1960s. A
few years earlier (say, in 1956), schoolboys had to make do on
pocket-money of a shilling a week (5p in new money), whereas
now they could earn £10 a week or more as soon as they started
work. This seems ludicrously low by the inflationary standards
of today, but it has to be set against an average national wage of
£13 a week in 1961, rising to £23 a week in 1968. I was earning
£18 a week in 1962 and considered myself relatively well-off.
After paying a very high rent, I was left with £6 a week to spend,

[19]

and was not obliged to deny myself some luxuries. One could have a decent restaurant meal with wine for £2–£3 once every couple of weeks and buy a good suit every few months for £9. For the young, spending-money of £5 a week was a sudden fortune, and since unemployment was under 2 per cent most young people had that spending power.

Bold signs of affluence on a grand level were multiplying year by year. There were jets flying across the Atlantic and motor cars available to all (I bought my first car second-hand for £7, and a new Mini cost only £500). Confectionery shops and grocery stores were closing all the time to make way for vast supermarkets imported from America, where the shopper helped himself to goods instead of being served from behind a counter. Terence Conran opened the first supermarket furniture store, Habitat, in 1964. And hire-purchase (or buying on the never-never) became widespread.

The most famous of the hire-purchase barons was John Bloom, who at the age of twenty-eight had made himself a millionaire within only two years. His commodity was washing-machines, which he sold direct to the consumer at an enticingly low price, with generous credit facilities. His success (or the appearance of it) made him a national figure whose activities were constantly recorded by the Press, and lent him such an air of respectability that he was able to lunch with the Queen. His glory was absurdly transient. In 1964 the Bloom empire collapsed and his name was in disgrace.

One ought to have learnt a lesson from John Bloom's demise, but this was not an age to learn from experience. Jim Slater, in partnership with Peter Walker, made a fortune simply by saying that he was going to make a fortune. His company, Slater Walker, dealt in shares and take-overs, turning his only asset, self-confidence, into a purchasable commodity. Slater's business acumen was not in question, but the existence of a business to harness it was as chimerical as the smile on the Cheshire Cat. Slater played with theoretic money. Some shareholders sold happily while the theory endured, and made large profits, others, clinging on through greed, lost fortunes. Jim Slater's stock market transactions were eventually the subject of investigation, and he too collapsed. There were to be hosts of Cheshire Cats grinning their way through the 1960s.

As more and more people found they had money to play with, the *Daily Mirror*, traditionally the working-man's newspaper, inaugurated a City Page to advise its readers how to invest their spare cash, an unthinkable development just a few years earlier. The biggest money-spinners were the new commercial television companies, which made vast profits purveying pulp to the masses (it must be said that the standard of their programmes improved a thousandfold before the end of the decade). The other pot of gold was to be made from property development, and the venal men who transformed the face of London with their hideous buildings, with wilful disregard for present or future aesthetic considerations, will answer for their appalling selfishness to generations as yet unborn. The one visible and immutable legacy of the Sixties is the destruction of a beautiful city sacrificed to the attractions of quick profit.

The young themselves, or some of them, showed extraordinary enterprise and, in so doing, effected their own transformation upon the 'scene', thankfully in a much more transient manner. Fashion underwent a fundamental revolution. Mary Quant, a student of Goldsmith's College, invented a sartorial sense which could appeal only to the young, and not be an adapted reflection of the taste of their elders. Mini-skirts, reaching from the waist down to only an inch or so below the modest parts, and looking more like a wide belt than a garment, astonished the older generation. More, they were sometimes made of PVC, a shiny substance which made the skirts appear permanently wet. There were even dresses made of paper. Innovation knew no bounds, and Mary Quant's contribution to its fine excess was rewarded with the OBE in 1966. To wear such clothes, models had need to be slim as never before, and after the reign of Jean Shrimpton as London's leading mannequin, there came Twiggy, a Cockney girl so skinny as to be almost skeletal. She would not have been given an audition in the 1950s.

For the men, there emerged a very young Scottish business-man called John Stephen, who specialized in clothing which was so cheap, in price and quality, that it could be discarded without tears after a week. This was revolutionary for men, who had until then cherished their suits over many years, keeping them carefully preserved to avoid waste. Stephen's fashions were remorselessly casual, as were those of more up-market designers catering to the rich young playboys. Scarves loosely knotted around the neck replaced the traditional tie, and velvet suits replaced the old-fashioned worsted variety. Top designers like Michael Fish appeared in public in ever more flamboyant garb, laying to rest the notion of men as dullards in dress, which had obtained with few exceptions since the First World War. There were special shops for the trendy, not known to, let alone patronized by, the excluded. Michael Rainey's 'Hung on You' and 'Granny Takes a Trip' in Chelsea, Rupert Lycett-Green's 'Blades' at the bottom of Savile Row, impudently challenging the taste of the world's most famous tailors on their very doorstep, were the shops to be seen in. John Stephen's chain of stores, aimed at the working class and the herd rather than the exclusive set, nevertheless made a mark which was not so ephemeral, for he changed one of London's streets. His first shop was sited in a dark and dreary little back alley leading nowhere called Carnaby Street, which I recall finding by accident one night after leaving the Palladium and thinking it was a perfect place to be robbed. Carnaby Street had some back entrances to offices, but nothing much to indicate familiarity with humans. When John Stephen had finished with it, and had opened a whole line of shops, it was colourful, cheerful and desirable. Now, of course, it is mentioned in so many guide books that tourists make a detour to see what is one of the prime sights of London.

Interior design likewise felt the influence of young men with new ideas. David Hicks and David Mlinaric made the greatest impact, their taste still visible in many a country seat as well as *hair*

Chelsea *pied-à-terre*. As for hair-styles, they altered with such manic rapidity and in ever more outrageous directions that the latest cut remained fashionable for barely a few weeks. The one change which endured was the trend towards shoulder-length hair for men, again something which had not been seen for half a century, and the one name which rose above all competitors was that of Vidal Sassoon, supported by the witty and inventive John Addey.

The normally lugubrious world of art-dealing likewise felt the influence of crazy innovation, and brought to public notice two gallery owners remarkable for their youth and enterprise, as well as a young peer to reassert the tradional role of the nobility in the patronage of fine art. John Kasmin and Robert Fraser were the new businessmen of the art world, both willing to take risks with taste and both equally at home amongst the trendies. Kasmin's brightest star was David Hockney, a restless artist who consistently sought new modes of expression and always succeeded. Hockney's precise perceptions and colourful blunt character brought glamour as well as distinction to his work. Fraser's artists were more bizarre in their experimentation, his galleries always packed with surprises. The peer was the Marquess of Dufferin and Ava, whose patronage was not merely financial but committed. His town house in Holland Park offered an unusual juxtaposition of richly comfortable traditional furnishings in one room, while across the hall was a room hung with gigantic canvases of eye-wearying blotches, stripes and splashes.

Artists who made their names during this period (and some who kept them) are too numerous to mention, and any half-list must be personal and selective. Bridget Riley's stark black and white patterns had undeniable impact, and seemed rather the result of design than creation, ordering not inventing. The craze for Pop Art, which turned to newspaper advertisements and comic strip cartoons for its inspiration, appeared to be the last refuge of those who could only copy. But it wasn't. From America came the impudent antics of Andy Warhol, who issued somebody

[23]

else's photograph of Marilyn Monroe in different colours, and who also took a film of the Empire State Building in New York which lasted several hours and consisted of one shot. Of course, Warhol did not belong to the London 'scene', but there were sufficient number of followers or disciples of his style ('style', in the end, was what he had, but that was all) for his influence to be felt. /

An artist whose name I have forgotten and purposefully chosen not to rediscover was the perpetrator of a widely publicized confidence trick or self-delusion, whichever one chooses to believe, in 1972. He ordered some building bricks from a brick merchant, piled them in two neat rows, put his name on one of them and sold them to the Tate Gallery as a work of art, despite the fact that it was obvious to all that human agency had played no part in the 'creation' of this piece, only in its packing and its purchase. Similar absurdities proliferated throughout the 1960s. I recall in the flat of a collector seeing a tooth-mug on a small shelf on the wall, with a mirror behind it. This was proudly shown off to me as my acquaintance's latest acquisition, bought for a tidy but not exorbitant sum. He took the tooth-mug down from its shelf and used it regularly, he said. Wasn't it magnificent that a work of art could also serve a *purpose*? The work was called something like 'object on a shelf'. In cold fact it was precisely that, a tooth-mug from a shop on a shelf on the wall, identical to thousands of others in flats all over the land. My friend had a healthy sense of humour in other matters.

These aberrations were never so widespread as to achieve general acceptance, but they had their champions, people who applauded the blurring of distinction between reality and art, and between what had always been called 'fine art' and the new commercial art. One critic went so far as to accuse Pop Art of 'regressive infantilism'. On a less arcane level, there was a degree of regret expressed that some artists should aim to appeal only to the aesthetically insensitive, to follow rather than to educate and enlighten. Their creations were the immobile equivalent of television soap opera, isolating and celebrating the familiar.

[24]

Television was itself claiming audiences of unimagined numbers, and not exclusively for rubbish. The birth of British television's international reputation for quality can be traced to the 1960s, and in particular, perhaps, to the series adapted from Galsworthy's *The Forsyte Saga*, subsequently shown virtually everywhere, even in Russia. The power of television was symbolically acknowledged by a famous breakfast at the Connaught Hotel (one of the most chic and expensive in London) given by David Frost on 7 January 1966. Frost was then a young man in his twenties whose only achievement was to appear regularly on television to question famous people. He was what Gilbert Harding used to call a 'tele-notoriety'. Yet he was strong enough to invite to his breakfast twenty of the most influential people in the land, including the Prime Minister, three newspaper editors, the Bishop of Woolwich, Lord Longford, the Chairman of EMI, the Head of BBC television and Professor A. J. Ayer. What is more, they all accepted. Well, nearly all; the one lofty refusal came from Paul McCartney of the Beatles.

These assembled luminaries ate kidneys, bacon and eggs, caviare, and drank not tea, but champagne. Their purpose, said Mr Frost archly, was to provide 'a chance for a few friends who don't always meet to gather and chat.' And, one might add, to keep the right side of Mr Frost. For once, Christopher Booker's harsh criticisms were entirely justified. Frost, he wrote, had 'an intuitive sense of television's power to recreate the world on its own unreal terms – to reduce everything and everyone, politicians and pop singers, philosophers and journalists, bishops and entertainers, to the same level, as bit players in a universal dreamworld.'

Television's unprecedented power to persuade, to cajole, and to induce conformity, was mercilessly exploited by the publicity men, who never before had been able to shape the preferences of several million people at once. That this power could be devastating in the wrong hands was mildly whispered, and on the whole dismissed as fanciful in a pluralist democracy. The exploiters were not about to waste their time and money, for

[25]

time is money, (so they said) thinking about moral responsibility. One housewife did think about it, and though Mrs Whitehouse got almost everything wrong, she managed to force attention upon the moral aspects of broadcasting and earn for herself a small honoured place in the social history of Britain.

Writers in particular were less concerned about the moral responsibility of television than the danger of its hypnotizing the viewer into a state of permanent apathy. Whereas reading a book or watching a play required participation by the reader and theatre-goer to make an experience shared with the creator, one could watch television for hours or days with no conscious effort and no noticeable effect. Writers were appalled by this inertia because it seemed to negate their very purpose; far from being influential, television ran the risk of being anaesthetical. N. F. Simpson said that people developed an immunity to it, scarcely remembering what they had seen; more probably, they had seen nothing at all, they had merely stared at it in a kind of catatonic gaze. Hence, as in so many other aspects of this meretricious age, content was very often sacrificed to presentation. At least the scope and purpose of television were opened to discussion in the Sixties, spawning many learned and worried articles in intellectual magazines, though there were always the guilty intellectuals, like R. H. S. Crossman, who stoutly defended the right of the masses to their trivia (and secretly wished he did not despise the trivia himself).

The single most surprising characteristic of the revolution in taste which took place in the 1960s was its domination by the style and habits of the young working class. Previous upheavals had been led from above, their direction dictated by the intelligent bourgeoisie. Now it was rather the mentality and attitudes of lower-class teenagers which spread upwards and outwards to stimulate, or infect, other classes and other age-groups. Britain did not suddenly become classless, but the cultures of different classes no longer clashed – they coalesced; the impetus came from envy of the confident relaxed style of working-class young-

[26]

sters who, in the vernacular of the day, were happy to 'do their own thing' and not care too much what other people thought about it.

In their book *The Permissive Morality* (1964), C. H. and W. M. Whiteley explained this phenomenon in terms so clear they cannot be improved:

> Formality is usually valued by ruling groups rather than by those ruled. Special sorts of dress for particular occasions, special manners of speech, special modes of courtesy, are cultivated by people who can spare the time and the money to elaborate their transactions in this fashion, and so mark themselves off from the vulgar mob who have not acquired such graces and do not know the proper thing to do. By contrast, the proletarian values mateyness as one of the prime values, and dislikes and distrusts anyone who puts on airs. In this respect the English people as a whole have gone over to the proletarian standpoint and are all trying hard to be just ordinary chaps.

Thus, the cause rather than the symptoms of 'Swinging London' was a generalized wish to emulate the carefree spontaneity of working-class youth and to shed formalized inhibitions which had for so long cast English social life in concrete. This had never happened before, and accounted for the beguiling sense of freedom which pervaded London from 1964 onwards. The English behaved like a team of cart-horses suddenly released from their shackles and cavorting friskily in an unaccustomed field of bluebells. No one could fail to notice and feel the change of air.

Not everyone was happy at the spectacle, even then. Peregrine Worsthorne fought valiantly to warn against what was coming. 'The class system is a reality in this country and likely to remain so for many decades', he wrote. 'To be classless is to be an alien, rootless, cut off from any truly intimate and satisfactory communion with any section of society.' Mr Worsthorne was quite right, but his anxiety was based on the fear that anyone should *want* to be classless. It is, as he said, an impossibility in England. The class system was not abolished; it was not even ignored; it was simply demoted to a lower level of importance as the proletarian Pied Piper led his cheerful way towards bright fresh horizons.

No single man could claim the mantle of the Pied Piper of the Sixties, and such is the disrepute now attached to the period that few would want to. The Piper turned up in many guises under different names and singing different tunes. However, since political leaders flatter themselves that they do actually lead, pride of place must go to the man of the moment, Harold Wilson, Leader of the Labour party and Prime Minister from 1964.

When Labour came to office the Tory party was, to put it bluntly, clapped out. Conservatives had formed the Government of the past thirteen years, the longest period of continuous office for over a century; and of the fifty years since 1914, they had been in government either alone or in coalition for forty of them. Harold Wilson had taken over the leadership of the Labour party in 1963 on the death of Hugh Gaitskell. A brilliant scholar and consummate politician, his air of craftiness did him no harm, at least to begin with. In comparison with Macmillan and Douglas-Home, he seemed to know what he was doing, to have plans and the ability to see them through to fruition. He talked of entering the technological age, of getting Britain moving, which was exactly right for the spirit of optimism, of cleaning away the debris, which then obtained. Seeing that young entertainers carried one of Britain's new banners of pride, wily man that he was, he consorted with young entertainers.

The Labour victory was the narrowest in the history of party politics. In a House of 630 members, Labour had an overall majority of only 4 seats, and their majorities in their 4 most narrowly held seats ranged from 7 to 53 votes. This meant that the votes of less than 200 people in the country secured the election. Nevertheless, much was expected of them, and much they intended. So ambitious were the reforms the new Government announced, that more than one Minister had to be firmly told by his Civil Servants that certain things simply were not possible. Hopes were raised by a buoyant mood. Bernard Levin wrote that he expected the new Government not to run away from its own sword, and to ensure that industry and initiative were rewarded, in order that Britain might catch up with other countries in the West. 'I for one,' he said, 'am not going to be fobbed off with the nationalisation of steel and the legalisation of private buggery.' How well the Labour Governments of 1964 and 1966 succeeded in their aims I am not competent to judge, but it did not require a political commentator to point out the mood of renewal and of exciting prospects which was apparent to anyone living then.

As one age of potential or promised greatness began, so another was symbolically closed with the death of the mighty Winston Churchill in 1965. His lying-in-state, the solemn impressive pomp of his funeral, the journey of his coffin on the River Thames, were attended by more Monarchs, Presidents, Heads of State and Prime Ministers than had ever gathered together in one place to honour one man in the entire history of human achievement. The President of the United States went so far as to order all American flags the world over to fly at half-mast, a mark of respect never before accorded to a foreigner. There could be no doubt that Churchill had been a unique figure, and it made his passing even more poignant to recognize that he had made Britain unique when he had directed her destiny, and that of the Western world, through sheer will-power. Britain no longer boasted that distinction, and one of the recurrent energies which underlay all the empty effervescence of the Sixties was the obscure but potent desire to hear Britain's voice trumpeted again.

One minor political movement had a major influence upon opinion which endures to this day and may justly claim to be a product of the Sixties' more thoughtful approach to man's place in the world. This was the Ecology movement, whose candidates habitually fared badly at elections, but which succeeded in fostering an awareness that if men continued to treat their planet with such ignorant contempt for the way in which it works, they would not need to wait for a nuclear holocaust to break it into smithereens, for it would be a large arid unproductive stone within a couple of generations.

The founder of the *Ecologist*, a monthly magazine devoted to spreading this particular word, deserves especial praise for his contribution. He was Edward ('Teddy') Goldsmith, brother to the more famous Anglo-French financier James Goldsmith, and possessed of much more charm. Teddy Goldsmith cared passionately about enlightenment, losing money for the cause as rapidly as his wizard brother accumulated it. He must claim credit, through his magazine, which though not widely read was constantly quoted in other journals, for bringing the dangers of pollution and spoliation of natural resources to public attention. This, together with the growth of health food shops (led by cranks) and the philosophy of the young 'hippies', helped to change habits. We have yet to discover whether he was too late with his message, or insufficiently messianic.

The death of Churchill removed the last link with a glorious past, giving those predisposed to gloom a splendid excuse for lamentation. The Sixties was a time for perpetual analysis of what was wrong with Britain, and why it should have become an embarrassment to refer to 'Great Britain' as if the name, perfectly appropriate in Victorian times, were now a hollow boast. As recently as the 1950s, London had still been the centre of the greatest Empire the world had ever known, represented on every continent and accounting for up to a quarter of the world's population. With astonishing speed, and for the most part with admirable dignity, the Empire was now being dismantled, and while the old saw this as a sign of humiliation, the young felt that theirs was the task of regeneration, that *their* attitudes and ideas would henceforth prevail. It was because these attitudes and ideas were so completely at odds with everything which had gone before that many people saw their influence in the 1960s as trivial, frivolous, destructive or negative. Not only was the mood different, but so were the moral precepts which supported it. What had been deemed wrong before was now proclaimed to be right, and vice versa. The suddenness of this upheaval was, of course, superficial; years of preparation had made it inevitable/ /The generation which grew up after the Second World War did not comprehend the virtues of self-denial and self-control which had fashioned the outlook of previous generations. It had previously been the responsibility of the individual to insure himself and his family against illness or unemployment and to make safe provision for the education of his children. He had therefore been obliged to foster prudence and if as a result of his labour and his savings he was able to provide for health and education, he had reason to feel pleased with himself. He had regarded them as rewards for industry/This Puritan ethic had no place in the England of the Sixties./To those who had grown up with the Welfare State it was unthinkable that one should buy education or health like a sack of potatoes, and I remember feeling utterly amazed and incredulous that in other countries, notably the United States, it was still necessary to pay for the privilege of reading and writing or for the misfortune of being ill; the one degraded education to the level of a commercial proposition, the other penalized bad luck. It was not so much that one considered education and good health each to be a 'right', which was logical nonsense, but that their provision was 'normal' in a civilized society. Countries which made no such provision were quite simply uncivilized. The new cause for pride lay not in maintaining an Empire but in treating citizens properly, giving them freedom from worry so that they might develop their individual talents.

Consequently, the notion that one should postpone one's enjoyment until one had earned it and paid first for all the necessities, became obsolete, and what erupted in the 1960s was a new ethic of pursuing enjoyment for its own sake and despising self-control as inhumanly oppressive. Even the achievers of the time, and there were many, were bent upon self-fulfilment today, not providential investment for tomorrow. Self-indulgence was respectable, even applauded, and had lost its taint of sin.

Political leaders sensed the new mood and pandered to it, each party promising more pleasure than the other. It was not until a quarter of a century later, under the harsh conservatism of Margaret Thatcher, that a politician dared propose a reversal towards thrift and self-reliance, or dared suggest there were things in life worth aspiring to beyond the satisfaction of whim.

The young did not see themselves as negative. Their hedonism was a positive response to the shallowness of political creeds and a revolt against the restrictions which, in their view, were left over from a less civilized period. They did not regard criminals as evil men who could choose to do good, but as sick men who needed to be helped. They did not feel compelled to give respect out of habit to individuals they disliked or traditions they deplored. Even on a superficial level, they welcomed the decline in formality between individuals. What possible purpose could be served by addressing a man older than oneself by his surname, as one did as a matter of course until the 1950s? (Those who inherited the habit cannot easily discard it; I still refer to my next door neighbour, whom I have known for nearly twenty years, as Mrs Brennan, though I can think of no reason apart from her being a few years older than myself; and I feel offended by strangers who answer the telephone at, say, an airline office, and introduce themselves by their first name.)

The question is, whether we should now view the Sixties' excitement as an insubstantial bubble of jollity which did more harm than good, or the symptom of a new national pride which did not last long enough. Were we positive or negative, frivolous or mature?

There is no categorical answer. Some manifestations of general ebullience were downright silly, and some consequences of upheaval were detrimental to social harmony. And yet, at the same time, this revolution in taste and manners brought a maturity which we cannot afford to denigrate, and advantages

[32]

◄ 2 ▲ 3

1   *Previous page:* Two sisters in topless dresses arrive at the film premiere of *London in the raw* 1964

2   Twiggy leaves Heathrow for the USA 1967

3   Terence Stamp and Jean Shrimpton arrive at the British Premiere of *The Collector* 1965

4   *Overleaf left:* Mary Quant displays her Order of the British Empire 1966

5   *Overleaf right:* Mrs Mary Whitehouse with a petition of 366,355 signatures against 'BBC dirt' 1965

◀ 6 ▲ 7

6   Two ladies with their copies of
    Lady Chatterley's Lover 1960

7   Stephen Ward's drawing of
    Christine Keeler

▲ 8

8   Harold Macmillan arriving at Euston
Station at the height of the Profumo
scandal 1963

which we still enjoy. It is above all in the area of moral perceptions that the changes can be most easily discerned. The next chapter deals with this subject, and demonstrates at once the inherent disparity between a more healthy view and some more unhealthy consequences. The new liberation was by no means all good. I then go on to show in subsequent chapters how these shifts in perception influenced other parts of British life; we at last saw that censorship was ridiculous, that legislation to control sexual preferences was absurd, and that hypocrisy was a stain on the national character which had to be removed./

Other chapters on the theatre in London and the domination of a culture based on popular music interrupt the theme, as does a consideration of how we came to recognize that the Royal Family needed to be respected rather than merely held in awe. The final chapter then looks at the largest moral problem we have ever had to face, nuclear bombs, and the evolution of CND to cope with it. In the end, it should be clear that the kaleidoscope of sins and boons which galloped through the decade left the country entirely different from what it had been before.

The New Morality

One cannot boldly identify or describe a change in the moral climate of a community. Such a change does not emerge spontaneously from a piece of legislation, nor can it obey the diktat of Pope or Prime Minister. It can only be measured by what obligations we demand of each other, and how we respond when those obligations are despised; or what conduct we regard as shameful, and what punishment we accord to those who behave, in the general view, shamefully. Once you have determined how far you may go before you are ostracized by your fellows, you know the boundaries of tolerance allowed by the community of which you are part. These boundaries shift and resettle according to the age of the individual and the 'feeling' of the times in which he lives. If the origin and nature of this change in climate are elusive, their effects are nonetheless felt by all who live through them. Anybody who was past infancy in London in the 1960s knows perfectly well, without necessity of proof, that he lived in a community which hurled down barriers and stretched the limits of permissible behaviour at a stunning pace. All moral obligations were considered harmful to the health of the individual unless they were self-imposed, so they were loosened; and as for the sense of shame, it was all-pervasive in 1958, and had virtually disappeared ten years later.

A man used to be ashamed if he broke off an engagement to marry. In the 1960s he might be expected to make several such promises and keep none. A young woman used to be ashamed if she was not a virgin when she married; in the Sixties, she would be more likely to feel shame if she went inexperienced to the marriage bed. Sexual activity had previously been a secretive thing, to snigger about when young and to indulge with the lights out when older; there was still, incredibly, a residual Victorian idea that ladies were not really meant to enjoy it, and some men still did not know that women *could* enjoy it. The film *Room at the Top* (1958) suggested for the first time that sex could be, indeed should be, gleeful, and the shock-waves bombarded schools and moral welfare people for months. It was an 'X' certificate, forbidden to people under the age of eighteen. In order to see such films, children had to resort to dressing-up in Dad's old clothes, and looking ridiculous (I remember once even wearing a false moustache, and my chin still as soft as marshmallow!), or 'bunking in' by a side door. If the film were an 'A', then you could stand outside the cinema and ask a stranger to take you in as his or her child, since such films were only forbidden to 'unaccompanied' minors. Anyway, we did see *Room at the Top* and were stupidly (in retrospect) excited by its daring. It would now be considered extremely tame.

The Sixties swept away all this stuffiness with the one idea, come from who knew where, that any moral rule which obstructed happiness or prevented people from enjoying themselves in a way which did not offend anyone else, was necessarily pernicious and must be abolished. As Christopher Booker wrote in the *Daily Mail* twenty years later, 'We believed that we were the first generation in the history of the world to recognise the true joys and values of sex.' Certainly it was the first generation since the war to decide that the mysteries of sex should be explored and discoveries made for the sheer fun of it. People copulated on the slightest pretext after an acquaintance of some minutes. Sexual partners were snapped up and discarded without ceremony, provided they had the newly-available contraceptive pill in their pocket or hand-bag. The first to chronicle the age, Jonathan Aitken, himself a man of twenty-four, commented sourly that his was 'the generation of non-emotional involvement, to whom sex is primarily a sport, a sensual entertainment for laughs and kicks.'

Aitken and other detractors of the Sixties failed to understand that non-emotional involvement did not *replace* emotional involvement, but existed alongside it. Love was not banished from the earth (or from London), but the notion that sex without love was wrong and sinful was mercilessly derided. There was sex-with-love, which was an emotional and spiritual coupling of deep intensity and such power that it could alter one's personality, and there was sex-without-love, which was none of these things but was enormously enjoyable. The 1960s made a mighty effort to rid sex of its guilty look.

The 'liberal progressive intellectuals' (so called by those who do not care for their views and manage to make two honest and admirable adjectives sound almost sinister) welcomed and encouraged these new attitudes. So did the churchmen, surprisingly, and the psychiatrists, understandably. It was perceived that clerics and shrinks tended to use the same language, recommending harmony and integration of the personality. Whereas the clerics had until then taken a harsh view of the road towards this harmony (self-denial, rigour, discipline, strength derived from misery), they began to agree with the psychiatrists that exacting moral standards produced strain and disequilibrium in the personality. 'The effort to be moral often appears in psychiatric writing as the main cause, even the sole cause, of mental unbalance,' wrote Dr Whiteley. It followed that a relaxation of moral standards would be beneficial, so that there was less to live up to and less damage caused by failure to be 'good'. It was not until much later that the danger inherent in this argument became manifest. The psychiatrist seeks to make a happy and well-balanced man of his patient. He is caught in a circular trap designed by Lucifer himself, for if he succeeds, he fails, and if he fails, he fails doubly. To make a man contented and harmonious is to make him placid, cautious, unadventurous, perhaps to rob him of his own unique personality, to emasculate him. This was the problem dramatized by Peter Shaffer in *Equus* (1973). The psychiatrist therefore succeeds in manufacturing harmony where there was disturbance, but fails his patient by symbolically killing him. If, on the other hand, he were to be true to his patient and allow him the passions and excitements which are essential to his personality, then he encourages unbridled licence, for there are as many private moralities as there are individuals, at least in theory. The Sixties played with these conceits, and left them unresolved.

The apostle of the drug culture, Dr Timothy Leary, inhabited what Diana Trilling called a 'sweeter moral universe', but it would be unfair to blame the whole orgy on Dr Leary and his supporters. Even before his name had been mentioned in London (he operated in the United States), the young were experimenting with their new ethical freedom to indulge their own passions with unprecedented abandon. 'The popular morality is now a wasteland,' said Professor Carstairs in his BBC Reith Lectures of 1962. 'It is littered with the debris of broken convictions. A new concept is emerging, of sexual relationships as a source of pleasure.'

The following year, *Time* magazine devoted an article to the phenomenon of England's sudden blossoming: 'On the island where the subject has long been taboo in polite society, sex has exploded into the national consciousness and national headlines.' 'Are We Going Sex Crazy?' asked the *Daily Herald*. 'Is Chastity Out-moded?' asks a school magazine for teenagers. 'Are Virgins Obsolete?' is the question posed by the solemn *New Statesman*. The answers vary but one thing is clear: Britain is being bombarded with a barrage of frankness about sex.

That frankness reached its peak, or nadir, depending upon your point of view, on 13 November 1965, on which momentous day the distinguished but mischievous theatre critic, Kenneth Tynan, uttered on television a word never before heard publicly. He was taking part in a programme devoted to a discussion of stage censorship. The Chairman, Robert Robinson, asked Mr Tynan whether he could countenance the possibility of sexual intercourse taking place on the stage of the National Theatre. This was his reply: 'I doubt if there are any rational people to whom the word "fuck" would be particularly diabolical, revolting, or totally forbidden. I think that anything that can be printed or said can also be seen.'

'That word' had a seismic effect upon the country. The BBC switchboard was jammed with telephone calls for hours. Jonathan Miller and George Melly apparently wrote eager fan letters of congratulations to Mr Tynan (for what?), and the Postmaster-General, Anthony Wedgewood Benn, was besieged with complaints. He said he had watched the programme but it was not his responsibility to comment upon it. The rising Wolverhampton housewife and busybody, Mary Whitehouse, told the world that she had written to the Queen demanding that Her Majesty make sure the word was never again used on the BBC. In all the uproar it was not easy to determine who made the silliest remark, there were so many contenders.

Why so much fuss? There was not a person in the country who did not know what 'fuck' meant, and precious few outside of monasteries who did not use it at some time or another. Even the absurd Mrs Whitehouse was familiar with the word, or presumably she would not have become so agitated. Undeniably, to hear the word spoken publicly produced a shock (which is not to say it was 'shocking'), especially after years of being told by one's parents that it was not polite to talk like that. But to pretend that fucking was a proper pursuit as long as it was called by a more decorous name was hypocrisy of cretinous dimensions, but hypocrisy, alas, to which the British had long been used. Therein lay the source of the trouble; while everyone knew that people had sexual congress and talked about it in non-medical jargon, it would not do for 'the masses' to join in, *even though* there was no secret that the masses used the word and others like it in daily conversation. Snobbery, the peculiar English disease, was at the root of public disquiet. It was simply improper for the word to be heard by people who might not know how to use it, who might think its use condoned, who might adopt it in the language they employed when speaking with their betters. The unacknowledged danger of licence was social anarchy. If Kenneth Tynan managed to break the hold of such notions, then perhaps he deserved to be congratulated after all. Yet, to my knowledge, we have not heard the same word pronounced on radio or television in the twenty years that have elapsed. People are able frankly to talk about 'making love' (which is not the same thing), and even to be shown doing so (genitals concealed), but no one since Tynan has advocated calling a spade a spade quite so bluntly.

British sensitivity about language was again demonstrated when the American actress Mia Farrow, who was settling in London, was accused of conduct likely to cause a breach of the peace because she had told someone or other in a public place that he or she should go and get fucked. In her defence, Miss Farrow said it was the nicest fate she could wish upon anyone. She was acquitted, another sign that England was growing up.

In New York, the trend towards freedom was going so far so fast that in one play the audience were invited to come up to the stage and engage in sexual relations with any member of the cast, and in another the entire cast was arrested after the performance and charged with public indecency, sodomy, and Heaven knows what else. We did not reach such vertiginous levels in London, but I do recall attending a performance in which the audience was made to close their eyes, walk through the cast, and be touched by members of the cast in a totally soothing and sensual way. It was very pleasant. (See Chapter Six)

We touch here upon the matter of censorship in the theatre, which also underwent a complete revolution in the Sixties, but will have to wait its place in the chapter. For the moment, it is fair to say that *Time* magazine's conclusion that the British were obsessed with sex was justified. That obsession was spectacularly fed by a sensational divorce case in Edinburgh, which filled the front pages of newspapers for weeks. The Duke of Argyll, 11th of his line, Chief of the Campbells, was divorcing his Duchess of legendary beauty once immortalized in the lyrics of Cole Porter, and threatening to cite dozens of co-respondents among the illustrious of the land. The people loved it, for it proved that even a nobleman could have his problems, and that dukes and duchesses cavorted between the sheets just like the rest of us. But it was amazing that this divorce should have held so powerful a fascination that it nudged off the page all other world news of perhaps greater import.

That the Argylls themselves suffered agonies of embarrassment at prurient interest in their affairs cannot be doubted. At one point, the Master of the Rolls (Lord Denning), faced with the problem of identifying a photograph of a naked man said to be one of Her Grace's lovers, and hindered by the fact that the head had been snipped off, instructed a Harley Street doctor to take a view of the genitals of a prominent Cabinet Minister to see if they matched. 'It has been demonstrated to my entire satisfaction,' wrote Lord Denning, 'that the "unknown" man in the photographs was *not* this Minister.' As Bernard Levin later wrote, it was extraordinary that two-thirds of the way through the twentieth century, and in a country as advanced as Britain, 'a judge should have been obliged to ask a doctor to examine the penis of a politician.'

Both litigants gave their version of events in the Sunday newspapers after the divorce was granted, and each tried to prevent the other from divulging secrets. The Duchess was called a whore in all but name, while the Duke was publicly chastised for breaking marital confidence for pecuniary gain, and asked to resign from his club (the worst calamity for a gentleman). The case served to illustrate the painful birth of Britain's new moral maturity, and the Argylls were the unlucky victims of the interlude between extreme conventionality and extreme licence. In truth, Margaret Argyll was no more promiscuous than any ordinary woman, but promiscuity in pre-Sixties measure meant more than two lovers in a lifetime. As for the Duke, it was said he was far too drunk to be able to deal effectively with the physical side of marriage.

All in all, it was, in 1963, a real-life drama far more absorbing than the current question whether or not the film star Richard Burton would leave his lovely Welsh wife Sybil for another film star, Elizabeth Taylor, whom the Press depicted as a collector of husbands. (He did, and Sybil remarried happily and settled in New York.)

Another indication of relaxed habits, albeit a childish one, was the sight of sudden, inoffensive and inexplicable nakedness in a public place. Hitherto, it had only been on New Year's Eve that one expected to see chilly frolics in the fountains of Trafalgar Square, but now it was possible to spy on a summer's day inconsequential bareness in the King's Road, Chelsea. A young lady took off all her clothes at a concert at the Albert Hall (she was in the audience, not the orchestra), for no apparent reason. Mr Levin again, rather ungraciously, commented that 'she had found it necessary to undress in public because she could find few to care whether or not she undressed in private.' I well remember having a quiet tea and cakes in Fortnum & Mason's on Piccadilly one Saturday afternoon. Fortnum's, it must be pointed out, is one of the two or three most select shops in London, where counter assistants wear black tie and tails, and customers habitually arrive in chauffeur-driven Rolls Royces. The tea-shop was packed with ladies in hats, chatting in low whispers, drinking tea with little fingers pointing in the air, and eating tiny cucumber sandwiches. A naked man rushed in, arms (and other things) waving, weaved in and out among the tables, then disappeared into the street. Nobody could claim not to have seen him. The whispers stopped for a moment, tea-cups paused in mid-air, everyone looked, then when he was gone, the ladies politely applauded. There was not even the faintest suggestion of an incipient scream.

The ladies in Fortnum's appeared indifferent, but I suspect they were rather proud of their unaccustomed tolerance; only a few years earlier they would have behaved quite differently. They were also far more understanding than they had been wont to admit, of the other women who could be found loitering in streets not far from Fortnum's (whores or slacks) or in exotic rooms with telephone and perfumes (the call-girls). Prostitutes were eventually banished from the streets, but the time when they were thick as flies in Curzon Street was only yesterday, and there was now a sudden interest in what they actually *did*, and how their lives were led. The answer to both turned out to be both surprising and hilarious.

It was once again the august intellectual magazine *Encounter* which broke the ice with an article by Wayland Young (Lord Kennet) entitled 'Sitting On A Fortune'. With his acumen and eagerness to paint a true picture Young dared to quote language which had never before been fit to print, of which the following is a choice example:

> There are all sorts of little gentle things you can do to a client so that with a bit of luck they come before they even get into me. When they do, I look ever so loving and gentle and say, 'Traitor.' Well, I'm not paid just to be a bag, am I? I'm paid to make them feel good.

That was paltry stuff compared with the stories he heard of the 'kinkies', men who like to dress up as maids and lick boots and be scolded, or have cream buns thrown at them. Young called this a 'market in illusion . . . where you can buy grunts and groans that are supposed to sound like love.' Love? No, there was scarcely any question of that. It was fantasy dredged from depths which no wife could understand, or would want to, as in this specimen:

> A client took me back to his place, and as soon as I got in the door there was a dirty great coffin standing open. He put me in a white nightie with a rosary in one hand and a Bible in the other and wreath of roses on my head. Then I had to lie down in the coffin. I thought, 'Is this a gag to get my money?' But no, I had my bag in with me. Then he started nailing the lid down, and all the time he was shouting out, 'You're dead now, God damn you to hell!' He'd told me his wife had died. He'd given me a big spanner to knock the lid up again, but I tell you I was wondering if I'd ever get out. I did, though, and when I looked round the place, he'd gone.

[42]

Wayland Young called that a piece of 'majestic oddness'. With the progress of the Sixties, however, it appeared less and less odd, as every placid individual discovered his own secret kink and, what was more, chattered about it happily. To have a simple sex life was *far* too boring. A curious development then took place, which would make a fine study for a social historian. As it became more widely known what antics prostitutes were required to perform to satisfy their clients (the Wayland Young article being so universally read or talked about that one heard stories from it at dinner-tables months later), and as these variations on coitus were attempted by those eager to experiment, so the prostitute was driven to yet more recondite performances until, by 1965, according to Jonathan Aitken, she was hardly required for sexual intercourse at all. Her main function, in some cases her only function, was 'correction', the administering of spankings upon an inert and submissive male. Ladies who made their fortunes with this speciality traded under names such as Miss Cord, Miss Swish, Miss Birchwood, or Sheila the Strong Armed Swede. Whores were no longer needed to satisfy men's dotty dreams, so much as to beat the dreams out of them.

The morals of the whore thus became generally adopted as the morals of the young generation of 'beatniks' and 'hippies', who while thinking to stretch the limits of personal freedom, in fact were laying the foundations of a new slavery. The dangers were recognized by some serious academics whose business was to study social tensions, but their books and articles were not widely read; and by impudent interfering women, whose voices were heard loud enough but whose arguments were so silly they went unheeded. The dangers sewn in the Sixties, with effects enduring many years after, may be summarized as follows:

1. As all rules of conduct were demolished, so all sense of security went with them. When there are rules which govern sexual behaviour, the individual knows what is expected of him and what is prohibited; even if he transgresses the prohibitions, he does so knowingly, and the prohibitions remain. But

[43]

when everything is permitted, as it was in the loose hedonistic world which earned the nickname the 'permissive society', the individual does not know where he stands, where he is anchored. One sexual partner may have different standards from another, whereas before they all had more or less the same conventions, with the result that the individual is perpetually floating in a soup of doubt and fear as to how people will respond to his conduct. Not for nothing was the phrase coined for London youth – the 'crazy mixed-up kids'. They were mixed up because they had no rules to guide them, and were not sure how to use their much-vaunted freedom. Dr Whiteley wrote, 'Thus neuroses of frustration are replaced by neuroses of bewilderment.' It was a revelation to discover that the removal of sexual frustration did not remove sexual anxiety.

2. Because there is nothing you cannot do, you are expected to do, or at least to try, everything. In this way, the new sexual freedom created more problems than it solved, for the individual inherited a new worry – would he live up to expectations? Would he be good enough? Would he be adventurous enough? Might he not be boring? Sexual freedom encouraged blatant competitiveness which was the enemy of ease and relaxation, and substituted the arousal of lust for the subtlety of courtship. The result was not richness, but impoverishment. These reflections did not occur to the Sixties generation; they were not examined until twenty years later, in books such as Celia Haddon's *The Limits of Sex* (1983). In 1963, on the contrary, there were no limits, and therefore no prizes.

3. The explosion in promiscuity naturally encouraged venereal diseases, and although they were contained, the germs had plenty of opportunity to adapt, evolve, and immunize themselves against drugs. Twenty years on, with a new, less controllable outbreak of disease, the effects are felt. In the homosexual community, the legacy of promiscuity has been the horrifying

collapse of all the body's system of immunity in the complaint (it is not a disease) called AIDS, which is both mystifying and mortal. As Professor Ryle wrote recently in the *Times Literary Supplement*, 'It can be argued that the true beneficiaries of the sexual revolution have been the viruses and bacteria that exploit the new vectors created by widespread promiscuity and unusual sexual practises.'

4. The generation which has no moral values has nothing to teach its children. Even when one accepts that morality is a private matter for each person to work out for himself, he still needs to work it out against an established code or background. The generation of the Sixties inherited such a code and rejected it; that of the Eighties has had no firm code to inherit.

5. It was thought, erroneously, that life was more enjoyable when impediments and difficulties were removed. We now know differently. Happiness derives from the encountering of difficulties and the successful overcoming of them, in other words, from achievement. This is as true in sexual matters as it is in mountain-climbing. Mr Aitken, writing in 1966, already spotted the truth. 'The swinger's water-coloured unemotionalism,' he wrote, 'that has destroyed the art of seduction and the thrill of conquest, and substituted the tedium of complaisant repetition, is merely a bore.'

6. The final consequence was the demise of the schoolroom as a place where order prevailed and where moral laxity was punished. Children set the standards, and teachers had either to acquiesce or be scorned. Speaking at Poole in Dorset in 1982, Dr Rhodes Boyson, Junior Education Minister and a former schoolteacher, allowed his anger, not for the first time, to pour forth in a torrent of hyperbole, which concealed nonetheless an acorn of truth: 'Children were brought up in a pathless desert where the world was to be exploited, not

served . . . there was a cheapening of human life and young people were brought up to be selfish, pleasure-seeking, or irresponsible. In schools we had child-centred education [Where else, pray, should education be centred?] which led to deprived children, lower standards, disorderly class-rooms, and defenceless and disillusioned teachers. Our present ills are the ripened and bitter crop of those seeds of the 1960s.'

There were, undoubtedly, many casualties of the permissive age, especially when moral laxity stretched so far as to allow, even to encourage, the wholesale use of dangerous drugs. The long list of youngsters, famous and unknown, who died from heroin, or 'speed', or hashish mixed with alcohol, makes depress-ingly sad reading, and even worse, the apparent reluctance of the young to learn from the mistakes of their heroes and heroines. Pop singers died, and pop fans went on drugging themselves. It was almost as if *every* experience had to be grabbed by a gener-ation bereft of discrimination or self-guidance, bent upon self-destruction as the ultimate 'high'. One girl may be allowed to speak for all of them. Edie Sedgwick was discovered by the American 'star' (it is difficult to know what else to call him) Andy Warhol, who placed her in a number of his unbelievably boring films. She was very quickly sucked into the world of indulgence, and onto the treadmill of pleasure, drugs, bliss, depression, more drugs, greater pleasure, ecstasy, and oblivion. She died, her body a ruin, at the age of twenty-eight. 'She liked walking very close to extinction, always,' said a close friend. 'She believed that to sit around was to rot.'

To listen to Edie's own voice is to hear the authentic echo of the Sixties, with its plaintive earnest naivety. It is, in every sense, pathetic:

Sex and speed, wow! Like, oh God, a 24-hour climax that can go on for days. I'd like to turn on the whole world for just a moment. I'm greedy. I'd like to keep the most for myself and

[46]

a few others, a few of my friends . . . to keep that superlative high, just on the cusp of each day . . . so that I'd radiate sunshine.

Of course, the majority of the young were not as reckless as this, and it would be foolish to castigate a whole generation, as some would wish to do, for the excesses of a few of their number. It may well be argued that the gains of the New Morality – an end to misery disguised as goodness and a freedom to explore the varieties of happiness – outweighed the perils. I myself would certainly take this view. The Sixties did not shirk the issues; this was a generation which welcomed debate and urged discussion. On no subject was the debate more comprehensive, or more enduring, or more relevant to the whole question of the New Morality, than that of pornography. It aroused passions and made fools of people who seemed to go berserk whenever the subject was raised. It made celebrities of nonentities. It closed theatres and muddied books. It was hopelessly confused, but it was, without doubt, the Big Issue of the decade. One hardly needs to turn up an index to know that it must be somewhere in the Sixties that this absurdity was penned: 'Pornography, the true pornography which seeks to excite and succeeds in so doing, is closer to poetry than it is to prose fiction.' (In fact, it was in 1963, and in a learned journal. The author was a poet and Professor of English at Yale University.)

At first, pornography was a rare item, smuggled in one's suitcase on a trip from Paris, or kept under the counter in Soho's shops. There were no blatant 'sex shops' selling aids to orgasm, and the only nudity available was in a decorous magazine called *Health and Efficiency* in which organs were definitely not tumescent and pudenda were hidden in shadow. Change in this field was rapid, and as the sex shops multiplied, so did views on the literature which they sold.

George Steiner, Fellow of Churchill College, Cambridge, was one of the first to cry halt. His objections to pornography were three-fold. In the first place, porn was boring and predictable:

The plain truth is that in literary erotica as well as in the great mass of 'dirty books' the same stimuli, the same contortions and fantasies, occur over and over again with unutterable monotony. In most erotic writing, as in man's wet dreams, the imagination turns, time and time again, inside the bounded circle of what the body can experience. The actions of the mind when we masturbate are not a dance: they are a tread-mill.

Secondly, much of the action encouraged by pornographic writing was impossible:

The notion that one can double one's ecstasy by engaging in *coitus* while being at the same time deftly sodomised is sheer nonsense.

Thirdly, the pornographer is too graphic. Unlike George Eliot, who leaves the reader to work out for himself what happens to Dorothea behind the bedroom door in *Middlemarch*, and thus achieves much greater excitement, the porn merchant has 'no respect for the reader whose imaginative means are set at nil.'

It was somewhat alarming that such matters should be the subject of frank discussion, but the very fact that they had for so long been taboo may be held to excuse Mr Steiner for getting so many things wrong. To call masturbation a 'tread-mill' was to pass judgement upon an action of which the writer disapproved, not to make any objective assessment of the activity. Repetitive it might be, but boring? It was precisely this new openness in referring to masturbation which made the 1960s, for some young people, so refreshingly healthy. From having been told that it was evil, sick, nasty and made you go blind, to now learning that on the contrary if you did not masturbate you were likely to suffer some psychological damage, was a leap of immeasurable dimensions. George Steiner was no doubt correct in arguing that pornography was tedious, but the young did not object to that.

Also, Mr Steiner betrayed the sorry lack of experience of his

[48]

generation in making the extraordinary assertion that it was impossible to enjoy being buggered at the same time as one was engaging in sexual congress of a more usual kind. The youngsters of the Sixties could have told him otherwise. And as for *Middlemarch*, Steiner's confident analogy took one's breath away. Of course George Eliot was a better writer than the porn merchant – one hardly needed telling – and of course her artistry allowed the reader to contribute his own creative imagination in interpreting her prose, but no one looked to pornography for *that*. One read pornography, when one could get hold of it, not to stimulate imagination, but to arouse libido. It was all very simple, except to the academics. George Steiner's one fair point, that widely-disseminated pornography brought a new servitude rather than a new freedom, tended to be lost amidst his misconceptions and his insistence on calling any erotic writing 'pornography'.

Maurice Girodias and Jean-Jacques Pauvert hurried to register their dispute with Steiner. Both being publishers of erotic literature, they had good cause to refute such reactionary ideas. Girodias had pioneered the brave publication in Paris of such writers as Henry Miller, despised in the 1940s, gradually recognized to be of true worth in the 1960s, and in the 1970s the Grand Old Man of American Literature. Pauvert published, also in Paris, a whole erotic library. The French looked upon Anglo-Saxon timidity in this regard as patently ridiculous but endearing, but people like Girodias and Pauvert saw it as more sinister.

Girodias pointed out that we should be free to choose our own reading matter according to our own tastes, however perverted they may appear to be to others. A modest proposal, one might think, but in 1965 thought by some to be revolting in its implications. He did not think that our reading habits should be dictated by a man like Steiner, who time and time again indicated that 'to him the couple is an adequate and sufficient erotic horizon.'

Pauvert was less polite, more trenchant in his criticism. The fact that pornographic books were tedious, he said, should not stop people reading them if they wanted to:

> When Steiner claims that our dreams are 'marketed wholesale' by pornographic literature, his remark is an interesting one but it can prompt the objection that literature has never done anything else but market dreams, and one wonders why this particular critic attaches more importance to his erotic dreams than to the other kinds.

Stung by this rebuke, Mr Steiner returned to the attack with a frenzy which bordered on the hysterical. He began with a sidekick at *The Olympia Reader*, which was 'literally packed with sadism' as was most of Mr Girodias's list, and one page was 'graced with an illustration which would lower the tone of a lavatory wall.'

Steiner's more subtle point, that pornography, if left unbridled, can breed the sort of mentality which allowed Nazism to flourish, was put forward with brutal directness:

> We live in a period in which files of naked men and women were made to masturbate to music or leap into cesspools to drown, and were drawn or photographed doing so, as they are drawn in *The Olympia Reader*. In the Christian literate heart of Europe, naked children were hanged on hooks (as they are hanged in the fantasies of Mr Burroughs*) while their parents were compelled to march past.

The whole question of sadistic pornography and its power to suggest activity which might not have been countenanced otherwise, in other words its power to corrupt, became a steaming issue with the arrest and conviction of the Moors Murderers, Ian Brady and Myra Hindley, who tortured and sexually humiliated children while recording their screams on tape, then buried them

* William Burroughs, *The Naked Lunch*.

[50]

on the Lancashire moors and had themselves photographed over the graves. It was a sordid and disgusting case, which even now arouses anger whenever it is proposed that Myra Hindley might be released from prison one day. The fundamental point for the enemies of pornography was, however, that Brady had a number of books by de Sade in his 'library', and, it was alleged, had submitted his victims to sadistic behaviour that he had first read about in books.

The fear produced by this revelation was manifest in the outcry which followed it. Pamela Hansford Johnson wrote a book, *On Iniquity*, devoted to the theme that the 'permissive' society had created monsters like Brady and Hindley, or at least made it possible for them to flourish, because the increasing availability of sadistic and pornographic writing actually encouraged the commission of crime by emulation. Her proposition was that a man might buy a copy of the collected works of de Sade, think 'Golly, this sodomy sounds like a good idea, and I rather fancy the bit about torture,' then would go out and find someone to practise on. In fairness, she did not put the matter quite so crassly, but that is what it amounted to. If Miss Hansford Johnson was right, and there were many who thought she was, then the way towards more, not less censorship was clearly indicated. She did not, however, consider the fact that other murderers equally repellent had committed their crimes in societies which could not be called 'permissive', nor that many such people could hardly read, let alone cope with the complex prose of the Marquis de Sade.

On the other side were those who thought the dangers of censorship far greater than any risk involved in free pornography. J. W. Lambert, Literary Editor of the *Sunday Times* (and one of the best-read men in England, with a knowledge and memory bordering on the encyclopaedic), averred that 'the appetites of people like Brady are formed long before any books can have influenced them. Their appetites will lead them to literature, not *vice versa.*'

The arguments for and against pornography were taken up by

virtually every newspaper and journal after Brady and Hindley were sentenced. An American professor of Social Philosophy, Ernest van den Haag, convinced of the harmful effects of such literature, subjected the arguments of his opponents to scrupulous logical analysis. He found that Mr Lambert's contention was unproven and unsupported by any evidence. 'At any rate,' he continued, 'the issue is not so much "appetites" – these are common enough although usually unconscious – but their translation into action. This translation can plausibly be fostered by literary, moral, or social support. I think it has been.'

Turning upon Kenneth Allsop, who had made the point that people who do not read sadistic literature commit sadistic crimes, Professor van den Haag dismissed the argument as irrelevant on the grounds that it was still desirable to eliminate one of the possible causes of sadistic crime, even if it was not the only cause. Allsop had also said that far more children were killed by motor accidents and aerial bombardment than by murderers. 'I am against traffic accidents and wars,' wrote the Professor, 'but I do not see why their occurrence argues for not controlling homicidal literature (or for it not being homicidal).'

Van den Haag experienced no difficulty in sorting out what was pornography and what real literature. The former used well-worn phrases and clichés in order not to encumber the main libidinous purpose with any aesthetic merit. 'A critic who is really incapable of distinguishing pornography from literature certainly has no business being one; a critic who is capable of making the distinction has no business testifying that he is not.' Mr Lambert and his cronies among the intellectuals were thereby chastised.

The burden of the Professor's positive contribution to the debate (as opposed to knocking down opponents, which was great fun and tried one's syntax wonderfully) was that there was no such thing as harmless porn.

I believe that pornography nearly always leads to sadistic pornography. By definition, pornography de-individualises and dehumanises sexual acts; by eliminating all the contexts it reduces people simply to bearers of impersonal sensations of pleasure and pain. This de-humanisation eliminates the empathy that restrains us ultimately from sadism and non-consensual acts.

This was very persuasive, and quite possibly true, but it begged the very questions which van den Haag accused the liberators of begging, i.e. that there was no evidence or proof to support this (admitted) 'belief', and that the implication that pornography 'nearly always' led to sadism was nonsense. It meant that every person who read pornography for fun (and there must have been a few million of these in Britain alone) suffered such disruption of his inhibitory factor that he was, as a direct result of his reading, a potential or almost certain psychopath.

J. W. Lambert, responding to what was clearly an attack, albeit in a polite monthly, said that people like van den Haag needed watching. He detected in the Professor a degree of disguised authoritarianism which was 'no longer acceptable in societies which have moved beyond the primitive'. He further castigated van den Haag's blinkered passion for absolutes and his fundamentalist head. Without naming her, he also allowed himself a swipe at Mary Whitehouse, whose voice was naturally heard piping away in the wings; worse than the distortion of academics, he said, was 'prurience disguised as righteousness'.

What was really at issue was not the nature or desirability of pornographic books, but their availability to anyone without the discernment to test and measure their effect, and it was always tacitly understood that the sponsors of control or abolition had in mind people who were too stupid to make these judgements for themselves. The debate about pornography concealed a peculiarly English complaint – snobbishness – and the move to ban erotic literature was an attempt to assert the inferior status of those who might be tempted to enjoy it. This in turn led to a frantic and at times risible campaign to enforce censorship. In the end, it was censorship which emerged from the

Sixties with a dirty face, not pornography, which had never made claims to purity in the first place. The death agony of the censorship lobby provided one of the most comic entertainments of the decade, and it is to this that we should now turn.

— 3 —

Retreat of the Censor

Novels with a dominant erotic dimension, and those which contain graphic descriptions of sexual activity, are now freely available at respectable bookshops throughout the country. Many of the authors are well known and enjoy high reputations. Had anyone been brave enough to publish, stock, or offer for sale a novel by, say, Harold Robbins before 1960 he would almost certainly have been sent to prison. For example, in 1955 a bookseller was sentenced by a local magistrate in Hornsey, north London, to two months' imprisonment for 'handling' a novel by D. H. Lawrence, *Lady Chatterley's Lover*. The fact that this was a major, if flawed, novel by one of the twentieth-century's finest writers was not held to be the point; it was indecent and obscene because it described on several occasions sexual congress between Lady Chatterley and her gardener Mellors and actually used the word 'fuck'. For this reason, Lawrence's novel had been for thirty years an outcast, unavailable, unbuyable, invisible, non-existent. You could buy it in Paris and, if you dared, smuggle it through Her Majesty's Customs into England, but the penalties were high. Lady Chatterley was a most suitable candidate to be the heroine of the Sixties censorship battle, and her unwitting producer and director was the Labour backbench Member of Parliament, later Home Secretary, Roy Jenkins.

The 1959 Obscene Publications Act was sponsored by Jenkins precisely in order to free literature from the shackles which kept pornography in brown paper covers. It was an attempt to distinguish between the frankly erotic and the genuinely artistic, to prise them apart, so that a work of art should no longer suffer

[55]

the same ignominious treatment as a book designed to assist masturbation. The distinction was to be made between those books which have a tendency 'to deprave and corrupt'* and those which do not, with the proviso that even those which might deprave and corrupt would not be proscribed if their publication were for the public good.

Unfortunately, the Act was badly drafted in a number of ways. The distinctions were not clear, the vocabulary susceptible to too many interpretations. It was left open to debate how one person might be depraved and corrupted by a book and another not, how the resulting depravity might be measured or proven, or what, in the end, obscenity actually meant. The most serious anomaly of all was inherent: that a book may deprave and corrupt and *at the same time* be for the public benefit. This concept gave the Act a logical club-foot over which it was to stumble so many times in the ensuing years that the battle between censors and liberationists in Britain became a long-running and wildly enjoyable comedy. 'The legal authorities of this country,' said Mr Jenkins five years later, 'can be relied upon to mishandle any issue touching the censorship of books. Unfortunately this record of ineptitude does not make them fight shy of this subject.'

From 1960 the law held in effect that a man may be guilty of a criminal offence if he published a book which a jury may *later* decide to be obscene or indecent; he could not know in advance if he was committing an offence or not.

The report of the Arts Council's Working Party on the Obscenity Laws (1968) put it this way:

Whereas any man who robs a cash-box knows (or could have ascertained) that he is committing a crime, a man who writes a book may have no intimation that he is at work on a criminal offence till the moment he finds himself condemned to prison for perhaps three years and to payment of a fine of unlimited

---

* This formula dates from 1868.

amount and of prohibitive costs. Which is a little late. He cannot inform himself in advance because the only issue to be resolved in court is, in essence, whether this particular jury's unbuttressed opinion of what is innocuous agrees with the writer's opinion. If it does not, then the writer has committed a crime.

Furthermore, the jury would be directed as to what was obscene or indecent by a judge whose ideas on such matters might be peculiar, to say the least. As late as 1965 Lord Chief Justice Parker made a ruling on the meaning of indecency which stands to this day:

> 'Indecent' means unbecoming and immodest, something that offends the ordinary modesty of the average man . . . If you are on the beach with your children and a woman takes off her clothes, that is indecent. We just don't do that sort of thing in this country. Or let us say you were attending an athletic or sporting event and the athletes, beautiful physiques though they may have, have not got clothing which fits properly, and as they perform you see their private parts. This is indecent.

With such opinions being expressed by the judiciary on 'indecency', it is hardly to be wondered at that their understanding of what made an 'obscene publication' was grossly archaic, and managed to turn Mr Jenkins' Act on its head. Only a long series of court cases over a period of eleven years could clarify the law and, let it be said, educate the legislators.

The first and most famous of these cases was the trial of *Lady Chatterley's Lover*, followed by *Fanny Hill*, *The Naked Lunch*, *Last Exit to Brooklyn*, and culminating in the *Oz* trial as the 1970s began. These were only the major ones. Piled together in one sentence like that, it suggests that the British must have gone out of their minds to start prosecuting *books*, of all things, and that there was little difference between the minds that could seek to ban these books and those other minds in Germany which had sought to burn them thirty years earlier. Yet that is exactly what happened.

Liberalization was slow at first, then accelerated, then sent all houses tumbling down in a matter of months. In 1960 the Folio Society published the classic *Golden Ass* by Lucius Apuleius, and got away with it because it was, theoretically at least, only available to members. (They had previously published Boccaccio's naughty *Decameron* and escaped censure – one reason being that the editions were too expensive to fall into the hands of the *hoi polloi*. A paperback would have been seized immediately.) Of the commercial publishers, the rashest was without doubt Anthony Blond, who in 1961 put out an anthology of friendship entitled *Eros*, which turned out to be a collection of prose and poetry all with a loosely homosexual theme. It escaped prosecution presumably because only the *cognoscenti* recognized its subject matter.

By 1964, there were glossy magazines on sale portraying semi-naked ladies in suggestive poses. Nothing about *Penthouse* or *Mayfair* could have been called pornographic, in so far as they contained no pictures of orgasm, or erection, or vaginas, merely cleverly posed portraits, but such was the British obsession with smut that the first magazine was chastised in Parliament by Mrs Anne Kerr, MP, and the second roundly attacked in *The Spectator* by David Holbrook. Mrs Kerr said, 'The House should be on record as opposing the dissemination of this type of vicious literature . . . perverted muck,' while Mr Holbrook opined that 'if *Mayfair* sells half a million, we must be a nation of masturbators'; he obviously thought that masturbation was either unusual or reprehensible or both.

By 1969 it was possible to bring out Philip Roth's amusing *Portnoy's Complaint*, in which the hero spends much of his time masturbating, in spite of Mr Holbrook's continued disapproval. Holbrook was, however, a stern but reasonable critic whose case was always cogently argued. One could not say as much for the posse of prudes who aligned themselves with him, such as Cyril Black MP, a man who gave the impression he was terrified of sex, and Mrs Whitehouse, who would not have been noticed but for her nuisance value to the hungry popular press. Between them, these two brought a number of private prosecutions whenever they thought the officials of the country were not moving fast enough to protect our morals, and if they were thwarted, they ignored the 1959 Act and manufactured grounds for trial under the 1953 Postal Act as well as older statutes concerning gross indecency, vagrancy and blasphemy. Mrs Whitehouse appeared to enjoy the fame that her mischief-making brought her, and to draw no lessons whatever from the fact that ultimately all her little 'victories' were swept aside, and the law with regard to published material now, twenty years later, operates as if she had never existed.

The Sixties were a period of turmoil and muddle in the field of censorship, as progressive steps overlapped with constraints still in force, so that one hardly knew where one was. At one point, the film of *Oh! Calcutta* was banned while the stage show of the same name depicting the same silly antics (nude bottoms and so on) could be seen by anyone in London. Similarly, Dingle Foot MP told the House of Commons how he had bought a copy of *The Perfumed Garden* at London Airport on his way out of England, and when he returned a few weeks later the book was confiscated by Customs officials.

To make matters even more confusing, really 'hard' pornography was available in Soho shops alongside fairly innocent stuff and aids to lust, such as vibrators and frilly knickers. It was only much later that the public discovered why. The Obscene Publications Squad of the Metropolitan Police, popularly known as the 'Dirty Squad', was far dirtier than anyone had imagined. Throughout the 1960s some police officers from the most senior downwards had operated a protection racket in Soho which permitted hard pornography to be imported and sold against regular and exorbitant pay-offs. Sporadic raids were made to keep up appearances, but the offenders were always warned by the police in advance what day the charade would take place, and the profits continued to pour into police pockets. Corruption was not exposed until 1977, when the culprits were finally brought to trial.

Theatre censorship was also laid to rest in the 1960s. Since 1737 the Lord Chamberlain, a member of the Royal Household, had been empowered to scrutinize every script for theatre performance, which had by law to be submitted to his office, and could either demand changes in the script before he would permit a public performance, or prevent its appearance on the stage altogether. There was no appeal against his decisions, and once a play had been passed by him, it could not be prosecuted. The Royal Court Theatre finally made a stand against this anachronistic potentate with Edward Bond's play *Saved* in 1964, and since there were few people who dared look so silly as to oppose the movement, the Lord Chamberlain's powers in this regard were abolished in 1968. (This did not prevent Mrs Whitehouse from bringing a private prosecution against *The Romans in Britain*, a play by Howard Brenton at the National Theatre, as late as 1982, claiming that the actors engaged in an act of gross indecency on stage by simulating buggery. She did not see the play in question, and dropped the prosecution after her counsel had made all his points and before defence counsel could reply to them.)

Nevertheless, it was in the field of published books that the main battle was to be fought, and once again the unspoken assumption was that paperbacks, which were cheap enough to be bought by the less discerning, needed to be controlled, whereas hardbacks (and theatre performances for that matter) were available only to a more prosperous élite and were therefore in less need of restrictions. In the trials which ensued, this was the principal subconscious preoccupation.

Lady Chatterley's Lover had circulated surreptitiously for a long time in foreign editions, and latterly in an American edition. D. H. Lawrence was highly respected in literary circles (it seems superfluous, even insulting, to write this now, but it was not by any means so in 1960), his work studied at universities. No course on Lawrence which included consideration of *Lady Chatterley's Lover* could offer copies of this book to students, as none legally existed, except in severely expurgated form. The situation was patently ridiculous, and someone sooner or later would have to do something about it.

In 1959 Weidenfeld and Nicolson had brought out a hardback edition of Vladimir Nabokov's funny and perceptive novel *Lolita*, which dealt with the infatuation of a middle-aged man for a pubescent girl. John Gordon screamed abuse at it as a 'dirty book', thus assuring it a wide market – indeed one critic said that Gordon was responsible single-handedly for making it a best-seller. Still, it was not burned in the streets. The climate seemed propitious for introducing Lawrence's notorious book to the public in an unbowdlerized version.

The most famous paperback publishing house in the English-speaking world, Penguin Books, had an illustrious record of making the great classics of literature available in cheap editions. 1960 would mark their twenty-fifth anniversary and, coincidentally, the thirtieth anniversary of the death of D. H. Lawrence. To celebrate the double event, they announced in the *Bookseller* of 9 January 1960 plans to publish eight of Lawrence's books, including *Lady Chatterley's Lover*. Allen Lane, Penguin's Chairman, had a shrewd idea that he would not only make publishing history but a pretty penny as well, and printed an advance of 200,000 copies. Then he tactfully sent a dozen copies to the Director of Public Prosecutions as a statement of intent, whereupon the DPP immediately declared he would prosecute. Penguin kept their stocks closely locked up pending proceedings, and prepared to do battle.

The saga may well have been short-lived had it not been for the chance which placed upon the scene a DPP of extraordinary obtuseness, Sir Theobald Mathew (the very same who thought he could 'stamp out' homosexuality), and a prosecuting counsel who matched him in antediluvian attitudes, Mr Mervyn Griffith-Jones. This advocate did not need to simulate indignation for his brief, as he manifestly believed Lawrence's book to be lewd and worthless, and that it was his mission to stem a tide of wickedness and reconfirm the proper values of literature. His only witness would be the book itself, since its degradation and iniquity must be obvious to anyone who had the misfortune to read it.

Defence counsel, Gerald Gardiner, had more subtle tactics up his sleeve. He would call 'expert' witnesses to testify that publication was for the general good, eminent academics who would underwrite its literary worth, and one schoolgirl who would declare that she had not been depraved and corrupted by reading it. Initially, 300 witnesses were on hand. This was eventually reduced to seventy, of whom half actually appeared in the witness-box.

The trial originally set for August, took place in November 1960, and lasted six days. It aroused intense public interest and was remarkable for the opinions expressed in court by two men, Griffith-Jones himself and the author of *The Uses of Literacy*, Richard Hoggart, who was called by the defence.

Griffith-Jones set the tone within the first hour; his opening address to the jury contained remarks so precious that they are even now resurrected as a warning to young men at the Bar:

> You may think that one of the ways in which you can read this book, and test it from the most liberal outlook, is to ask yourselves the question, when you have read it through, would you approve of your young sons, young daughters – because girls can read as well as boys – reading this book. Is it a book that you would have lying around in your house? Is it a book that you would wish your wife or your servants to read?

John Sutherland has aptly called this 'a lapse so grotesque it has gone into folklore.' Five of the jury had difficulty reading the oath! It was unlikely that any of them had so much as *seen* a servant. Nor surprisingly, there was a rumble of laughter in court. A recent chronicler of the Sixties, Francis Wheen, has written that 'the atmosphere was that of a small and private club, whose members fear that the riff-raff may be let in.'

Unchastened, Griffith-Jones went on to list the number of

times certain offensive words occurred in the text (he did not disclose whether he had counted them himself). There were, he told the jury, 30 'fucks' or 'fuckings', 14 'cunts', 13 'balls', 6 'shits', 6 'arses', 4 'cocks' and 3 'piss'. The inference was that any book which would use such language could not be for the public good, while the astonishment of those present arose from the realization that counsel had apparently read the book quite unaware that it was a work of clear literary merit. He dealt with *Lady Chatterley's Lover* as if it were trash, which was precisely what the Obscene Publications Act of 1959 had been designed to prevent; he even grew indignant at the number of times the word 'womb' was mentioned.

So confident was Mr Griffith-Jones in the purity of his case that he told the amazed courtroom that he did not intend to call any witnesses at all. (It was only much later that news leaked out that he had been unable to find a single professor or author of distinction willing to testify that the book was without literary merit. One wonders what thoughts crossed his mind when he knew that he was alone in the world with the percipience to understand that Lawrence was a base pornographer.) Mr Gardiner, on the other hand, produced authors, clerics, dons, journalists, who paraded into the box to sing the praises of D. H. Lawrence so fulsomely that it became embarrassing. Under cross-examination, they produced some choice moments.

The Bishop of Woolwich, for example, contended that every Christian should read *Lady Chatterley's Lover*, and young people especially would find it a useful guide in preparation for marriage. The love-making which Lady Chatterley so energetically enjoys with her gardener was described by the good bishop as 'an act of Holy Communion.' This was all too much for Mr Griffith-Jones, who never expected to see the day when adultery would be defended by a prince of the Church; it became increasingly clear that in his eyes the prosecution should really be directed against Lady Chatterley for allowing herself to be possessed by someone other than her husband.

Not only that, but her gardener to boot! The second theme

of the trial, that such goings-on should not be admitted between people of different classes, constantly underlay the questioning. Richard Hoggart, like D. H. Lawrence himself, was an author and lecturer of working-class origin. When, at the request of defence counsel, he read out long passages of Lawrence's powerful musical prose in a manner which left no doubt as to their beauty, the entire courtroom stilled to a silence so concentrated that one could hear a feather float. This demonstration thoroughly confused Mr Griffith-Jones, who had been busy reading other passages like a smutty-minded schoolboy. Mr Hoggart delivered his final, cruel *coup de grâce* when, echoing the Bishop of Woolwich, he declared that D. H. Lawrence was a 'puritan'.

Lawrence's puritanism had been evident as early as 1929. 'Genuine pornography,' he wrote, 'is almost always underworld, it doesn't come out into the open. You can recognise it by the insult it offers, invariably, to sex, and to the human spirit. Pornography is the attempt to insult sex, to do dirt on it. This is unpardonable.'

Poor Mr Griffith-Jones! The court was left with the impression that he was the one 'doing dirt' on sex, not Lawrence, and that he deserved the rebuke from Mr Gardiner, who said, 'There are minds which are unable to see beauty where it exists, and doubt the integrity of purpose in an author where it is obvious.'

The jury found Penguin Books not guilty. Two million copies were then sold within twelve months, and nearly seven million have been sold to date. It was not however true that Lady Chatterley made Allen Lane a millionaire – *that* he was already.

The trial of Lady Chatterley was an important event, and a signal pointing towards the tone of the decade to come. Within a very short time it would seem unthinkable that the British had tolerated censorship well into the second half of the twentieth century, or had pilloried a citizen of whom they should have been proud. But there was some way to go yet. The debate about Lady Chatterley did not evaporate with her acquittal, but spluttered on for a year or more. Dr F. R. Leavis, the foremost living authority on Lawrence, had declined to appear for the defence. He kept his reasons to himself, but the rumour circulated that the great critic both distrusted the motives of Penguin Books and feared for the outcome of the trial. He suspected that huge profits rather than the defence of literature were the true attraction, and he worried lest the publicity might result in Lawrence's being associated forever after with his least representative book. In this he has been proved right. But at least some of those who read Lady Chatterley for the juicy bits may have enjoyed the rest and gone on to discover the real core of Lawrence's work.

That there were still some, in relatively high places, who persisted in denigrating Lawrence was demonstrated by an hysterical letter from the bizarre Edith Sitwell, published in the *Times Literary Supplement.* It is a beautiful item, managing to display the arrogance and vanity of the woman, as well as her neurosis, in a very few lines. 'The public canonisation of that insignificant dirty little book *Lady Chatterley's Lover* was a signal to persons who wish to unload the filth of their minds on the British public. As the author of *Gold Coast Customs* I can scarcely be accused of shirking reality, but I do not wish to spend the rest of my life with my nose nailed to other people's lavatories.'

Edith Sitwell had nursed for years an abiding hatred of Lawrence which distorted her judgement. Lawrence had based some aspects of the character of the cuckolded Sir Clifford Chatterley on Edith's brother Osbert Sitwell, very accurately and perceptively as it happens, but what stuck in Edith's gullet was that an upstart from the slums should presume to use real writers as 'material' instead of keeping their places, and then to mock the character for his sexual misfortune and his class. Thus, in *Taken Care Of* she had written that *Lady Chatterley's Lover* was 'a very dirty and completely worthless book, of no literary importance' and Lady Chatterley herself was 'that nasty little nymphomaniac'. One wonders why the prosecution did not approach Dame Edith to appear as their one witness. She would surely have grabbed the opportunity, but whether her hysteria would have done the prosecution any good is another matter.

By far the mightiest repercussion of the Chatterley trial was the contribution to the debate by John Sparrow, Warden of All Souls Oxford, a man of so few words that his article on Chatterley was almost the first occasion anyone had seen his work in print. *Encounter* magazine published in 1961 a series of articles by such luminaries as Rebecca West, Andrew Shonfield, Katherine Ann Porter and Raymond Williams. The sediment had settled, it seemed, and there was nothing more to say, when Sparrow popped up in February 1962 with his piece 'Regina v. Penguin Books Ltd: An Undisclosed Element in the Case', which had the effect of pouring vinegar on an ant-hill. With the suppressed glee of a schoolboy about to create mayhem with his catapult, the Warden told us that he had, almost accidentally, stumbled across a most important fact, namely that everyone had misunderstood Lawrence's book; that no one had seen what the gardener Mellors was really up to when he was in Lady Chatterley's company; that, in short, prosecution and defence had got it all wrong.

Towards the end of the book there is a passage to which reference was made in court in Mr Griffith-Jones's closing speech. He did not explain it, merely commented that it was 'not very easy, sometimes, not very easy, you know, to know what he is driving at.' Was counsel too shy to elucidate? Or did he really not know? Mr Sparrow certainly knew, and, impishly, he told us. The passage in question was referred to as 'the night of sensual passion'; and it contained an unmistakable description of Mellors buggering Lady Chatterley.

Now, Mr Sparrow did not suggest that Lady Chatterley was an unwilling participant, nor that she failed to enjoy the experience. What he did suggest was (a) that Lawrence sinned against his own principle of not 'doing dirt' on sex by describing it frankly, since on this occasion he used elliptical phrases which smacked of innuendo rather than honesty; (b) that none of the thirty-five expert witnesses appeared to have understood Lawrence's intentions at all, if they missed such a fundamental point; (c) that

[66]

the verdict may well have been quite different if they had so understood it. Sparrow did not want to propose that the verdict *ought* to have been different, only that it would most likely have been so. 'The shock to the jury might have been greater,' he wrote, 'if the true nature of Lady Chatterley's love had been put squarely to them. It may well be that the policy of silence on this crucial point saved the day for the defence.'

Against all expectation, however, Mr Sparrow did not have the last word. That belonged to the novelist Colin MacInnes, who in a reply to Sparrow, written, it seemed, in white hot fury and with scarcely concealed contempt for the Warden, the courts and everyone else who played their squalid game, cried out for a stop to this pernicious belittlement of a great artist. His points were several, and were expressed with mounting vehemence. First, it was foolish and insulting for lawyers to arrogate judgement upon a work of art:

It is a total betrayal of a writer of Lawrence's gifts and intentions to presume to defend his art on grounds other than those chosen, at great human sacrifice, by himself: that is, in terms of artistic truth. The only possible reply of anyone asked to appear as a 'defence witness', and who had some understanding of what art is, and what law, was to refuse to dishonour Lawrence (and their own critical reputations) by even considering the proposal.

The seventy 'experts' who were prepared to go into the witness-box and the thirty-five who actually did, were equally guilty of traducing Lawrence's talents, and equally stupid not to see that was what they were doing. The net result of the trial was that everyone in the country now recognized *Lady Chatterley's Lover* as a 'dirty book'. 'It would have been better had the book remained "banned" . . . than that Lawrence's vision should have been defended in terms acceptable to an obscenity law and to a semi-literate courtroom.'

Secondly, it was even more despicable to draw attention to

[67]

any one aspect of the sexuality of a character as if it were more significant than the characterization itself. The human body being the shape it is, doubtless every sexual possibility was practised, had been practised and always would be practised, and so what? 'No Englishman, since the puritan occupation of our country, can write of sexual matter in an acceptive spirit: that is, with a simple recognition of physical fact prior to any consequent judgement of behaviour: and no Englishman can read such a writer in this spirit either.' It was Lawrence's achievement that he managed to transcend these self-inflicted wounds, to dismiss them, ignore them. No wonder Mr MacInnes was angry, for the whole pantomime of the Lady Chatterley trial had shown that Lawrence, thirty years later, was still wasting his time, that the English were still as intelligent in sexual matters as a thirteen-year-old schoolboy.

And now, along came Mr Sparrow, not to redress the balance, not to breathe some sanity into the proceedings, but to add a whiff of his own to the excrement. That is not how MacInnes put it, but that unmistakably is the impression he gave of his feelings. 'On the decisions of this hateful trial,' he wrote, 'a one-man court of criminal appeal, in the person of the Warden of All Souls, has now passed adverse judgment; and pronounced it in terms this court itself would thoroughly understand . . . the "witnesses" insulted Lawrence by making him out a literary sex maniac whose intentions were nevertheless honourable, and their scourge, the Warden, continues the good work by concentrating even more superfluously on the witnesses' failure to spot one specialized aberration.'

MacInnes concluded with the withering remark that none of this infantile academic sniping actually mattered. 'Who cares if dons, barristers, and pedants make idiots of themselves when they speak and write of art?' Well, MacInnes cared for one, and beneath the invective lay the knowledge that it did all matter, though it ought not to. He hoped that the younger generation, growing to adulthood in the Sixties, would at last look with maturity upon the work of D. H. Lawrence and love his books not because they occasionally spelt out wicked words or from time to time depicted a scene of love-making, but because they celebrated life.

If anything must emerge with credit from the whole Chatterley saga, it is this *cri de coeur* from Colin MacInnes, now mostly forgotten, but still deserving to be read in its entirety. For it correctly identified the pathetic English obsession with the sinfulness of sex as being at the root of all the nonsense (and which is why, incidentally, the working classes were meant to be protected for their own good by their betters, who understood sin), and it heralded, or hoped it heralded, a new age when such antics as the Chatterley trial would be held to scorn. That age has thankfully come, but the rest of the Sixties were to be spattered with yet more book-trials, in which the innocent as well as the salacious were dragged through the ludicrous system, before the lesson was finally learnt. One can only guess at the frustration of people like MacInnes, whose voice seemed to disappear unheeded into the ether.

Still there were the happy faces of the literary entrepreneurs, who gloried in the commercial success of notoriety, to balance the sour tight-lipped anger of the artist. Penguin Books Ltd, as they passed their two-millionth sale of Lady Chatterley, carried the inevitable enticement on the covers of Lawrence's other books, 'by the author of *Lady Chatterley's Lover.*'

The next loose woman to be reprimanded by a British court was the naughty eighteenth-century whore Fanny Hill. Though celebrated in the history of literature, John Cleland's *Fanny Hill: Memoirs of a Woman of Pleasure* had, amazingly, never been published in a legitimate edition. The first appearance of the book, in 1749, had been clandestine, and all subsequent editions were likewise either shady or expurgated. The paperback publisher Mayflower announced that it would publish the first real edition of *Fanny Hill* in 1963. As with Penguin and Lady Chatterley, they made their intentions known to legal authorities and awaited developments. Alas, they did not proceed as expected. The apostles of restriction were not going to be thwarted again, by submitting their case to a jury, where there might be men of reason and intelligence who would refuse to do their duty. There were other ways. *Lady Chatterley's Lover* had been prosecuted under Section 2 of the 1959 Obscene Publications Act, which sought to penalize offending publishers; Section 3 of the Act was designed to catch 'specialist' booksellers, and judgment in such a case could be passed by a magistrate acting alone, not before a jury. So Mayflower Books were left in peace, and a Mr Gold of Tottenham Court Road, who had a peculiar shop selling jokes and magic tricks for children at one end of the counter, and pornographic publications at the other, was selected as the putative offender.

Police officers found copies of *Fanny Hill* in Mr Gold's shop and took one to the Bow Street magistrate, Sir Robert Blundell, who thereupon issued a search warrant. One hundred and seventy-one copies of the article were seized from Mr Gold's shop, and he himself summoned to appear before Sir Robert in December. Mayflower protested that this could mean they would face (or rather individual retailers would face) prosecutions in various parts of the country, for whatever Sir Robert Blundell's decision, it would have effect only in the area within his jurisdiction. That was, however, beside the point. Under the 1959 Act, the magistrate was acting properly in bringing charges against a retailer, and the frustrated publishers could do little but watch and weigh the consequences. It befell Mr Gold to show cause why the seized copies should not be destroyed.

Prosecuting counsel was again Mr Mervyn Griffith-Jones, who again had to declare that he did not intend to call any witnesses (presumably because he could not find any). His attack concentrated solely upon the allegation that *Fanny Hill* was a book which would tend to deprave and corrupt. Griffith-Jones had a cleaner task this time, for there could be no nonsense about the holiness and purity of the author's purpose (as there had been with Lawrence), it being clear for all to see that Cleland wrote a frankly titillating tale. But that he, or Sir Robert Blundell, should think this innocent romp could corrupt even a half-witted virgin, beggared belief. Fanny is made to describe her experiences in language which is at once coy and humorous, as though she were saying, 'Come on, chaps, sex is to be enjoyed and not to be debated in this solemn fashion. What's the matter with you?' In vain Mr Griffith-Jones would search the book for the 'fucks' and 'balls' he so condemned; here he would only find 'mighty members' and 'tender passages'; this did not, however, discountenance him. He managed to count twenty-seven occasions in the book when sexual intercourse (or 'copulation' as he preferred to call it) took place, so he had his statistic after all.

The defence was conducted by Jeremy Hutchinson, who called seven 'expert' witnesses from the world of literature. The first was Peter Quennell, poet, critic, and literary historian. Perhaps bearing in mind John Sparrow's revelations about Constance Chatterley's 'night of sensual passion', Mr Quennell said that Fanny Hill was 'an advocate of the pleasures of straightforward sex and when she describes deviations she makes it clear that she does not approve of them or considers them inferior substitutes for straightforward enjoyment.' Mr Quennell also thought *Fanny Hill* was of historical interest, being the literary counterpart of Hogarth's *The Harlot's Progress*, and that it represented a step in the emancipation of women, for Fanny claimed the right to have her own pleasure considered, as well as her lover's.

Mr Griffith-Jones asked Quennell if he would list some passages which he considered of historical interest, which he duly did, for the next day's hearing, producing forty such passages. Griffith-Jones was not convinced that people who bought the book would do so for the enlightenment it brought to their social history.

The next witness, H. Montgomery Hyde, thought the book a work of literature and not an example of pornography; having just written a history of pornography, Dr Hyde might be supposed more able than most to make the distinction. Karl Miller said *Fanny Hill* was as rich as *Moll Flanders* by Defoe. The fourth witness to be called was the inconoclastic Marghanita Laski, who had had to read the book for review some time earlier. She had expected, she said, to be disgusted and miserable after reading it; 'but I was surprised that I felt cheerful and felt I had read a gay little book.'

Miss Laski returned to the theme time and again, that Fanny Hill was 'jolly', 'refreshing and pleasing', all of which had little effect upon Mr Griffith-Jones, who must have learnt to distrust academics like venereal disease. He asked Miss Laski how the book could be of social value historically, and she obliged by pointing out several words used by John Cleland before anyone else, not that Cleland had invented them, but that he was the first to put them in print; such as 'settee bed', 'tea-time', 'birthday suit', 'well-to-do'.

Crown counsel's irritation with academics was made perfectly plain with the next witness, Professor Iain Watt, whose evidence maintained that not many people would actually get through *Fanny Hill* since it required intellectual attention. 'If that's all you have to say,' remarked Mr Griffith-Jones, 'we will leave it.'

Anthony Storr and Robert Pitman were the final witnesses. On the fourth and last day, Mr Hutchinson reminded the magistrate of his ominous duty. 'Owing to the fact that these proceedings have been brought under the forfeiture provisions,' he said, 'you are here sitting alone in effect to decide whether the ordinary reader on this side of the Atlantic should be allowed to read this novel by John Cleland.' He also could not resist, like others before him, pointing out that it was Mr Griffith-Jones who represented the pornographic mind, not John Cleland: 'If you start from the premiss that sex is dirty and in itself is depraved, then of course you speak as Mr Griffith-Jones did of the "kicks" in the book and "hot passages" and so on.'

Sir Robert Blundell was not one jot overwhelmed by his duty. Not even bothering to invite Mr Griffith-Jones to address him in reply to Mr Hutchinson, he took just over one minute to declare his decision that the order to forfeit and destroy the books should proceed. Police removed the 171 copies from the court and burned them. In Brighton, Sheffield, Birmingham, Manchester, local police forces took their cue from the sage of Bow Street and sent uniformed officers into local bookshops to confiscate Cleland's bawdy novel. No one appeared to be embarrassed by this cretinous display of British hypocrisy; the Profumo scandal was in full swing, and the expensive edition of *Fanny Hill* (at 2 guineas, in contrast to Mayflower's paperback at 3s 6d) continued to be placed on sale unmolested. The implications were blatant and crude, yet lost on the most perceptive men, such as Peregrine Worsthorne, who wrote, 'It would surely be odd for a society pledged to monogamous marriage to allow any citizen with a few shillings in his pocket to buy *Fanny Hill*.' All right, of course, for the citizen with a few pounds in his pocket. (Incidentally, *Fanny Hill* promotes the virtues of monogamous marriage – there is no adultery in it whatever.)

Twenty years later, *Fanny Hill* may be bought in most book-shops in a paperback edition with impunity to the retailer and safety to the reader.

William Burroughs' *The Naked Lunch* was never formally prosecuted in Britain, for reasons which are far from clear. It is not literature, like *Lady Chatterley's Lover*, nor is it honest bawdy, like *Fanny Hill*, but devoid of almost any graceful feature or any merit whatever, it must be one of the most crassly written and unpleasant novels in circulation. Its only purpose, it would seem, is to shock, in which it succeeds handsomely. There are passages of frankly nauseating horror, in which bodily discharges are described in repetitive fashion, and the anus is the star attraction. Apparently, a copy was sent to the Director of Public Prosecutions at the end of 1964, and he decided to take no action. There was a cheeky rumour in London at the time that the DPP's office employed a civil servant whose sole duty was to read books all day and advise the DPP whether or not to prosecute. This official's only and certain test was to observe if he felt the stirrings of an erection to result from what he was reading, in which case he would deem the book obscene. Well,

The Naked Lunch clearly produced no such signs of tumescence; the fact that the functionary probably chucked up in the lavatory was not held to be strong enough evidence of arousal.

There was real substance to the rumour. 'A Treasury Solicitor was asked privately what guided him in recommending a book for prosecution,' reported the Arts Council's Working Party. 'He replied – in confidence, so he must remain anonymous – that the test he used was whether the book made him feel randy. "Entirely subjective," he said, "but what else is there?"'

The Naked Lunch is worth a mention when talking of censorship, nonetheless, because it was scrutinized in the pages of the *Times Literary Supplement* for weeks on end, and afforded all and sundry an opportunity to show their colours. The list is too long to examine here, but it did demonstrate into what knots the 'experts' can entangle themselves when attempting to defend a book. The whole process is absurd anyway – that a book should be 'defended'; it should be read or used to protect the table from coffee-stains. Miss Mary McCarthy may be allowed the only voice in this debate, as illustrating the sort of things a lady of letters might say when pushed into a corner:

> Seen in terms of space, history shrivels into a mere wrinkling or furrowing of the surface as in an aerial relief-map or one of those pieced-together aerial photographs known in the trade as mosaics. The oldest memory in *The Naked Lunch* is of jacking-off* in boyhood latrines, a memory recaptured through pederasty. This must be the first space novel, the first serious piece of science fiction – the others are entertainment ... The sexual climax, the jet of sperm, accompanied by a whistling scream, is often a death spasm, and the 'perfect' orgasm would seem to be the posthumous orgasm of the hanged man, shooting his jissom into pure space.

* American slang for masturbation.

The reader will look in vain for some clue that Mary McCarthy is pulling his leg.

The last major case involving the prosecution of a book was Hubert Selby Jnr's *Last Exit to Brooklyn*, another American import published in Britain by Calder & Boyars in 1966. It is, in the view of this reader at least, virtually illiterate, but it does have some power to upset and is *au fond* a severe moral tract. The one scene which caused most concern was the murder by repeated rape of the prostitute called Tralala. Tory backbenchers worked themselves up into a frenzy about this book, led by Sir Charles Taylor and Sir Cyril Black, and were bitter with frustration when the DPP decided not to prosecute. Sir Cyril would not take that lying down.

Sir Cyril Black was already well known as an energetic busybody and enemy of freedom. His voice was constantly heard inveighing against the advertising of alcoholic drinks, the opening of fun-fairs on Sundays, the activities of homosexuals, the sale of contraceptives from automatic machines, even the excuses made by psychiatrists to avoid the recommendation of stern discipline. In the sarcastic words of one commentator, he was 'a man much preoccupied with other people's sins, and is in the fortunate position of knowing what causes sin and what prevents it. His knowledge is derived from the scriptures and, ultimately, from God; and it never seems to occur to him that he may be mistaken.' Sir Cyril was not taken very seriously, but he was, it could not be denied, a wretched nuisance.

Sir Cyril now discovered another loophole in the 1959 Obscene Publications Act. Under Section 3 it was possible to take out a private prosecution, which meant in effect that any member of the public could apply for a search warrant to empower a police constable to seize articles which he, the individual, thought obscene; thus one person could with patience cause a book he disliked to be banned throughout the country. The application would be heard before a magistrate, and there was no right to a trial by jury. This was what Sir Cyril Black set out to do.

The magistrate before whom he made the application was

[75]

none other than Sir Robert Blundell, who had taken sixty seconds to condemn *Fanny Hill*. He read *Last Exit to Brooklyn* and ordered copies to be seized. Calder & Boyars bravely announced that they would under no circumstances cease publication; they evidently believed in the novel.

When the case was heard at Marlborough Street magistrates' court, there were on this occasion witnesses for the prosecution, including the erstwhile tolerant H. Montgomery Hyde, and the publisher Robert Maxwell, who said the book was filthy and likely to undermine the morals of the young. Asked by defence counsel if he would ban the *Decameron*, Maxwell replied, 'What is the Decameron?' Counsel for Black was Michael Havers, eventually to be Attorney-General. Havers had difficulty with the prolific author Anthony Burgess, who appeared as witness for the defence, and said that *Last Exit to Brooklyn* was the very opposite of obscene, because it did not arouse one to lustful thoughts or action, but rather turned one right off!

The magistrate, Leo Gradwell, himself a well-read and tolerant man, decided the book was obscene and ordered the seized copies to be destroyed. There was uproar in the House of Commons over the decision, which it was said made Britain the laughing-stock of the civilized world, and the publishers made up their minds they would take no notice of the magistrate's decree, and thus invite further prosecution. The DPP duly said he would prosecute, and the defendants at last had the right to trial by jury, which they elected to exercise. The subequent trial, in November 1967, lasted eleven days, was studded with expert witnesses of star quality on both sides, and represented the last death agony of the censorship lobby. Once more, experts had some astonishing things to say. The poet A. Alvarez thought that *Last Exit* was a masterpiece. The all-male jury disagreed. They returned a verdict of guilty, and Sir Cyril Black was noticed, quite justifiably, to smirk.

The Revd David Sheppard (later Bishop of Woolwich) had admitted that he may have been depraved by the reading of *Last Exit*. He agreed to meet the Arts Council's Working Party. 'In the event,' they wrote, 'he impressed us deeply, but not as an awful example of depravity. On the contrary, he left us with the feeling that, if this was a depraved man, then society had little to fear and much to gain by his multiplication.'

Calder & Boyars lodged an appeal, and the Appeal Court judges overturned the verdict in July 1968. Sir Cyril had done a service, however, for which there were many who would thank him. The loophole in the law which enabled men of uncertain judgment to force their views upon the world at large was closed by Parliament.

It would of course be misleading to suggest that the decade of the Sixties forever stilled the voices of those who would tell us what we can and cannot read. They are still about. What it did was to give those voices a microphone, so that their rhetoric could be heard and exposed, and ultimately subdued. The three great trials of books demonstrated at last that no such trials should occur, and in the matter of literary censorship, as in so much else, Britain came of age between 1960 and 1968.

The idea of censorship was seen to be much more offensive than the books, 'dirty' or otherwise, which it sought to control. It was better to live in an open society where books which depicted scenes one person might not enjoy could still be read by another; where the nastier sides of human behaviour were not concealed by ignorance, but were exposed by detailed scrutiny; where personal decisions were allowed, and the expression of unpopular views not suppressed. It came to be seen that re-pression could deprave and corrupt. The idea that no one should be permitted to read a book which might influence the conduct of a psychopath was also discredited. Laws which hinged upon the idea of incitement to anti-social behaviour were made to look less weighty. 'Every advertisement for gin unquestionably contravenes the Obscenity Acts,' said the Arts Council.

The words of John Stuart Mill in *On Liberty* might be held to have particular reference to the censorship debate of the 1960s:

[77]

The peculiar evil of silencing the expression of an opinion is that it is robbing the human race; posterity as well as the existing generation; those who dissent from the opinion still more than those who hold it. If the opinion is right, they are deprived of the opportunity of exchanging error for truth; if wrong, they lose, what is almost as great a benefit, the clearer perception and livelier impression of truth, produced by its collision with error.

— 4 —

Profumo

When Macaulay made his celebrated and sagacious observation that 'We know no spectacle so ridiculous as the British public in one of its periodic fits of morality,' he thought he had witnessed the worst of such fits in the claptrap uttered on the iniquity of Byron. But even he would have been astounded by the fearful explosion of piety in the summer of 1963, when a respected, hardworking and decent cabinet minister was brought to his knees to grovel in disgrace because he had been to bed with a pretty and sexually stimulating nineteen-year-old girl. All kinds of other excuses were made for his ritual destruction, viz. that he was a liar and a risk to the security of the realm, but at bottom he was ruined for having done what men had done before him, have done since, and were doing at the very time they were chastising him, namely succumbing to the charm of illicit romance. This grave crime was treated so seriously that it affected the health of the Prime Minister, almost brought down the Government, filled the newspapers for days on end almost to the exclusion of everything else, caused the suicide of one man and the imprisonment of the girl at the centre of the *affaire*, and made Great Britain the wonder and laughing-stock of the world.

The malefactor was J. D. 'Jack' Profumo, Secretary of State for War in the Conservative Government led by Harold Macmillan, a post he had held since 1960, and before that Minister of State in the Foreign Office. He was forty-eight years old, and had served in Parliament since the age of twenty-five, first as MP for Kettering 1940–45, then as Member for Stratford-upon-Avon from 1950. He had also had a distinguished military career, being mentioned in despatches, and was a Baron in the peerage of the late United Kingdom of Italy. He is the 5th Baron Profumo, but of course as an Englishman he was never known as anything other than Mr Profumo. More to the point, he had married in 1954 a very popular actress, Valerie Hobson, star of many jolly and innocent post-war British films, and more especially, star at the Theatre Royal, Drury Lane of Rodgers and Hammerstein's musical *The King and I*, which had played to packed houses. Before 1963, only political journalists were familiar with the name of Jack Profumo, whereas the whole country knew Valerie Hobson. That, alas, would be so drastically altered by events that the name of Profumo would pass down into the history of British mores, while that of Valerie Hobson, once so great, would be eclipsed by the scandal and is today unknown by almost everyone under the age of forty.

It was Mr Profumo's grotesque misfortune that his sins came hard upon others which had embarrassed Macmillan's Government in 1962. An Admiralty clerk, William Vassall, had been found guilty of spying for Russia and had been sentenced to eighteen months' imprisonment. The Fleet Street papers, in some ways the best and in many other ways the worst in the world, had mercilessly pounced upon a Junior Minister, Thomas Galbraith, suggesting by loathsome innuendo that his relationship with his employee Vassall was rather more intimate than it should be. Vassall was an admitted homosexual; the inference of this manufactured gossip was plain and damaging. In the light of Fleet Street's vendetta, Mr Galbraith offered his resignation which Mr Macmillan, unaccountably, accepted. Galbraith obviously thought the gossip would damage the Government he served, but as there was no foundation whatever to the stories which circulated, and as the journalists who invented them subsequently went to prison rather than divulge the identity of their (non-existent) sources, Mr Macmillan ought to have had more faith and more resilience. He was still, a few months later, mindful of this sad error of judgment when the Profumo scandal broke, and this explains to some extent why the poor Edwardian

[80]

gentleman was made to take egg on his face for a second time.

Now for the story, in all its simplicity. Not the least preposterous aspect of the unholy fuss which ensued was the fact that the events which made heads tumble occurred *two years before*. On 8 July 1961, Mr and Mrs Profumo arrived to spend the weekend as guests of Lord Astor at his great country house, Cliveden. After dinner, it being a warm evening, the party strolled down to the swimming-pool, where they found another party frolicking in the water, including a young woman called Christine Margaret Keeler who at the time had no clothes on. Some good-natured laughter followed, and no one took much notice, except Mr Profumo who had been entranced by what he saw.

The party in the pool consisted of Stephen Ward and some girls, Miss Keeler among them. Ward rented a cottage on the Cliveden estate, a favour granted to him by a grateful Lord Astor, whose occasional aches and pains Ward had helped to alleviate. Ward was an osteopath who charged fees for curing the rich and gullible of their ailments by prodding and pulling their limbs. Among his clients were Sir Winston Churchill, Douglas Fairbanks Jnr, Elizabeth Taylor (the film star, not the novelist), and J. Paul Getty. Stephen Ward was also an accomplished artist, commissioned by the *Illustrated London News* to draw sketches of the famous, and he had drawn six members of the Royal Family, including the Duke of Edinburgh and Princess Margaret. He had even made a sketch of the bemused Mr Macmillan, who had been unaware that he was sitting, as Ward had made the drawing from the Strangers' Gallery at the House of Commons.

Stephen Ward had several faults, though no more than the average man. He was a persistent social climber who gloried in his acquaintance with people of eminence and wealth. A fifty-year-old bachelor, he liked to impress young women with his connections and entice them to be his mistress, always with success. It was said that his house in London was furnished with a two-way mirror through which he could observe the sexual performances of his friends, and that he provided 'popsies' for some of them. He also had some sympathy, not supported by much information or experience, with Soviet Russia. Above all, he was indiscreet. The combination of these individually innocuous faults was to bring tragedy to half a dozen people.

Miss Keeler was Ward's current mistress. He had known her since she was 14, 15 or 16 (accounts differed) and she was now living with him at his London house. She was an extremely pretty girl, who had sensibly turned her attractiveness to advantage and led a very exciting life, beyond anything she could expect as reward for her natural deserts. If part of the price was to share the occasional bed with some of Stephen's friends, it was one worth paying. She did no harm to anyone, and must be considered one of the victims of that summer madness in 1963.

Another of Stephen Ward's friends arrived at Cliveden on Sunday, 9 July 1961. This was Captain Ivanov, a diplomat at the Soviet Embassy and an agent (it was supposed) of the KGB. Ward had been introduced to Ivanov by the editor of the *Daily Telegraph* at the Garrick Club, and the two men had quickly become good friends. On that Sunday, Ivanov drove Christine Keeler back to Ward's house in London several hours before Ward himself returned and, presumably, engaged in some amorous activity with her while they were alone; he never became her lover, though there were few people in London who would believe *that* once the scandal had broken.

As soon as he was back in London, Mr Profumo arranged through Stephen Ward to meet the seductive Miss Keeler, and the disastrous affair began. Profumo bought her presents, took her out (once borrowing another minister's car), and entertained her in his own house on one occasion when his wife was away. It was not long before the Security Service got wind of the fact that the Secretary of State for War and the Russian diplomat shared a mutual acquaintance with Stephen Ward, which might just conceivably be dangerous. Ivanov had apparently intimated to Ward that the Russians knew the United States Government intended to arm Western Germany with nuclear weapons, and suggested that Ward might be able to find out more. So the

Security Service asked the Secretary of the Cabinet, Sir Norman Brook, to have a quiet word with Profumo by way of warning. Security did not, apparently know that Profumo was engaged in an affair with Miss Keeler, which in any case was not their business; they had to protect the safety of the realm, not scrutinize the moral behaviour of ministers. Mr Profumo suspected otherwise, and took the warning as a sensitive hint that he should cease the relationship. Immediately after this interview, he wrote Miss Keeler a letter to put her off:

Darling,
In great haste and because I can get no reply from your phone. Also something's blown up tomorrow night and I can't therefore make it. I'm terribly sorry especially as I leave the next day for various trips and then a holiday so won't be able to see you again until some time in September. Blast it. Please take great care of yourself and don't run away.

Love, J.

Bernard Levin's comment on this letter is, 'the earth is littered with pieces of paper on which men have written things that they must have known as they wrote them would destroy them, figuratively if not literally, if they ever came to public knowledge.' At any event, with this letter Mr Profumo virtually ended a liaison which had lasted barely four weeks. He did not see Miss Keeler again after December 1961. That was, or should have been, the end of the matter.

And indeed it was, as far as Mr Profumo was concerned. Throughout 1962 he got on with his work and lost no sleep at all over his indiscretion. Unfortunately for him, the other dramatis personae were busy making mistakes which had nothing whatever to do with him, but which would eventually drag him into the vortex of their trivial disasters.

Stephen Ward fancied sleeping with a black woman. He asked Christine to procure one for him, and she duly asked around the Westbourne Park Road area amongst black men whom she knew and from whom she occasionally bought a 'joint' (marijuana cigarette). One of these was Aloysius 'Lucky' Gordon, whom she liked enough to desert Ward for. Ward, meanwhile, replaced Miss Keeler with another teenage girl, Miss Marilyn Rice-Davies ('Mandy'). Christine then met another black man, John Edgecombe, and moved in with him. Jealousy between the two men, Gordon and Edgecombe, led to violence and eventually to arrest. Miss Keeler was left penniless and worried. She had now, one other asset apart from her looks; she had a story to tell the newspapers, a story which involved a very prominent man; perhaps that would provide her with enough to live on for a few months.

Other things were happening on Stephen Ward's side. The Cuban Missile crisis, when the Russians despatched nuclear weapons to Cuba and the American President, John F. Kennedy, had to force the ships that carried them, by persuasion and threat, to turn back, threw Mr Ward into a panic. The last of all wars might be imminent! Mandy Rice-Davies said he was hysterical, obsessed. *He* was in a position of influence, he must use that influence to save the world. Through Captain Ivanov he could pass crucial messages. Ward offered his services to the Foreign Office, who politely and firmly refused them; Ward was clearly too unstable and confused a man to be of much use, and it would have been folly to ask him to get Ivanov to defect. Stephen Ward's flirtation with Communism was more than likely merely a reflection of his desire to be with important people. Ivanov flattered and charmed him, made him feel that he was at the centre of affairs, whereas he was in reality nowhere near the periphery. Stephen Ward's influential friends used him, but never trusted him. As long as he was intoxicated with the proximity of power, he could not see the truth; that was his tragedy.

At the beginning of 1963, events accelerated, tension increased. Christine Keeler's lover, John Edgecombe, had fought with 'Lucky' Gordon and slashed his face with a razor, causing a wound which required 17 stitches. He had also pursued

Christine to Ward's house in Wimpole Mews, where she was visiting Mandy Rice-Davies in order to escape his attentions, and taken a gun. When she refused to come out, he fired at the lock, then fired at her in an upstairs window. Both incidents now led to charges against him, and his trial was due to take place at the beginning of February. Miss Keeler would, of course, be the main witness against him.

By now, however, she was active in spreading abroad the story of her plight. At the beginning of the year, only a handful of people knew she had been for a short time mistress of the Minister of War. By March, everyone in Parliament and in Fleet Street had heard about it. At a party she met a former MP called John Lewis, and told him. He repeated the story to George Wigg, MP, a man who did not care for Profumo and would not weep if he were discredited. Christine also told the story to two newspapers, the *News of the World* and the *Sunday Pictorial*. The latter bought it for £1,000, of which £200 was to be paid immediately. In return, she gave them the hand-written letter from Mr Profumo beginning 'Darling'.

When Stephen Ward heard what was going on, he told his lawyer, who told the Solicitor-General, who told the Attorney-General, who told Mr Profumo. Profumo asked to see the Head of Security with a view to having publication stopped, but this could not be done. He lunched with Lord Astor and Stephen Ward to discuss the implications, and he was certainly a worried man.

The most alarming aspect of the story was Keeler's assertion that Stephen Ward had asked her to ascertain from Profumo the date of delivery of atomic weapons to Germany, so that he could pass on the information to Ivanov. It was nonsense, but the fact that it was said, and might be published, would be hugely damaging. The public which devours newspaper gossip would be perfectly prepared to believe that a nineteen-year-old girl could pause from satisfying her lover to ask, 'By the way, darling, what about those bombs?'

Frantic efforts were made at the end of January to pay Miss

Keeler to keep quiet, even to spirit her out of the country. She was asking for £5,000. As more and more people heard the rumours, Mr Profumo had to face several of his colleagues to deny them. He saw the Chief Whip, the Attorney-General, the Solicitor-General, and the Prime Minister's Private Secretary. To all of them he averred in the strongest possible terms that there was no truth in any of the rumours, that he had not even touched the girl, let alone slept with her. The use of 'darling' as a term of endearment was commonplace amongst theatrical folk and held little meaning. All these men were impressed by Mr Profumo's evident determination to sue for libel any newspaper which published such rumours; they felt he must be certain of his ground to be so bold. But it is odd, and has never been properly explained, why not one of them asked to see the 'Darling' letter and judge its content for himself.

Christine Keeler then did something which made the ghastly denouement inevitable. She disappeared. Since she was due to appear as chief witness at the Edgecombe trial in a day or two, and since the gossip of her relationship with Profumo was the talk of Fleet Street, it was very easy to put two and two together and conclude she had gone away to make life easier for the Minister, and further, that he had organized her disappearance to save his skin. He had not. She went to Spain with a friend and lived very simply in a remote fishing village until the Press managed to track her down and she fled to the Madrid police station in despair. No one explained what made her leave England in the first place, but I suspect she was by now very scared indeed by the rumpus she had caused; she could have had no idea how severe would be the repercussions.

The *Sunday Pictorial* (still mindful of the mistakes made over Mr Galbraith) decided the story was too hot to handle, and cancelled the contract. The *Daily Express* on the other hand plunged in head first with a front-page story which, as journalists habitually do, they invented, to the effect that Mr Profumo had been asked to resign. He hadn't, but that did not detract from the sensational effect of the front page.

Now at last George Wigg dared to say in Parliament what most people were thinking – in Parliament because there he was protected by the special privilege accorded to members of the House of Commons and could not be sued for libel – and demanded that the Home Secretary either categorically deny the rumours that were spreading, or set up a Select Committee to enquire into them. The Labour MP Barbara Castle added her voice, pointing out that it was the duty of anyone who knew the whereabouts of Miss Christine Keeler to inform the police, or justice would be wilfully thwarted. This was tantamount to an accusation against Mr Profumo, and it could not be ignored. The fact that it was made late at night (just before midnight) did not diminish its impact, for among the few members in the House at the time were the Solicitor-General, the Attorney-General, and the Home Secretary, all intimately interested in the outcome.

It so happened that the Home Secretary in 1963 was one of the daftest and most incompetent men ever to reach high office. Mr Henry Brooke had proven time and again that he could be trusted to mishandle any crisis, to say the wrong thing, or to say the right thing in an unintelligible way. He was one of Mr Macmillan's least happy appointments. Mr Brooke recognized that he would be required to reply to these disguised allegations against a member of the front bench, but he did not know what to say. The Chief Whip, the Attorney-General and the Solicitor-General hurriedly drafted a form of words, which Brooke then recited at the Despatch Box, to the effect that honourable members should make their nasty insinuations outside, if they had any proof, and not there like cowards.

The Chief Whip saw Mr Profumo late that evening. 'I must ask you point blank,' he said. 'Did you or didn't you?' 'I didn't,' replied Profumo. The Chief Whip told him he thought he, Profumo, would have to make a personal statement, but for the moment he should go home to bed. Mr and Mrs Profumo found their house besieged by reporters at nearly 1 a.m. and had to fight their way through to the front door. They took sleeping pills and went to bed.

Back at Westminster, the Chief Whip and the leader of the House discussed the matter further. If they did not act quickly, the Sunday newspapers would go berserk with enthusiasm. The rumours should be stopped without delay. The Prime Minister was telephoned, and he agreed that a personal statement in the House of Commons was called for. Meanwhile, other Ministers joined the extraordinary late-night discussion, until there were five of them in all, and they determined to bring Mr Profumo back to the House, no matter how late it was, to settle things once and for all. There was no answer to his telephone, so they sent round a messenger who, at 2.45 a.m., dragged the groggy Minister from his bed, still half flattened with sleeping pills, and waited while he rustled around for a clean shirt.

The point of this meeting was to draft the statement which Profumo would make later that day. Curiously, it was thought advisable that Mr Profumo's own solicitor should also be woken and summoned. It is usual to keep one's mouth shut and open it when the solicitor tells one, only when one has something to hide, so the solicitor's very presence was suspicious in itself. By 4.30 a.m. the text of the statement was finally agreed, his colleagues having persuaded Mr Profumo that he could not get through it without at least mentioning Christine Keeler, and they all went home. Mrs Profumo had sat up waiting for her husband's return.

It did not occur to anyone, throughout the night, to call the Home Secretary, Henry Brooke. Or perhaps it did occur to some, who dismissed the thought as an intrusive complication. Brooke was better off in bed, where he could not do anything awkward. Yet he was the Minister whose responsibility was most closely involved, especially if, as would later be claimed, there was a security aspect to the affair.

On Friday morning 22 March 1963, Mr Profumo made his catastrophic statement to the House of Commons. The Prime Minister had seen it shortly before, and had approved. He naturally knew about the rumours over the past weeks, and had accepted Profumo's declaration that they were without foundation.

The statement denied that Profumo had anything to do with the disappearance of the witness, admitted that he knew Stephen Ward slightly and that he had met Captain Ivanov twice. The crucial sentences, inserted against the wishes of Mr Profumo who would rather not have mentioned her at all, were these:

Miss Keeler and I were on friendly terms. There was no impropriety whatsoever in my acquaintanceship with Miss Keeler.

The Prime Minister had no reason to disbelieve Mr Profumo, as the convention of the House which requires strict honesty in a personal statement was so honoured that no one would dare traduce it. There were some present, however, who had their doubts. That afternoon, the Profumos were in the Queen Mother's party at Sandown Races, and in the evening were observed dining at Quaglino's.

It looked for a while as if the ruse had succeeded. Christine Keeler obligingly told the Press that Mr Profumo's statement was quite correct, and when Profumo sued the French *Paris-Match* and the Italian *Il Tempo* for suggesting otherwise, he was awarded damages. There was one actor in the drama, however, who was not happy. Stephen Ward felt he was about to be lined up as the scapegoat. Police had started an investigation into his activities and the nature of his relationship with the girls who were at different times sharing his house in Wimpole Mews. In a desperate effort to have the investigation halted, Ward wrote to all and sundry, including the Prime Minister, implicitly stating that he knew enough about Mr Profumo's friendship with Miss Keeler to spill the beans. He had an interview with George Wigg to the same effect. Of course, nobody could or would do anything to interfere with police investigations, but Ward's alarm communicated itself to the Press and resurrected the rumours, now embellished by fantasy (and envy, more than likely) to form constructions of glorious absurdity. It was openly said over drinks in Fleet Street that nine High

Court Judges were involved in sexual orgies organized by the likes of Stephen Ward, and that a Cabinet Minister waited at table at a dinner party wearing nothing but a mask and a pinny. The Leader of the Opposition, Harold Wilson, told the Prime Minister that he was worried about the security aspects of the affair, and was assured by Mr Macmillan that the Security Service had kept watch on events since the beginning. Nevertheless, he would instruct the Lord Chancellor to make an enquiry into the Ward–Ivanov connection. As soon as this happened, at the end of May, Mr Profumo knew that his days in Parliament were numbered. It was pointed out to him by the Chief Whip that if the enquiry revealed any disparity between its findings and Mr Profumo's statement to the House, the Government would be severely embarrassed. On 31 May, Parliament adjourned for the short recess, and Mr and Mrs Profumo went to Venice for a holiday. There, he told his wife for the first time that he had indeed indulged in a sexual liaison with Christine Keeler. They together decided to return to London immediately, by train and boat to avoid the attention they might receive at London airport.

On 5 June, Jack Profumo resigned. His letter to the Prime Minister (who was holidaying in Scotland and was just about to take a jaunt with his wife to Iona) demonstrated with clarity that all perspectives on the affair had become hopelessly distorted. At the time of his personal statement on 22 March, he wrote:

Rumour had charged me with assisting in the disappearance of a witness and with being involved in some possible breach of security. So serious were these charges that I allowed myself to think that my personal association with that witness, which had also been the subject of rumour, was, by comparison, of minor importance only. In my statement I said that there had been no impropriety in this association. To my very deep regret I have to admit that this was not true, and that I misled you, and my colleagues, and the House. I ask you to understand that I did this to protect, as I thought, my wife and family, who were equally misled, as were my professional advisers. I have come to realize that, by this deception, I have been guilty of a grave misdemeanour and despite the fact that there is no truth whatsoever in the other charges, I cannot remain a member of your Administration, nor of the House of Commons.

Mr Profumo also talked of his deep remorse, as well he might, for the stories were now so out of hand that it was suggested Mr Macmillan knew all along what was going on and connived in the deception.

No novelist could have so cleverly designed the confluence of circumstances which brought before the Old Bailey on this very same day, 5 June 1963, one of Christine Keeler's lovers, Lucky Gordon, on a charge of causing actual bodily harm. The chief witness was, of course, Miss Keeler herself, who could not move now without causing a stampede of journalists and voyeurs. Gordon conducted his own defence, and claimed he had contracted venereal disease from Miss Keeler, whereupon she shouted her protests from the back of the court and had to be removed, weeping copiously.

Other developments, tumbling upon each other, seemed to have been guided by fate as an ever more threatening crescendo towards the climax of the Government's possible collapse. Two days after Profumo's resignation, on 7 June, the Director of Public Prosecutions was in conference with counsel to discuss the case against Stephen Ward, when word reached him that Ward was about to leave the country within days. On that intelligence, a warrant was issued immediately, and Ward was arrested in the street on 8 June, a Saturday. His application for bail was refused on police suspicion that he would interfere with prosecution witnesses, so he spent his remand in Brixton Prison. Ward's great and famous friends were now as strangers to him in his moment of disgrace.

The Prime Minister left Scotland on 9 June to face the crisis in London. As the *Annual Register* put it, 'In the dawn of Monday 10 June, Mr Macmillan emerged from his overnight sleeper at Euston and marched grimly down the platform. The toughest, bitterest week of his premiership was before him.' The House of Commons would debate the affair on 17 June, and it promised to be the biggest show in London. Nobody suspected for a minute that Mr Macmillan relished it. Yet he was good humoured enough to be overheard at the University of Sussex in Brighton, on 11 June, saying, 'Aren't politics fun? And they always seem to come out right in the end.' Those were bold words.

On the same day, politicians on their various engagements turned their speeches to Profumo when they saw journalists gather. Mr Healey wanted to know how much the Prime Minister himself was hiding. Mr Wilson declared that he was not interested in the intimate life of a Cabinet Minister, only in the danger to the country's security, a theme he would consistently stick by while, naturally, mentioning Mr Profumo's wickedness at every opportunity in order to disclaim interest in it. Lord Lambton thought the affair was a 'severe blow to those who expected truth and honesty from the Tory Party,' which was doubly ironic; first, because there were few who had such high expectations of Conservatives, then or since; secondly, because Lambton would himself be the offender in another sexual scandal a few years later. In other words, humbug was spread thick over every utterance that week, and if the damage to Mr Profumo, Miss Keeler and Mr Ward was final, so too was the damage done to the public's perception of politicians. In that regard, at least, Profumo's offence was rendered insignificant against the Tory Party's self-destruction in hypocritical piety.

The chief culprit was Lord Hailsham, who was interviewed on a television programme called 'Gallery' on 13 June. I remember it well, and recall a slight feeling of alarm when it looked as if the noble lord was about to have an apoplectic fit in full view of us all. 'A War Minister cannot afford to have dingy companions or squalid vices,' he said. 'A great party is not to be brought down

because of a scandal by a woman of easy virtue and a proven liar
... he lied and lied and lied, lied to his friends, lied to his
solicitor, lied to the House of Commons ... if I thought the
Prime Minister knew he was lying, I should begin to lose my
faith in human nature.' Lord Hailsham averred that if he had
known, he would not have stayed in the Government for five
minutes, 'or I would have seen him [Profumo] out.' Again in the
words of the *Annual Register*, Hailsham 'waded knee-deep in
moral precepts'; it was a 'moody and idiosyncratic' performance.
The Bishop of Southwark, Dr Stockwood, intimated that Hailsham should see a psychiatrist, and Antony Greenwood, Deputy
Leader of the Labour Party, said, 'Anyone would think lying was
unheard of in the Conservative Party.'

J. Enoch Powell, the Minister of Health, was profoundly
troubled for days as he considered whether or not he should
resign on the moral issue; he even thought the whole Government
should resign. A keen and strict constitutionalist, as well as a
man with deep religious convictions, Powell was most hurt by
the lie to Parliament; however trivial the subject, the principle
was all.

The Times thought so, too, and wrote a stern editorial which
produced days of correspondence sometimes covering four whole
columns; no one subject had monopolized attention to such an
extent since the Abdication of Edward VIII. Some writers were
indignant about the 'crippling blow at basic decencies on which
society is founded' or lamented that 'the prestige of this country
has been severely damaged.' Others were most anxious to show
that the scandal could have blown up in any ranks, not just
Conservative ones. Some were angry at the nauseous, self-
righteous, sanctimonious tone of the rest. A. C. B. Chancellor
pleaded for less hysteria and less hypocrisy. 'There, but for the
grace of God, go very many of us,' he wrote. William Devlin
pointed out that Mr Profumo had not lied about things which
mattered, only about things which didn't. 'The only question he
answered incorrectly was one that should never have been put
by any public body.'

The rest of the world looked on with amazement. As President Kennedy was due to visit England within weeks, and even stay as guest in the Prime Minister's home, the *Washington News* saw fit to declare that 'we can think of no better time for an American President to stay as far as possible away from England.' What did they mean? That the President might be contaminated? As Jack Kennedy was an incorrigible womanizer, with more mistresses than Mr Profumo would have dreamt of, this was irony of a rich order. The French, as always, had a more sensible view. *Le Monde* wrote, 'In many countries, deeming themselves no less civilized, Mr Profumo's errors would not have created a scandal comparable with that which shakes Britain today.' One detected that the French were rather amused by it all.

The most adult and charitable attitude came from Her Majesty the Queen. Mr Profumo's disgrace was so total that his name was removed from the Privy Council, and his public denigration so loud that he was prevented from handing over the seals of office to the Queen in personal audience, as any retiring Minister traditionally does. John Cordle MP led the attack. 'I was appalled,' he said, 'that our beloved Queen should be so wrongly advised as to give an audience on Tuesday next to the former Minister of the Crown.' (Cordle could not bring himself actually to mention the man's name.) In order to save the Queen embarrassment, Mr Profumo sent the seals of office to Buckingham Palace by messenger. But we have it on Bernard Levin's word that Her Majesty did not feel so sullied by events as Mr Cordle imagined, for she wrote a pleasant letter to Mr Profumo, thanking him for his work in her Government and expressing sorrow that his career should have ended in such an unhappy way.

The stage was set for ritual expiation by means of the House of Commons debate on 17 June. The Prime Minister spent the weekend of 15 and 16 June alone at Chequers, his only visitor for lunch on Sunday being the Chief Whip. (He did not see the Home Secretary, Henry Brooke, who had summoned a naval frigate to bring him back from Guernsey in time.) The debate itself was held in a packed house. Queues had formed outside for entrance to the Strangers' Gallery, some people waiting all night, but the gallery was mostly full of the wives and friends of Tory and Labour members in their Sunday best, who would not vacate their seats for anyone.

The debate was opened by the Leader of the Opposition (a post he had held for only four months), the Rt. Hon. Harold Wilson, who took the opportunity to deliver a rousing piece of oratorical bombast. 'This is a debate without precedent in the annals of the House,' he began, arising from 'disclosures which have shocked the moral conscience of the nation.' His main charge against the Prime Minister was one of 'indolent non-chalance' in not keeping abreast of the gathering drama and not dealing with it effectively much sooner.

Wilson piled on the epithets in an attempt to make clear that this disaster could only have befallen the Tories, with their distorted materialistic values. 'What we are seeing is a diseased excrescence, a corrupted poisoned appendix of a small and unrepresentative section of society that makes no contribution to what Britain is, still less to what Britain can be.' The implication, that the Tories were not morally fit to govern (if they habitually produced such 'excrescences'), would in the next years grow into a fundamental shift in political perceptions, allowing Labour for the first time in a generation to be regarded as the natural party of government, and the Tories the outsiders.

When Mr Macmillan got up to reply, there was little doubt that he was a profoundly shaken man. He said:

What has happened has inflicted a deep, bitter and lasting wound. I do not remember in the whole of my life, or even in the political history of the past, a case of a Minister of the crown who has told a deliberate lie to his wife, his legal advisers, his ministerial colleagues, not once but over and over again, has subsequently taken legal action and recovered damages on the basis of a falsehood. This is almost unbelievable, but it is true.

What greater moral crime can there be than to deceive those

[95]

naturally inclined to trust you, those who have worked with you, served with you and are your colleagues? I find it difficult to tell the House what a blow it has been to me, for it seems to have undermined one of the very foundations upon which political life must be conducted.

This may sound a trifle naive, but if the Prime Minister was putting on a show, he made sure he did not turn in a matinée performance. In one of the most plaintive moments of a speech which not only invited, but implored sympathy, Mr Macmillan said that none of the five ministers in late-night colloquy had asked to see the 'Darling' letter because they could not believe Profumo would be so mad as to lie about its contents when it might be published at any moment. Moreover, Mr Profumo had sufficiently explained that the word 'darling' held no significance in theatrical circles. 'I believe that might be accepted,' said Mr Macmillan. 'I do not live among young people very widely.'

(This now legendary remark has enabled Macmillan to maintain the image of himself during this debate as a stag at bay, bewildered by the world he was being asked to comment upon. He even managed to lose his place in his notes at one point. It does not take into account that his wife's sister-in-law was Adele Astaire, the dancer, who presumably did not tailor her language within the family to encompass only the vocabulary of an Edwardian gentleman. Mr Macmillan was not entirely a stranger to theatrical ways, any more than he had passed his seventy years without ever hearing a man tell a lie.)

The Prime Minister included a rotund declaration: 'I know I have acted honourably. I believe I have acted justly. And I hope that when they have heard my account members will consider that I have acted with proper diligence and prudence.'

There were not many in the Chamber who would give him so much credit. From his own Tory benches, Nigel Birch made the point that most of those present had known Profumo for years. 'I must say that he never struck me as a man at all like a cloistered monk, and Miss Keeler was a professional prostitute. There

▲ 9

9   Lord Denning with some of the files of
     evidence for his report on the Profumo
     affair 1963

10   *Overleaf left:* Lord Arran at the Premiere of
     Dr Strangelove at the Columbia Theatre
     1964

11   *Overleaf right:* M.P. Leo Abse arrives at the
     House of Commons dressed in a Victorian
     suit of his own design 1963

◀ 12 ▲ 13

12   David Frost searches through the papers
      for material for *That Was The Week That Was*

13   The *Beyond the Fringe* team at the Fortune
      Theatre in 1961

▲ 14 15 ▶

14   Judi Dench as Sally Bowles in Harold
      Prince's production of *Cabaret* 1968

15   Mick Jagger is driven to Brixton Prison to
      begin a three month sentence for a drugs
      offence 1967

16   *Overleaf left:* Cliff Richard cutting his first
      long playing disc at the age of 18

seems to me to be a certain basic improbability about the proposition that their conduct was purely platonic. What are whores about?' Mr Birch thought the time had come for Mr Macmillan to relinquish office himself.

George Wigg stood up and bluntly called Lord Hailsham 'a lying humbug,' for which gross impertinence he ought to have been chastised by the Speaker, but he was not. Lord Lambton returned to the Prime Minister's responsibility. 'I can see the Prime Minister putting the telescope to his blind eye and saying, "I cannot see any of these things." That is what I find it so difficult to forgive.' Mr Parkin said that since everyone had known the truth for months (which was an exaggeration), how was it that the Government did not know?

Mr Reginald Paget, on the Opposition benches, had the most trenchant remarks of the day. His sympathy was with Mr Profumo. Nobody had really believed Profumo's story, yet Lord Lambton had been the only Tory to admit it. For the rest, 'They were satisfied with a lie if he could get away with it. That is always the attitude of the Tory Party.' As for the unsavoury show of Lord Hailsham on television, it was 'a virtuoso performance in the art of kicking a fallen friend in the guts,' and Hailsham's moral indignation was contemptible 'when self-indulgence has reduced a man to the shape of Lord Hailsham, sexual continence involves no more than a sense of the ridiculous.'

The debate concluded at 11.00 p.m. Punishment of the miscreants was by no means over. There were still Ward and Keeler to dispose of, to be publicly excoriated in order that the British might feel clean again. Miss Keeler was the easier victim, for she was young, unconnected, and female. In the House of Commons she had been called a 'professional prostitute' (which she wasn't) and mention had been made, without checking the evidence, that she had been offered a job in a night-club for £5,000 a week. Harold Wilson claimed he felt insulted: 'I say to the Prime Minister that there is something utterly nauseating about a system of society that pays a harlot twenty-five times as much as it pays its Prime Minister, two hundred and fifty times as much as it pays its Members of Parliament, and five hundred times as much as it pays some of its ministers of religion.' That was heady stuff coming from a man whose own private life was, at any rate as far as the public knew, blameless. Yet there were some voices raised in Miss Keeler's defence, even if the newspapers did not allow them much space. She could not be called a 'harlot' simply because she was known to have had sexual congress with married men. Her solicitors issued a very dignified statement after the House of Commons debate, largely ignored but shouting with truth even after twenty years. 'Those who speak of her without charity,' it said, 'seem to take no account of her youth nor of the fact that since the age of fifteen her manifest immaturity has been consistently exploited by a so-called adult society.'

Lord Denning, too, in his report on the whole affair months later, spared a word for Christine Keeler which demonstrated all too clearly his own humanity and tolerance. 'Let no one judge her too harshly,' he wrote. 'She was not yet 21. And since the age of 16 she had become enmeshed in a net of wickedness.'

These voices notwithstanding, Christine Keeler became something of a national spittoon, as notorious as Nell Gwyn and as evil as Lucrezia Borgia. Blame for the scandal was heaped upon her, and desire for retribution was eventually assuaged when she was sentenced to nine months' imprisonment for perjury committed during the trial of Aloysius 'Lucky' Gordon. Having served her purpose, she more or less disappeared from public view, although news of her marriage was reported in the newspapers, and she was recently tracked down to a council flat in Chelsea where she lives with her grown-up son.

Then there was Stephen Ward. His trial at the Old Bailey began barely a month after the House of Commons show, on 22 July, the prosecution counsel being none other than Mervyn Griffith-Jones, scourge of the hedonist, who had made a fool of himself chastising Lady Chatterley and Fanny Hill, and now positively relished the task of humiliating what he called 'a thoroughly filthy fellow.' The charges included that of living off immoral earnings, for which there was no evidence whatever, Ward being a relatively poor man who had to borrow money from Lord Astor. Providing 'popsies' for the rich did not amount to the same thing as running a call-girl business, and money did not change hands. (Mr Profumo never paid Christine Keeler, though he gave her presents and once lent her £20 to help her mother.) On the same day that the trial of Ward began, an exhibition of his drawings, including some of the Royal Family, was opened at the Museum Street Galleries. Ward turned up at the gallery after a day sitting in the dock (he had since been released from custody on bail of £3,000).

The trial lasted eight days. On 30 July, the Judge began his summing-up, and had not finished when court adjourned. On 31 July, Stephen Ward was found at his house in a deep sleep, having taken an overdose of barbiturates. He was removed to hospital, the Judge continuing his summing-up in the absence of the defendant. The jury found him guilty of living on the earnings of the prostitution of Christine Keeler and Marilyn Rice-Davies. In an uncharacteristic outburst of intolerance, John Sutherland makes reference in his book *Offensive Literature* to 'filthy flagellant Ward on his deathbed . . . sentenced while in terminal coma.' In fact he was never sentenced; the Judge postponed this pleasure until the defendant's recovery, but he died on 3 August. He had left fourteen suicide notes, in one of which he wrote, 'I am sorry to disappoint the vultures.'

Mandy Rice-Davies, at the première of *Cleopatra* on the same evening (the Elizabeth Taylor–Richard Burton film which started the famous romance), said, 'Whatever he has done or admitted, he never deserved to get into this awful mess.' Lord Astor, brave man, paid tribute to Stephen Ward's powers of healing. 'Those who were fortunate enough to have been treated by him will remember him with great gratitude. His readiness to help anyone in pain is the memory many will treasure.' It was a pity tributes like this should have come too late; at the trial Ward was completely alone, his friends having deserted him. The Judge took trouble to point out in his summing-up that no one had come to testify in his favour, and it was surely this realization, cruelly emphasized, which drove him to take his own life that night. Stephen Ward had been socially ambitious, had used young women selfishly, and was not, to many, an attractive man. Yet the penalty overtook the fault. At his funeral there were no less than fifty dozen white roses sent by an anonymous group of people with a card reading, 'In memory of a victim of British hypocrisy.'

In the intervening years there have been many to agree with the use of this harsh word, most strident among whom was Bernard Levin in his book *The Pendulum Years*, where he talks of 'a massive exercise in hypocrisy, perhaps the most staining episode of the entire decade.' Levin noted that there lurked within most of us 'a response of fierce joy to the shame and pain of others,' and there was even some masochistic element in contemplating the degeneracy of Britain as if it were an echo of Gibbon's vision of the death throes of the Roman Empire.

For others, it was not so much the hypocrisy of reactions which offended as the frivolity of the interest. There were so many other more important matters to claim public attention, yet they were all submerged beneath this great tide of fascination with the shiftiness and depravity of people in authority. It certainly made politicians as a whole appear less than great, and undermined their ability to command respect as a right. The young, who were about to inherit the earth as 'Swinging London' became their exclusive domain, saw little reason to excuse themselves for excess when at least they were frank about their pleasures and tolerant of those pursued by others. People under twenty-five, on the whole, sympathized with Mr Profumo and reserved their scorn for the jackals who tormented him. Levin put it succinctly when he wrote, 'Men are never so firmly bound to one way of life as when they are about to abandon it, so that fanaticism and intolerance reach their most intense forms just before tolerance and mutual acceptance come to be the natural order of things.'

One final act in the drama was in keeping with the Grand

Guignol atmosphere of the whole summer. Mr Macmillan decided that a full-scale enquiry was called for into the circumstance surrounding Profumo's resignation, and the possible consequences for national security. He appointed Lord Denning, Master of the Rolls, to undertake the task on 21 June, only four days after the Commons debate. Not only is the Master of the Rolls one of the highest legal offices in the land, head of the Court of Appeal and Supreme Court of Judicature, but this incumbent, appointed in 1962, was a Judge held in the highest respect and the warmest regard. Denning was essentially a simple man who kept his country brogue and brought native common sense to complex problems. He also had a straightforward control of language which made lawyers occasionally listen to his judgments for the sheer beauty of simple prose and elegant exposition. If anyone could sort out truth from rapidly congealing legend, Denning should be the man.

Throughout the summer, he interviewed everyone connected with the case, and many on the periphery, covering 160 persons altogether. Press anticipation of his findings was so eager that he had to allow photographers in to take pictures of him at his desk, an unprecedented piece of show-business for a government report.

Even more astonishing was the actual publication of Lord Denning's Report (as it was simply and characteristically called) on 26 September. In order to help newspapers get copy for some morning editions, Her Majesty's Stationery Office took the unique step of opening at midnight, copies being legally available at one minute past. None of the staff who co-operated in this useful gesture could have been prepared for what ensued, as both television channels sent cameras and arc-lights and news commentators for special late-night programmes, after normal hours for closing down the TV service, in order to cover the event. Not only that, but crowds of people filled the pavement and the street to be among the first to read the report, jostling and pushing as soon as the doors opened. The sedate Stationery Office can have experienced nothing like it. Over 100,000 copies were sold in the first twenty-four hours, a record unequalled by even the most salacious novel.

Much has been made of the raciness of Lord Denning's Report, as if somehow the substance were rendered void by the style. Certainly it reads at times like a detective story. Chapter and paragraph headings are unexpectedly perky ('Christine Asks for £5,000', 'Mr and Mrs Profumo Go Home'), the language is frequently colloquial as well as suspenseful, and Miss Keeler is referred to as 'Christine', like a personal friend. Perhaps Lord Denning enjoyed the challenge of telling a story well.

Not enough, however, was said about Denning's conclusions, both stated and implied, or his restraint. Enquiring into rumours was, he said, a dangerous business, for anyone could start a rumour and the person so slandered was condemned on the principle that there was no smoke without fire, even when the smoke was synthetic. Denning heard lots of rumours; this is how he dealt with his response to them:

> When the facts are clear beyond controversy, I will state them as objectively as I can, irrespective of the consequences to individuals: and I will draw any inference that is manifest from those facts. But when the facts are in issue, I must always remember the cardinal principle of justice – that no man is to be condemned on suspicion. There must be evidence which proves his guilt before he is pronounced to be so. I will therefore take the facts in his favour rather than do an injustice which is without remedy. For from my findings there is no appeal.

What if he were accused of a 'cover-up' or 'white-washing'? He gives his answer in advance, firmly and finally:

> While the public interest demands that the facts should be ascertained as completely as possible, there is yet higher public interest to be considered, namely, the interest of justice to the

individual which overrides all other. At any rate, speaking as a Judge, I put justice first.

Thus the Denning Report was in some ways as much a portrait of its author – his humanity, compassion, his loathing for unfairness and for excessive power – as a chronological account of events. For example, on the question as to whether the Security Service should pry into any man's private conduct, Denning says, 'It would be intolerable for us to have anything in the nature of a Gestapo or Secret Police to snoop into all that we do, let alone into our morals.' By 'us', he indicates that he means 'most people in this country'; Lord Denning was perfectly aware that there were some, excluded by this definition, but in positions of power, who would not agree. This was his way of giving warning that ordinary folk (of whom a judge is one, and the Sovereign another) would not tolerate such abuse. He positively rejoices in the limits placed upon the power of the Security Service:

> They have no special powers of arrest such as the police have. No special powers of search are given to them. They cannot enter premises without the consent of the householder, even though they may suspect a spy is there. If a spy is fleeing the country, they cannot tap him on the shoulder and say he is not to go. They have, in short, no executive powers. They have managed very well without them. We would rather have it so, than have anything in the nature of a 'secret police'.

This was nothing less than a statement of faith.

As to the persons involved in the drama, Lord Denning was always ready to give benefit of doubt, slow to chastise. We have already seen that he said of Miss Keeler, 'Let no one judge her too harshly.' He forbears to rebuke Stephen Ward (called 'filthy' by men of less wisdom), and while establishing that Mr Profumo did in fact lie and did in fact commit adultery, he insists upon also giving space to the man's good character:

[103]

No one can doubt that a man with such a record was entitled to the confidence of his colleagues and of the country: and it should not be assumed by anyone that he would give away secret information. Whatever indiscretions he may have committed, and whatever falsehoods he may have told, no one who has given evidence before me has doubted his loyalty.

Denning also paid tribute to the steadfastness of Mrs Profumo. What of his conclusions? First, there was no security risk whatever. The Russians sent Ivanov packing as soon as they saw clouds gather, and he left empty-handed. Second, even if Mr Profumo lied about his adultery, the men in Government should have known better than to believe him, when all the circumstances pointed in the opposite direction. So the Government was at fault, and by implication the Tory ethic of solidarity was in question:

> The conduct of Mr Profumo was such as to create, amongst an influential section of the people, a *reasonable belief* that he had committed adultery . . . It was the responsibility of the Prime Minister and his colleagues, and of them only, to deal with this situation: and they did not succeed in doing so.

But Denning's severest strictures were not widely reported in the Press, for they were directed at the Press itself. He strains not to lose his temper when pointing out that the scandals arising out of Profumo's resignation were invented, expanded and commercially exploited by newspaper editors: 'Scandalous information about well-known people has become a marketable commodity. True or false, actual or invented, it can be sold.' Newspapers compete with each other to buy it. Sometimes the laws of libel prevent some parts of the story from being printed; the bits left out do not die; they circulate in Fleet Street, then in Westminster, then in London clubs and public houses; they cross the Channel and back again, each time growing in sensational content. Thus are reputations ruined.

John Profumo has led a useful life since his disgrace. For six years he did not appear in public at all. Between 1968 and 1975 he worked at Toynbee Hall, devoting his abundant energies to the less privileged. In 1975 the Queen conferred the CBE upon him. He is a prison visitor and a member of Boodle's. Looking back, it seems scarcely credible that his life should have been so drastically altered by such a commonplace mistake. Today, men in higher office than he held tell lies as a matter of course, and pass unchallenged. And no one would think to suggest that a man conquer his lust when tempted by a pretty girl.

Lord Denning thought that 'something should be done to stop the trafficking in scandal for reward.' It has yet to be done, and still it is the newspapers who are the real liars and the real victors. For no one can punish them.

— 5 —

Homosexual Law Reform

The way in which books were placed on trial, and the harsh treatment of Mr Profumo demonstrated both how silly and how vindictive British attitudes towards moral questions had been. When those attitudes were turned to the existence among us of homosexual men, they had actually become downright cruel. Before 1967 it was not possible in England for two men to comport themselves freely within the home of either one of them without a very real risk of imprisonment. If they were tied by bonds of affection, they were criminals each time they gave it physical expression. Sexual contact between them meant, in the archaic language of the time, that one was 'committing an offence' against the other, and when the offence went so far as the act of love, one or both of them could be sent to prison for life. Even when writing letters to each other, they had to be circumspect in the language they used, for the police were empowered to invade their homes without warrant and without notice, ransack their possessions, and use any private letters which contained terms of endearment as evidence in court of 'unnatural passion'. Making his maiden speech in the House of Lords in 1965, the Marquess of Queensberry (with powerful irony the great-grandson of Oscar Wilde's merciless mad persecutor) said, 'I believe these laws will be changed, and that when my children are grown up they will be amazed that laws of this sort could have existed in the middle of the twentieth century.'

He was right. Those children are now grown up, and the whole of their generation can scarcely believe that this state of affairs was not an Orwellian fiction but a cruel fact. There were something like one and a half million men in Britain who were denied the individual freedom one expects in a civilized society, and which they could enjoy anywhere else in the Western world with the exception of the still more backward United States of America. These men could choose either to suppress their sexuality and lead a life of total abstention, or to indulge in furtive criminal behaviour on a regular basis. Most pretended for safety's sake to choose the former, while pursuing a parallel clandestine path towards the latter. Tensions resulting from the fear of being found out were omnipresent and grotesque, but of course not all homosexual men could be charged and tried, for they would have filled the existing gaols thirty times over. The danger was that any one of them could be selected as an example to deter the others.

The struggle to alter the law was long and hard, fought against a background of astonishing public ignorance. A Gallup Poll of the 1960s showed that 93 per cent of the population thought that homosexuality was a disease, and it was commonly assumed to be contagious. A young man who came into contact with a homosexual was supposed to be in grave moral danger, notwithstanding the fact that it was he, the younger man, who more often than not had seduction in mind. The dread of sweeping contamination gave rise to the most virulent prejudice, and it was generally deemed better not to discuss the subject lest these slumbering angers be unleashed. Until the Wolfenden Report of 1957 the word 'homosexual' was rarely uttered in public, and when a case came before the courts it was not unusual for ladies present to be warned that the evidence was likely to be shocking and that they should therefore leave the building; for the most part, they did.

Some measure of the ignorance which prevailed may be gleaned from books published at the time. In *Against the Law* (1955), Peter Wildeblood admitted on the first page that he was homosexual. It now seems an unnecessary confession, but he was the first to make it in print, and it was then thought to be amazingly bold. (Wildeblood had just served sentence after a particularly sensational case, otherwise he would certainly not have had the courage to lay himself bare in this way.) He also found it necessary to explain that homosexuals were by no means easily recognizable; indeed, most people thought they could 'tell one a mile off' by the limp wrist and the mincing walk. That this appalling ignorance continued into the 1960s, apart from in some medical and psychiatric paperbacks which were snapped up and devoured in the same hungry way that children used to pore through medical books looking for dirty words, is attested by a study of homosexuality by Bryan Magee published in 1966. The chapter headings of *One in Twenty* speaks volumes for the gap in education which Magee's book intended to fill. 'What do male homosexuals do?', 'What lesbians do', 'Can homosexuals change?', 'Who are the homosexuals?' That such questions should be asked now, only twenty years later, would appear ludicrous, but such was the climate of intolerance that they were treated very seriously, and Magee's book was one of the contributing moves towards reform.

At the same time, there were people whose standing in the community suffered if they so much as suggested that reform was a good idea. The distinguished writer and lawyer Dr H. Montgomery Hyde may serve as an example. Between 1950 and 1959 he sat in the House of Commons as the Ulster Unionist member for North Belfast, during which time he was an outspoken and fearless campaigner for a number of reforms, including the abolition of the death penalty and the liberalization of laws concerning homosexuality. It was this last concern which cost him his seat, as his constituency association refused to readopt him as their candidate in 1959 on the grounds that 'We cannot have as our Member one who condones unnatural vice.'

This kind of attitude was alarmingly widespread. In the House of Commons a Conservative backbencher, Mr Godfrey Lagden, gave his opinion that 'in the general run the homosexual is a dirty-minded danger to the virile manhood of this country,' while in the Upper House there were many voices to support Mr

Lagden. Field-Marshal Lord Montgomery said that a weakening of the law would 'strike a blow at all those devoted people who are working to improve the moral fibre of the youth of this country,' and Earl Winterton, in an earlier debate, had predicted the end of British influence in the world if men were allowed to dally with each other in this loathsome way. 'I am convinced,' he said, 'that the majority of British people agree with me that few things lower the moral fibre and injure the physique of a nation more than tolerated and widespread homosexualism.'

Newspapers, also, tended to favour continued persecution. One columnist in particular, Mr John Gordon of the *Sunday Express*, carefully nurtured his reputation as the scourge of the thinking man. 'Perversion is very largely a practice of the too idle and the too rich,' he wrote. 'It does not flourish in lands where men work hard and brows sweat with honest labour.' As was usual with Mr Gordon, what he wrote was demonstrably untrue, but this did not induce his editor to sack him, presumably because such views accorded with his readers' prejudices. In fact, there were among men convicted of homosexual acts ten times more labourers and factory workers than there were 'idle and rich' men of independent means. But Gordon's intemperate outburst perfectly described the mood of Britain before the social upheaval of the 1960s, and identified one of the root causes of Britain's isolation – snobbery. Just as, in the Lady Chatterley trial, it was tacitly assumed that Lawrence's book was safe in the hands of the upper classes but would sew corruption like a forest fire if read by servants and wives, so the love (or even lust) of one man for another was thought to be limited to graduates from public schools and would lead to degeneracy if practised by lorry-drivers and farmhands. Absurd though it now seems, this was the attitude which literally terrorized homosexuals into silence and dissemblance until the mood gradually changed as the decade progressed. Gilbert Harding said that life would be much easier if everyone who had indulged in a homosexual act were to turn an appropriate shade of blue, for there would be so many tinted people walking the streets that one would quickly see the idiocy of a law which sought to incarcerate such people. The law was applied with shameful ferocity, and before we chart its destruction as one of the major reforms of the 1960s, we need to journey briefly into the history of this legislation and the climate which it engendered.

The Act which first made homosexual behaviour criminal was passed in 1533, in the reign of Henry VIII. It was sandwiched between an Act for 'the avoiding of receipts in callendering worsted' and another 'against killing of young spawn or fry of fish,' and there is evidence that it was motivated by political rather than moral considerations, as a means of removing some power from ecclesiastical courts. It stipulated that the 'detestable and abominable Vice of Buggery' be adjudged a felony punishable by death and forfeiture of property. It was re-enacted several times in subsequent years, and subjected to legal clarifications in 1631 (in the trial of the Earl of Castlehaven, when it was declared that emission of seed was sufficient to constitute buggery, whether or not penetration had taken place), and again in 1828 (when the judges decided that proof of penetration was required in order to show that an offence in criminal law had been committed). Under this Act, all men who engaged in anal intercourse were liable to suffer death, and in practice many did, the last execution for the offence being recorded in 1836. Finally, in 1861, the punishment was reduced from death and forfeiture of property to life imprisonment, and with this modification the Act of 1533 remained on the Statute Book until 1967.

It was a much later Act of Parliament which was to cause all the mischief and leave in its wake a long line of what Oscar Wilde aptly called 'monstrous martyrdoms'. Exactly a hundred years ago, in 1885, the Criminal Law Amendment Bill was moved by the government as the direct result of public disquiet aroused by the campaign of the journalist W. T. Stead to draw attention to juvenile prostitution and white slavery. The Bill was not remotely concerned with homosexuality. Its purpose was to provide protection for women and girls and to control brothels, and its main legacy was to raise the age of consent for adolescent girls from thirteen to sixteen, where it remains today. It was in all respects a beneficial and admirable Bill.

Having passed through all its stages in the House of Lords, the Bill went to the Commons, where after the Second Reading it was referred to a committee of the whole house. The committee stage was taken late at night on 6 August 1885.

At this point, the Liberal-Radical MP Henry Labouchere tabled an amendment to insert a new clause, to the effect that:

> Any male person who, in public or in private, commits, or is party to the commission of, or procures or attempts to procure the commission by any male person of, any act of gross indecency with another male person, shall be guilty of a misdemeanour, and being convicted thereof, shall be liable, at the discretion of the court, to be imprisoned for any term not exceeding one year with or without hard labour.

Another member rose to point out that the proposed clause had nothing whatever to do with the subject under discussion and should not lie within the scope of the Bill before the House, but the Speaker ruled that at this stage any amendment of whatever nature could be introduced. The amendment was accepted on behalf of the Government by the Attorney-General, who increased the proposed penalty from one to two years, and there was no further debate upon it. What was later to be notorious as the 'Labouchere amendment' was passed by a thinly-attended House of Commons in the early hours of the morning just before the summer holidays, without anyone appearing to notice its import or implications. One wonders if Labouchere himself was aware what he was up to; as the editor of *Truth*, a magazine not unlike the modern *Private Eye*, he had a keen social conscience and an ambition to protect rather than restrict freedoms, and was altogether the most unlikely person to be author of such a punitive measure. The Criminal Law Amendment Act (1885) became law on 1 January in the following year. Under it, Oscar

Wilde was convicted, serving his full term of two years without remission.

Three conditions of the Labouchere amendment could have been foreseen as pernicious with a moment's thought. First, there was no age limit mentioned, so that the clause could not be said to have been designed for the protection of minors. Any man of whatever age could be accused, no matter how responsible or discreet he might be or however loyal to his partner. Secondly, he was committing an offence even if his actions were restricted to the privacy of his home and were unknown to anyone else. Thirdly, the reference to 'any act of gross indecency' was so imprecise that it could be held to include (and was so held) simple masturbation or, still less, touching the genitals. Even the Henry VIII Act of 1533 did not make *all* homosexual activity a crime, but specified sodomy as the object of its attention. Now, for the first time in English criminal law, any kind of sexual embrace between men, at any time or in any place, could be termed 'an act of gross indecency' and be punished with two years' imprisonment (the full severity of the 1533 legislation, prescribing life imprisonment for buggery, was still in force). The Labouchere amendment was in every sense a retrograde step.

Many of the sentences passed in the following eighty-two years were inexplicably harsh and made one question the moral sanity of those who imposed them: a man of twenty-five charged with an act of indecency committed nine years earlier, when he was sixteen; a boy who joined the Air Force at the age of nineteen, served two years, then faced charges dating back to his schooldays in an orphanage, his career and self-esteem destroyed. Even as late as 1963, when the movement for reform was already under way, the Lord Chief Justice sentenced a twenty-two-year-old labourer and a twenty-four-year-old United States airman to three years for buggery and indecency, with the remark, 'Whilst there is no question of corruption, both prisoners being grown-up men, I am not going to condone such action between consenting adults.'

The law had not truly been applied in all its force until the appointment in 1944 of Sir Theobald Mathew as Director of Public Prosecutions. Mathew was a Catholic with puritanical sympathies, who took a lively personal interest in the elimination of 'vice'. He was given energetic support years later when Sir John Nott-Bower became Metropolitan Commissioner of Police, declaring that it was his avowed intention to 'rip the cover off all London's filth spots.' This was in 1953, two years after the sensation caused by the defection of Burgess and Maclean to Russia amid squeals of alarm that they had been permitted to hold sensitive positions when all the world knew (or at least everyone in the Foreign Office knew) that they had been homosexual.

The Home Secretary instructed the police to institute 'a new drive against male vice,' a task they undertook with unseemly relish. A senior officer from Scotland Yard was despatched to America to confer on methods with the Federal Bureau of Investigation, and there followed a wave of prosecution against the famous and the distinguished in an effort to show that the new men meant business. One of England's finest actors was cruelly exposed and held in public contempt. The writer Rupert Croft-Cooke was found guilty on the evidence of two men who declared that they wished to withdraw charges exacted from them under police pressure but were not allowed to do so. Homosexuals were invited to turn Queen's evidence and make accusations on the promise of immunity from prosecution simply to increase the incidence of such cases before the courts, and junior constables were seduced by the prospect of early promotion if they could notch up several arrests of 'queers'. No method was too sordid for the police to engage in, no evidence too tainted to be presented before a jury. It was a liability to have one's name in the address-book of any man suspected of homosexuality.

Young policemen were selected for their handsome appearance to act as *agents provocateurs*, with instructions to enter public urinals and behave in such a way as to attract the attention of men and invite them to fondle. Many did in fact engage in some homosexual activity before they revealed their identities and arrested their partners. Since there were as many homosexuals in the police force as there were in other professions, quite naturally, the situation sank to the depths of tragic farce where a man might enjoy the company of another one day and return the next day in uniform to make an arrest.

Soon after the passing of the 1885 Act it was nicknamed the Blackmailer's Charter, and in 1953/4 the blackmailers, with the connivance of the Police Commissioner, had their *annus mirabilis*. It was a matter of unequivocal certainty that if a man reported to the police that he was being blackmailed for alleged homosexual offences, he would be charged with those offences, no matter how stale and ancient, and was likely to serve a longer term in prison than his persecutor. Not surprisingly, few would take the risk, preferring to lose their life's savings rather than face obloquy for themselves and their families. Many, indeed, were married men, which made the threat of exposure even worse, since the gulf between reality and public understanding was so great that no one could conceive a 'queer' being in all other respects a normal man.

By far the most heavily reported cases were those involving a peer of the realm, Lord Montagu of Beaulieu, at the end of 1953 and in 1954. In the first case he was charged with committing an unnatural offence against boy scouts, and with indecent assault. The police were so determined to get him that they tampered with his passport (or let us say that his passport was tampered with while it was in police possession) in order to prove him a liar when questioned about his movements, and thus influence the jury's level of trust in his answers on other matters. He was acquitted on the first charge, but the jury disagreed on the second, so a re-trial was ordered.

While this was pending, the Director of Public Prosecutions brought new charges against Lord Montagu, Peter Wildeblood and Michael Pitt-Rivers, including one of conspiracy to commit acts of indecency. Details of these charges were released to the

Press before any of the accused was allowed to consult with his solicitor, thus making it quite impossible for Montagu to be fairly treated at his re-trial on the earlier charge. Police searched the homes of the accused without a warrant, and read Lord Montagu's private letters from his fiancée. The evidence against all three men was provided by rogues who traded for immunity, and in the subsequent trial the real English vice was laid bare by counsel's accusation that Lord Montagu had associated with people who were 'infinitely his social inferiors'. The three defendants were found guilty, Pitt-Rivers and Wildeblood being sentenced to eighteen months, and Montagu to twelve months.

Crowds gathered outside the courtroom in Winchester, some to jeer, others to see what a homosexual looked like. The whole business was unwholesome in the extreme. Cockney schoolboys who wished to taunt each other gave up the accusation of being queer, calling out instead 'so-and-so is a Montagu.' Such was the effect of hysterical publicity upon the name of a respected and useful member of the community. But in the long term the Montagu case was to prove the turning-point, for it revealed that the law with regard to homosexual behaviour in England had not advanced one inch since the prosecution of Oscar Wilde and that police methods had, if anything, deteriorated. Some public reaction was measurably in sympathy with the three defendants, although it would take Parliament another thirteen years to catch up. There were a sufficient number of people in positions of responsibility who felt shame for what had happened for the first suggestions of reform to be whispered.

The first voice raised was, to the surprise of many, from the Church of England. Even before the Montagu trial, the Church's Moral Welfare Council had published a pamphlet entitled *The Problem of Homosexuality: an interim report*, which proposed that homosexual behaviour should no longer be regarded as criminal, and pointed out that 'the homosexual is capable of a virtuous love as clean, as decent and as beautiful as one who is normally sexed.' Immediately after the trial, the *Sunday Times* defected from the general antipathy of the Press to print a leading article which suggested that the British attitude to sex between males was riddled with hypocrisy and called for an enquiry into the subject, the case for which was 'overwhelming'. Other newspapers and periodicals followed suit. Even John Gordon, of the *Sunday Express*, was incensed by the revelation that police inspectors were empowered to ransack a man's home without a warrant. The resistance of bigots was as firm as ever, but not strong enough to withstand the tide, and only one month after the public humiliation of Lord Montagu, the Home Secretary bowed to pressure and agreed to set up a Departmental Committee, under the chairmanship of Sir John Wolfenden, to investigate the law and make recommendations.

The Wolfenden Committee took three years to prepare its report, from 1954 to 1957, but since its recommendations were not accepted until ten years later, it may properly be regarded as belonging in spirit to the reforms of the 1960s. There were fifteen members of the Committee, drawn from legal, ecclesiastical, political and medical disciplines, and it called over two hundred witnesses, both expert and lay, to assist its deliberations. Nobody could say with any certainty how many men in Britain were affected by the law as it stood, as there had been no authoritative study on the incidence of homosexuality, but there had been two comprehensive works published in America, by Dr Kinsey and colleagues, on the sexuality of the human male and the human female, in 1948 and 1953.

The Kinsey Reports were well known in Britain by virtue of their prurient exploitation by the Press, but they were not so easy to obtain. One of the books was actually confiscated in Doncaster (Yorkshire) by order of magistrates who thought it likely to 'deprave and corrupt,' and a doctor went so far as to write in a professional journal that 'it would have been a cleaner world if Kinsey had stuck to his rats.' The Wolfenden Committee, however, took Kinsey as a serious and reliable source, finding that his controversial figure of 37 per cent of American males who had indulged in some homosexual activity in their lives, to the point of orgasm, could be safely translated, with reservations, into English terms.

Wolfenden came to some conclusions which, at the time, seemed startling. The Committee found no evidence to support the view that homosexual conduct led inexorably to the degeneracy of a nation, nor that homosexuals represented a greater security risk than drunkards, gamblers, or promiscuous heterosexuals (the truth of which is not, even now, as widely accepted as it should be). They saw no reason to suppose that a law which prohibited homosexual conduct succeeded, or ever could succeed, in reducing that conduct, and that the law was therefore both useless and derisory. On the other hand, those who thought that homosexual conduct was repugnant would continue to do so whether or not the law was changed. Even more importantly, the Committee repudiated the frequent contention that homosexuals made a habit of seducing youth; there was no evidence that an adolescent seduction had any lasting effect upon a boy's eventual orientation, but there was ample evidence that criminal proceedings arising from such an incident, with attendant publicity and domestic drama, could be extremely harmful.

Part I of the Committee's report dealt with female prostitution, Part II with homosexuality. It declared unequivocally that personal behaviour in matters of sexual interest should be the private responsibility of the individual and not the business of the law. Further, it was ludicrous that the activities of two men together might render them liable to life imprisonment if those activities took a particular form (under the 1533 Act), but to only two years behind bars if they took another form (under the 1885 Act) which might be no less repugnant to ordinary people. Therefore, they recommended that *all* homosexual behaviour between consenting adults should no longer be an offence under the law.

The Wolfenden Report, like the Denning Report a few years later on the Profumo affair, became something of a best-seller. It represented, after all, the first real information to be publicly available on a mysterious, taboo subject, and the British are not a people who enjoy being kept in the dark. Wolfenden set in motion the drive towards education, and to him must belong the initial credit for changing the law. It was generally said that Sir John had written most of the Report himself, and its persuasive, restrained, elegant tone, that of a sensible and sane man trying to shovel off years of debris from an essentially simple subject, earned universal approval. There was scarcely a voice dissenting as articles poured forth in the Press welcoming the Wolfenden proposals. It seemed that at last Britain was ready to shake off an embarrassing hypocrisy.

The Conservative Government, on the other hand, behaved as if they wished they had never heard of Sir John Wolfenden and his irritating report, and clearly hoped that if they did not mention his name, he and his proposals would be forgotten. The Government did not intend to act in any way on those proposals, still less to introduce legislation which might actually carry them out. Silence and neglect were to be their watchwords. The Home Secretary, R. A. Butler, stated that there was 'at present a very large section of the population who strongly repudiate homosexual conduct and whose moral sense would be offended by an alteration of the law which would seem to imply approval or tolerance of what they regard as a great social evil,' after which nothing more was said by anyone. Wolfenden was well and truly shelved.

Privately it was suggested that, though the Report was full of good ideas, and while *of course* the law would have one day to be changed, it was far too early for such a drastic revolution. The country simply was not ready. The notion that reform was good in itself but would get better if delayed was a novel one. The truth was that the Government was nervous, even frightened, not so much as a body of legislators, but as a collection of men.

One man who was most certainly not afraid to face up to the implications of the Report was Lord Longford, who has the credit in this long saga of being the first to bring the matter to the attention of Parliament. Longford introduced a debate in the House of Lords on Wolfenden three months after the report's publication, without pressing his motion to a division. It afforded the first opportunity to test opinion in the light of the new awareness. Ten peers spoke in favour of Wolfenden's recommendation, eight against. Among those who resisted were the septuagenarian Earl Winterton, already quoted, and the Lord Chancellor Lord Kilmuir (who, as David Maxwell Fyfe, had been the Home Secretary who had set the police their task of eliminating homosexuality by whatever means they thought most effective). On Lord Longford's side were the Archbishop of Canterbury, and one of the most respected and most overtly 'masculine' peers in the country, Lord Brabazon of Tara. Having pointed out that all sexual intercourse is in cold logic rather unattractive, whether it involves men and men or men and women, Brabazon spoke eloquently for tolerance and an open mind; in fact, he was trying to shift the minds of his fellow peers into a different gear, not merely convince them reasonably, but unshackle them emotionally:

> I feel myself [he said] that to have on the Statute Book of this great country imprisonment for life for one act of homosexuality between men is almost going back to the time when people were hanged for stealing five shillings . . . If there is one thing I deplore more than anything else, it is the inclination in some quarters to indulge in witch hunts.

The Commons, however, remained sluggish on the issue. Despite attempts by such men as Robert Boothby and H. Montgomery Hyde to summon interest, the Government was determined that Wolfenden should be emasculated by neglect. They would not provide time for a debate. Over a year passed before they relented, allowing the House to debate the recommendations of the Wolfenden Committee at the end of November 1958.

This was the debate which produced such ill-natured hysteria from Mr Lagden, and shallow indifference from most other members. On the Labour side, Anthony Greenwood said it was tragic that a still greater toll of human misery would have to be exacted before the law was changed, but even he felt it necessary to add that he spoke only for himself, not for the Labour Party. The closing speech for the Government stated categorically that the 'instinct' of the public and of both Houses of Parliament was to reject Wolfenden. No vote was taken, as the motion 'That this House takes note of the Report' was specifically designed to avoid one, and thus spare members the awkward dilemma of making a stand one way or the other.

By now it was clear that pressure would have to come from outside Parliament. Accordingly, the Homosexual Law Reform Society was established to argue for new legislation and to further educate the public. Their undisclosed primary purpose was naturally to educate Members of Parliament. Nowadays, when there is a proliferation of organizations, all of which have kidnapped that useful and beautiful word 'gay', it is difficult to imagine how bold it was of anyone to inaugurate such a society, especially one which had the temerity to use the word 'homosexual' in its title for all the world to see. It was immediately suspected by the ignorant of fostering 'buggery clubs', and it had somehow to manage a low profile with a loud voice. Of necessity, many of its officers used pseudonyms, for their careers and their very freedom would have been at risk had their identities been known; police harassment continued unabated.

The Homosexual Law Reform Society arose out of a letter to *The Times* on 7 March 1958 calling for the early implementation of the Wolfenden recommendations and signed by, amongst others, Noel Annan, Lord Attlee, A. J. Ayer, Isaiah Berlin, Robert Boothby, C. M. Bowra, Julian Huxley, C. Day-Lewis, J. B. Priestley, Bertrand Russell, Stephen Spender, A. J. P. Taylor, C. V. Wedgwood and Angus Wilson. The initiative for forming the Society was taken by a lecturer in English Literature at the University of Wales, Mr. A. E. Dyson, who approached the signatories of this letter and invited them to be on the Honorary Committee of the proposed Society. He also enlisted the support of both the Archbishop of Canterbury and of York. Kenneth Walker, a distinguished surgeon and sexologist, was made Chairman, while the Secretary was an Anglican clergyman,

Andrew Hallidie Smith. In the early days, the fearsome burden of work involved in keeping the issue alive both by writing to all and sundry and by consulting the MPs of all parties was undertaken in private homes. By 1964, when the momentum towards reform was becoming urgent, the Society had tiny offices in Shaftesbury Avenue and had changed its personnel. The new President was A. J. Ayer, the Chairman C. H. Rolph, and the Secretary Antony Grey. It was Grey (a pseudonym) who acted as spokesman and chief negotiator and who gradually grew established in the public mind as the moving spirit.

Grey soon realized that MPs' reluctance to tackle the question responsibly was due to their fear of unpopularity among their constituents ; in other words, quite understandable self-interest. Evidence of this came through his letter-box occasionally, as indignant correspondents (who were obviously someone's constituents) declared implacable hostility to his aims. One writer finished with the remark, 'I would sign my name to this letter but people like me have to be protected from people like you.'

In the years that followed, the work of Antony Grey was largely submerged by the quite proper recognition for the parliamentary efforts of Lord Arran in the Upper House and Leo Abse in the Commons. But Arran and Abse would have been unlikely to summon such arguments as they did without the field-work of Grey, who in turn would have floundered without the public forum which his parliamentary sponsors could command. Grey's task, to turn the tide of public opinion in order to make reform more palatable to hesitant MPs, was herculean.

The General Election of 1959 returned another Conservative Government, and R. A. Butler was again appointed Home Secretary, in which capacity he received a delegation from the Homosexual Law Reform Society and told them once more that legislation was premature. However, there was to be a debate on the Wolfenden Report at last, in June of 1960, and he would be happy to review the situation after that.

A Labour MP and future Minister of Health, Mr Kenneth Robinson, introduced a motion calling upon the Government to 'take early action' on the recommendations of the Wolfenden Committee. The motion was defeated by 215 to 101, on a free vote, but it was perhaps significant that all but one of the speakers from the Labour benches supported the motion, while every single voice from the Conservatives opposed it.

Two years later, in March 1962, Mr Leo Abse introduced his Sexual Offences Bill for the first time, having drawn lucky on the ballot for Private Members' Bills. It was an exceedingly modest document. Mr Abse thought it wiser not to seek to implement the principal recommendation of Wolfenden (to legalize acts in private), but to advance gingerly, by asking Parliament to agree that all prosecutions for offences involving consenting adults in private should be authorized by the Director of Public Prosecutions. The Bill also sought to minimize the danger of blackmail by prohibiting prosecution for offences committed more than twelve months earlier, and to make mandatory the provision of a psychiatrist's report for first offenders. The opponents of reform were in force to kill even these lukewarm proposals, which one of them called 'Wolfenden watered down,' and they contrived to prolong artificially the preceding debate so that there was only one hour at the end of the day to attend to Mr Abse's Bill. Accordingly, it was 'talked out' and abandoned. The decade of the Sixties did not begin at all auspiciously for homosexual men, who might with justice think that London could hardly be a 'swinging' place for the likes of them.

Meanwhile, the process of education undertaken by the HLRS continued, and they were able to discern tiny shifts in attitude as Britain advanced into its new era. For one thing, they earned the support of Sir Thomas Moore, 'Father' of the House of Commons and a usually reactionary Tory Member. For another, the Director of Public Prosecutions issued a directive to Chief Constables in 1964 asking that they consult him in future before bringing any charges which involved private behaviour. Then the General Election of October 1964 returned a Labour Government with the promise of a new atmosphere in public life. But the Government's majority was so small that the HLRS thought it imprudent to press for reform when the likelihood of success was still not great. A new election would have to be held soon, and it would be better to save one's energies for a more stable Parliament.

Nevertheless, the reformers were lucky to gain the support of their ultimately proudest champion, Lord Arran, in the early days of the new Parliament. Lord Arran was never on the Honorary Committee of the HLRS, but he approached them and announced that he intended to introduce the Wolfenden recommendations in the House of Lords as soon as he was able. The decision to grasp this particular nettle was therefore taken independently by Lord Arran, not as a spokesman for the HLRS, and their views did not always coincide. But, as Antony Grey has written, 'There is no doubt that the main Parliamentary credit for achieving homosexual law reform is his.' Arran's Sexual Offences Bill was debated in the House of Lords on 24 May 1965, and when the division took place he carried a majority in favour of 94 against 49. The Third Reading of his Bill on 28 October of the same year was carried by 116 votes to 46.

The significance of these votes was not lost upon the homosexual population of London. It was the first time that a majority in either House had declared in their favour. It was about this time, in 1965, that London was assuming its festive role as home of the world's adventurous and creative youth, and there was a noticeably more relaxed atmosphere in the Earl's Court pubs where homosexuals habitually congregated, even if their association outside the pub had to be furtive, and the danger of blackmail persisted.

Leo Abse sought permission to bring in a similar Bill to Lord Arran's in the Commons under the Ten-Minute Rule, but was refused. In the following year, however, a Conservative MP, Humphrey Berkeley, was able to introduce a Private Member's Bill and take it to a vote on Second Reading on 11 February 1966. It was carried by 166 votes to 109, a majority of 57. Thirteen members of the Cabinet voted in favour of the measure, not including the Prime Minister, Harold Wilson, who did not vote either way. This was again a breakthrough, for now the House of Commons had perceptibly shifted in mood. It is not without interest that the Commons *followed* the Lords in their progress towards reform, rather than led them, an uncomfortable paradox to swallow for those apologists of Labour's crusading zeal. Unfortunately, Wilson called a General Election in March 1966, which meant that all matters pending had to be dropped, and the whole business would need to be started again from scratch in the new Parliament. At least there was only one more mountain to climb.

For the third time, Lord Arran introduced his Bill in the House of Lords only a matter of days after the General Election of April 1966. The Bill's Second Reading took place on 26 April, the Third Reading on 16 June, on both occasions being carried by a comfortable majority. Hostility to the Bill from Lords Montgomery and Dilhorne could not disguise the trend of opinion behind Lord Arran, who had the pleasure of announcing to their lordships that Admiral of the Fleet Earl Mountbatten of Burma gave his wholehearted approval to the measure. Lord Arran worked closely with Antony Grey of the Homosexual Law Reform Society in getting the Bill through ('Fathering William', they called it), as for both of them it was not only an important experience, but an unusual one. Lord Arran was not accustomed to pushing legislation through the complex and tedious processes of Parliament, and was therefore very willing to accept the offer of Government help. Harold Wilson's Government was very clever in this regard: they did not sponsor the Bill, or take it over, but officially remained neutral. On the other hand, they provided government draftsmen to prepare it, and government time to hear it, so that they could have some influence on its content, and could claim it as their own if it proved to be popular in the country. If being kind to queers helped maintain the Government's 'image' as an enlightened and civilized body of men, so be it. If on the contrary it made them seem effete and slack, they could always claim that it was not their Bill at all, but a Private Member's.

One could understand their anxiety. It was by no means easy to judge the popular mood. The heroes of the young were looking increasingly androgynous, with shoulder-length carefully styled hair arranged by a ladies' hairdresser. Six years had passed since the American pianist Liberace had to stand in a British courtroom and deny that he was homosexual, in pursuit of his libel claim against the *Daily Mirror* which had suggested that he was. Those six years now seemed more like sixty, and though entertainers did not make gratuitous and embarrassing confessions of their sexuality, nor did they strain unduly to conceal it. Privately, discussion was much more open than it had ever been before, and homosexuals could behave with the same freedom as heterosexuals in 'picking up' someone at a party, without attracting too much police attention. Had the police returned to their pre-1964 selective persecution, there would have been uproar. The task of educating Joe Public was practically completed before Fathering William entered its final stage.

There was no room for complacency, however. When Canon Montefiori was rash enough to suggest at a meeting in Oxford that Jesus Christ might have been homosexual, he earned a sharp rebuke from the Archbishop of Canterbury, Dr Ramsey, and a cold reception in the Press. This kind of extravagance awoke precisely those fears which opponents of reform could prey upon; namely, give them an inch and they will take a mile! The Tory MP who said reform would not cleanse the national bloodstream but would corrupt and poison it did, after all, represent a certain point of view which the reformists would ignore at their peril. Lord Arran was keenly aware of this, and therefore much more flexible in his response to Government advice than Antony Grey, for whom nothing less than *total* reform would suffice. Grey was the polemicist, Arran the pragmatist.

Leo Abse, who again introduced an identical Bill in the House of Commons under the Ten-Minute Rule, was also a pragmatist with many years' experience in the art. He knew just how far one could go without touching sensitive nerves among MPs which could push into reverse all the progress made so far. With the new, younger, House of Commons, Abse could count upon the support of about 60 Conservatives for the first time, and he was not going to compromise this support by demanding too much of it. Privately, he accepted the Freudian view that everyone was essentially bi-sexual, and he knew well enough that the most vociferous opponents of reform were often those men who were most likely to succumb to the temptations of what they regarded as sin, but it would be folly to air these views in debate. Abse skilfully steered his Bill through all its stages with rational, dispassionate argument, avoiding any discussion of morals which might quicken thinly concealed fears. His cautious approach did not endear him to Antony Grey and the HLRS, who urged him to be more radical.

For example, the Government wanted the age-limit for homosexual conduct with consent to be fixed at twenty-one. Antony Grey, probably correctly, considered this to be impossibly high, and thought it odd and incongruous that girls should be protected by the law up to the age of sixteen, while boys should be regarded as being in need of protection and unable to know their own minds until they were twenty-one. He suggested that young men of the future would not be able to understand or forgive this anomaly. Abse, on the other hand, perceived that the attraction felt by many heterosexual men for the charm of an adolescent boy would make them look with horror upon any measure which sought to legalize sexual relations between men and boys; it was effectively their own potential which frightened them. Rather than initiate a dangerous discussion as to when a boy became a young man, Abse willingly accepted the twenty-one age limit, thus ensuring that the main provisions of the Bill could proceed with the minimum of impediment and the maximum of speed.

Tactical considerations again ruled the day when the Service Ministries requested the insertion of a new clause exempting merchant seamen (as well as servicemen) from protection under the Bill. Mr Abse acquiesced, even though the hastily drafted wording of the new clause made legal nonsense. (As a result of this clause, a merchant seaman may not lawfully engage in any homosexual act with another merchant seaman, either from the same British ship or from another British ship. If, however, he has homosexual relations with a passenger, or with a foreign merchant seaman, he is protected by the law.) As Mr Abse subsequently wrote, 'I could not take seriously their attempts to prevent buggery in the Merchant Navy. In practice, there were ships where it was tolerated and those where it was not, and men with homosexual dispositions rarely made the error of joining the wrong ship.'

The last lap of Leo Abse's Sexual Offences Bill was a nail-biting experience. The third reading was set for Monday, 3 July 1967, and it went on all night long. Abse knew that he would have to keep at least 100 supporters awake in order to move the closure and pass the Bill, and during the seven separate divisions which took place during the night the numbers fell at one point to 103. It required only four Members on his side to collapse and go home for the Bill to be lost. In the event, they hung on, and history was made as dawn rose on the morning of 4 July, with a majority for the bill of 85 votes.

Before it could become law, the Sexual Offences Bill had to pass through its remaining stages in one session. Therefore, Lord Arran was called upon to introduce it for the last time in the House of Lords. This debate was notable for a remarkable speech by Baroness Wootton, who did not intend to contribute but was so taken aback by Lord Dilhorne's intransigence that she rose without notes to deliver this extempore observation:

What are the opponents of this Bill afraid of? They cannot be afraid that these disgusting practices will be thrown upon their attention, because these acts are legalised only if they are performed in private. They cannot be afraid that there will be a corruption of youth, because these acts will be legalised only if they are performed between consenting adults. And obviously, they cannot be afraid, as they might be afraid in the case of illicit heterosexual intercourse, that such action will result in irresponsible procreation. I can only suppose that the opponents of this Bill will be afraid that their imagination will be tormented by visions of what will be going on elsewhere.

Surely, if that is so, that is their own private misfortune, and no reason for imposing their personal standards of taste and morality on the minority of their fellow citizens who can find sexual satisfaction only in relations with their own sex.

Arran concluded the debate by paying tribute to Antony Grey, who had done more than any other individual to bring this problem to public attention. Royal Assent was given on 27 July 1967, whereupon the Sexual Offences Act immediately became law throughout England and Wales (Scotland and Northern Ircland had to wait another fifteen years).

There was no dancing in the streets, no marches of celebration, no ostentatious braying by the victorious. Gradually, homosexual men began to be less fearful of admitting the nature of their domestic life in casual conversation, less anxious that there might be a policeman at the front door at any time. Some coffee-houses opened, like the Gigolo in King's Road, Chelsea (beneath the Casserole Restaurant), where men could congregate in peace and make friendships in freedom. But there was no awful prose-lytizing; that did not emerge until many years later with the Gay Liberation Front and like organizations who could not remember how inconceivable it was to be gay and 'gay' before 1967. In the Sixties, the mood was one of quiet relief, not stridency.

Of course, the new law was not perfect; laws seldom are. Two anomalies have already been mentioned, (a) that a merchant seaman may have sexual relations with a stranger who is a passenger on his ship, but not with a friend who is also a merchant seaman, and (b) that a man may not consent to homosexual activity until he is 21. In fact, the law for people between 16 and 21 is perhaps worse than it used to be in some respects. Two men aged 20 can still be sent to prison for two years even should their conduct take place in private, while a man of 21 is liable to five years' imprisonment if he indulges in any homosexual act with a man of 20, even in private and with both parties consenting. That a boy can be guilty under the law of rape at the age of 14 but incapable of knowing his sexual desires until he is 21 is plainly ludicrous. In practice, as the years go by the police are less and less inclined to meddle in private affairs. (In just the same way, life imprisonment remains the penalty today for a man who commits buggery with his wife, but it is the convention not to enforce this law.)

Another real difficulty has been the legal definition of 'in private'. Originally, the Wolfenden Committee intended this to be left to the courts to decide, as they do when a heterosexual display is alleged to be offensive to public decency. But the Bill's opponents forced their own narrow definition upon Mr Abse, with the result that as the Act stands behaviour is only 'in private' when no more than two people are involved. Three homosexual men in a room together must legally remain chaste, but if a woman is present and consents to whatever conduct they propose, then they are free to indulge in sexual activity within the law.

After the Act became law, Lord Arran expressed anxiety lest it might be abused, implying that no one should suddenly feel free to flaunt homosexuality, but should remain discreet. His fears in the long term proved justified, in so far as there have sprung up since 1967 a number of discothèques where on certain nights hundreds of men openly flirt and fondle. The irony is, however, that nobody minds any more, and if the discothèque is successful, heterosexual couples frequent it as well and show no signs of shock. So the legacy of the Sixties in this regard is rather greater than the sponsors of the new law intended; it is nothing less than one more indication of the belated maturity of the British people in their contemplation of sexual mores. The Act which changed the law heralded a revolution in attitudes which changed the British character. Even the guardians of public morals (always self-appointed) concede that homosexuals are no different from the rest of us, and if they attempted to revert to former attitudes, they would now be laughed to scorn. That is an achievement which cannot be measured in votes.

One aspect of homosexual life did not change. The 'rent-boys' who hung around Piccadilly offering themselves for money still do so, and probably always will. They are mostly part-timers, supplementing their income when the need arises, and they are there, as they always were, of their own free choice. Their clientele are those men, heterosexual as well as homosexual, who feel such guilt within themselves that they need to be furtive, whatever concessions the law may make in their favour, and they, too, are probably permanent. The conclusion of Simon Raven's celebrated and (at the time) alarming article on the renters ('Boys will be Boys', *Encounter*, November 1960) remains as true today as it was then:

Wolfenden may suggest this, the Church may propose that, Mr John Gordon deplore the other thing: but the law of supply and demand is engraven in brass, and is not to be erased by the abstract and irrelevant indignation of catch-penny public moralists.

6

The Theatre

For Christopher Booker it is 'indisputable' that 'there is no clearer window on the psychic health of a society than the condition of its arts.' With this in mind, one can deplore theatrical products not because they are badly written or boring, but because they display symptoms of an illness in 'society', whatever that is. For G. Wilson Knight, it is the other way around; the theatre does not show symptoms of the illness, it is there to correct or cure it. The new dramas which emerged after 1956 'exist to bring new health to the insane paradoxes of a decaying culture.' This accords nicely with Molière's old-fashioned but still persuasive view that the theatrical purpose is to point out the cruelties and follies of mankind and thereby help us to put them right. Mr Booker and Mr Knight agreed that 'society' was ill; so did most of the playwrights of the period.

Personally, I remember the Sixties as a Golden Age in the theatre, not so much for its innovation or its diagnostic brilliance, as for sheer professional perfection, whether in modern plays or in the classics; and it is mostly, I'm afraid to say, the classical productions which delight the memory twenty years later.

First, however, we should test how the so-called 'Kitchen Sink' dramas have earned their right to speak for the age. They were certainly vocal, and manifestly different from anything which had gone before. As early as 1955 we had seen Beckett's bewildering *Waiting for Godot* at the Arts Theatre, offering a new kind of entertainment which was compulsively watchable and meant very little. Samuel Beckett, Irish born and French educated, showed the way towards a new drama of form in which content was recognizable only by the playwright, a way to be followed very shortly by our own Harold Pinter. But the true Kitchen Sink variety did not occur until John Osborne's *Look Back in Anger* in 1956. Does anyone know who first coined the phrase 'kitchen sink' to refer to this new crop of plays? It was apt as a contrast with the 'drawing-room' comedies of Noel Coward and Terence Rattigan, plays in which no character looked as if he had just got out of bed, nobody swore, and everyone had his own tailor and hairdresser. The plays of Coward and Rattigan were acute and often profound, far more so than some of the poor things which followed them, but they earned the contempt of the new generation because they were so obviously contrived, and always took place in the drawing-room. From now on, plays would be set in the kitchen or the scullery, where life really was lived, and people would be real, not stereotyped. It went without saying, of course, that 'people' meant working-class people, the sloggers and toilers whose voice had never been heard on stage and whose disappointments needed expression.

The set for *Look Back In Anger* actually included a kitchen sink over which the middle-class heroine, berated and humiliated by the hero throughout the play, was made to labour (that is, when she was not ironing). I did not see the very first, now historic, production at the Royal Court Theatre on 8 May 1956, applauded by the critics Kenneth Tynan and Harold Hobson, with Kenneth Haigh as Jimmy Porter, Mary Ure as Alison, and Alan Bates as Cliff. Later the same year it moved to the Lyric, Hammersmith, this time with Richard Pasco as the acerbic Jimmy Porter; both the actor and the theatre were curiously appropriate, as Osborne (himself an actor) had written his play while sharing a tiny flat in Hammersmith with Pasco, and a number of the references it contains to shops can be identified in Blythe Road (future historians, please note). This production I did see, and was entirely captivated by the sweep of Pasco's vitriolic verbiage. The language was powerful, and definitely 'angry'; but the character was so tiresome I simply did not believe anyone would have put up with him for five minutes.

One thing was immediately clear. Jimmy Porter's anger was born of class and directed at class. He felt despised by, and in turn contemned, the upper classes who, without chins and with silly voices, had everything their way. Moreover, they were not very bright, whereas the working classes had more native intelligence and more honesty. They required the articulacy of a Jimmy Porter to be their advocate. Unfortunately, he was so disillusioned that he no longer gave a damn what he said or whom he offended. Kitchen Sink drama was, then, to be remorsely proselytizing on behalf of a clearly defined ideal: working-class emancipation. (G. Wilson Knight went so far as to see Porter as a modern Hamlet, with Cliff his Horatio, but it was difficult to see what they had in common apart from being two sets of friends.)

When *Look Back in Anger* was voted Best Foreign Play on Broadway in 1958, the new drama had arrived. It spawned about it a number of like-minded youthful dramatists and writers collectively known as Angry Young Men. Apart from Osborne, they included novelists Kingsley Amis (*Lucky Jim*) and John Braine (*Room At The Top*), both now Complacent Old Men who consider working-class boys to be louts; playwright Arnold Wesker, who did genuinely try to bring the working-classes into the theatre, and failed only because of their lethargy, not his; and a young observer of mankind with the apparent learning of Socrates, Colin Wilson, whose book *The Outsider* was quickly adopted as the expression of youthful ire and became the most surprising best-seller of the post-war years.

Wilson's book was in effect a long philosophical essay in the manner of Albert Camus, dealing with people who were observers of life rather than participators, not, as the psychiatrists would maintain, because they were neurotic, but because they saw and understood too much of life's essential absurdity without being able to do anything about it. They were outsiders because they were too intelligent, and included such as T. E. Lawrence and Van Gogh. Just as Camus had written that the absurdity of human existence did not absolve the intelligent man from proper action, even though he knew such action would be useless, that the very act was the only dignity he had left and which he could still choose, so Colin Wilson said attention must be paid to the outsiders, their counsels heeded, or else we should never understand the psychological condition of modern man and would flounder forever. To say Colin Wilson became a cult figure would be to understate. He was treated like a film star or pop idol. He could not emerge from his front door to buy some eggs without finding an army of press photographers waiting to capture his image. Of course, it was a romantic image; he was young, scruffy and working-class, and lo! he had written a masterpiece. No doubt Wilson enjoyed the glamour for a while, as all celebrities do, no matter what they may say to the contrary, but after a while it became oppressive, and he had to escape. When it was suggested he was organizing orgies on Hampstead Heath and his girl-friend's parents were pestered, he and the lady in question went to stay in a remote part of Devon where photographers might not locate them, fell in love with the place, and have stayed ever since. (There is still a warning on the fence that visitors are only admitted by appointment.)

The Outsider is a fascinating book today, and will survive the tawdry attention it received on publication. But all Angry Young Men were meant to read it. Some wrote their own treatise entitled *Declaration*, which allowed them to vent ferocity in all directions. There were contributions from John Wain, Lindsay Anderson, John Osborne and Kenneth Tynan. Colin Wilson, instead of remaining aloof from this schoolboy tantrum, made a contribution. (In subsequent years, he has devoted a great deal of time and energy to the study of murder, which he considers a manifestation of the outsider's frustration.)

Working-class themes from working-class writers required working-class actors to present them. Now that we have become used to BBC announcers making a mess of the English language, presumably by command, it is difficult to recall that just before 1960 these announcers were the admiration of the English-speaking world, and every actor who aspired to the great heroic parts had John Gielgud as his beau idéal. A working-class accent had been such a severe handicap that it could cripple one's career. From 1960, it was quite otherwise. New young actors with *real* voices (i.e. ones that ordinary people used) emerged in triumph. Albert Finney from Salford, Lancashire; Tom Courtenay from Hull, Yorkshire; Peter O'Toole from Leeds, Yorkshire; and later (in films), Michael Caine from Camberwell, South London. Their rise was part of the Sixties' respect for working-class talent, but I doubt if it would have come about so quickly without the plays on proletarian themes which were then so much in evidence. Some whispered that Michael Caine was a fraud, because his first (and best) film role was the upper-class officer in *Zulu*, but he was a genuine Cockney; he was at the same school as myself, Wilson's Grammar near Camberwell Green, where he was known as a rather dull chap with a name something like Michael Micklewhite.

Another working-class playwright who, sadly, has not yet fulfilled the promise of her first work, was Shelagh Delaney from Salford. Her *Taste of Honey* was first produced at the Royal Court in 1959 and later made into a film with Rita Tushingham and an unforgettable portrayal of a sympathetic little queen by Murray Melvin. There were also the anarchic and linguistically liturgical plays of Brendan Behan, an Irish drunk first brought to attention by the pioneering Joan Littlewood at her theatre in the East End of London, with *The Quare Fellow*. English drama could not survive for long, however, if it remained quixotically glued to the class system. Osborne's and Wesker's plays could ironically become as unrepresentative of English life as Coward's and Rattigan's had been before them. There were other strands emerging which have proved more enduring. One, in a category all by himself, was held by Harold Pinter, a writer whose plays have continuously held audiences spellbound by releasing them from the obligation of having to work out what was happening on stage; they are like prose-poems of inconsequential delight with a mysterious undercurrent of menace. Another type of drama, in the hands of Robert Bolt and Peter Shaffer, sought to examine the human condition in the hope that understanding might palliate some of its worse consequences. Neither of these strands in new drama was restricted by consciousness of the English class system.

Finally, there was the work done on classical theatre both at the Old Vic and at Stratford-on-Avon which reached heights in the 1960s as yet unparalleled. Because they were not 'new' they have avoided the gloat of nostalgia and have been written about much less, but they were the real achievement of the decade. As a postscript, one should not forget also the unique experience of the World Theatre Season at the Aldwich; once a year Peter Daubeny brought the best of theatre from all over the world and in all languages to London, and in spite of audiences having to wear headphones if they wanted to hear a translation, an encumbrance one might have thought intolerable, the season was regularly sold out. (I did not understand a single word of one of the finest performances I ever saw, by the Spanish actress Nuria Espert; the great French tragedienne, Edwige Feuillère, was a regular star for whom audiences queued all day at the Aldwych. Our debt to Peter Daubeny has never been properly acknowledged.)

If we look at what was available in 1960 (or, more precisely, what this particular theatre-goer remembers most clearly, for the selection in this chapter is a resolutely personal one), we can see these various strands developing independently of one another and each acquiring a considerable audience. It may be platitudinous to say so yet again, but London audiences seem able to vary their taste and attempt any theatrical experience that comes along; the same people will struggle with Ibsen, be patient with Shaw, giggle with Ayckbourn or sit glum-faced through Beckett. (This is not true of concert-goers; the faces at the Festival Hall and Wigmore Hall are never seen inside a theatre.) On 27 April there opened at the Arts Theatre a play by Harold Pinter which would prove to be a landmark. This was *The Caretaker*, with Alan Bates, Peter Woodthorpe and Donald Pleasance giving weird, uncanny interpretations of ordinariness and at the same time suggesting that nothing was ordinary, that the threat of unknowability lurked in every human being. It later transferred to the Duchess Theatre, where bewildered audiences were subjected to an odd and lingering experience.

Over at the New Theatre (now called the Albery) in St Martin's Lane the first night of *Oliver* took place on 30 June. Based on Dickens' novel *Oliver Twist* and written by former pop-song churner Lionel Bart, it was an immediate and joyous success. No difficulties, no profundities assailed the audience. On the contrary, not only was the story simple, sentimental and familiar, but it gave us an excuse for pride. Here, at last, was an English musical which did not fall flat on its face. Until then, the successful musicals had all come from New York (*Carousel, The King and I, Oklahoma*), and English attempts had always been clumsy. Only two years before, in 1958, Wolf Mankowitz's brave satirical show *Espresso Bongo* had limped home, proving an embarrassment for its star, the classical actor Paul Scofield. *Oliver* did not boast wonderful music, but simple memorable tunes (the *on dit* went around London that Lionel Bart has artfully played some Mozart back to front and set words to it), and an adorable hero in young Keith Hampshire, who sang a number all by himself on stage, as well as a hateful villain in Ron Moody's portrayal of Fagin. The latter is still occasionally to be seen playing the part twenty-five years later; not so Mr Hampshire! The real star of *Oliver* was the designer, Sean Kenny, who created a revolving wooden set which so expertly conveyed the 'feel' of Dickens' squalid yet exuberant London that it received a warm ovation all to itself.

At the Haymarket was John Gielgud's melodious Shakespearian recital *Ages of Man* to remind us that there was no greater actor in our time to illuminate the rich poetry and wisdom of Shakespeare's lines with his lyrical voice – and I nurse the hope that someone will persuade him to do it again before he retires. While at another theatre, the Cambridge, the rough cadences of our newest actor, Albert Finney, were enticing audiences to Keith Waterhouse and Willis Hall's *Billy Liar*, when Finney left the cast, he was replaced by an even newer name, straight from acting school, Tom Courtenay. The next year saw the same happy juxtaposition of old and new, experimental and established. At the Lyric, Hammersmith in February was Brendan Behan's remarkable *The Hostage*, and at the Aldwych another recital, this time by four actors, called *The Hollow Crown*, which virtually gave a history lesson in British monarchy in the most entertaining manner imaginable; once again, what it really celebrated was the versatility and reliability of English actors.

Just to prove that the old-fashioned Broadway musical was not dead, the Palace Theatre showed Oscar Hammerstein's last creation, *The Sound of Music*, which cheekily defied a uniformly hostile Press to run for years. The critics found it trite and embarrassing, the public disagreed; as its subsequent popularity in a film version with Julie Andrews demonstrated, the public was right. In its way, this also served to illustrate one of the strengths of London theatre, namely that audiences will make their own choice and find their own level despite advice from their betters, a healthy circumstance which does not obtain in New York. No one could say that people went to see the plays of Wesker, Pinter and Osborne because newspapers told them to.

Arnold Wesker's plays were enjoying especially success at this time. *Roots*, with Joan Plowright and Charles Kay, had transferred from the Royal Court to the Duke of York's, and now *The Kitchen* was put on at the Royal Court in June 1961. Their relentless but affectionate realism touched a chord which has not been heard since. Wesker was followed at the Royal Court by Osborne's new play in July; this was *Luther*, starring Albert Finney and directed by Tony Richardson, Osborne's third success in a row. (*The Entertainer* had received the unexpected accolade of a central performance by Sir Laurence Olivier, who *asked* to play the part.) Nevertheless, the finest jewel of the year was not a new discovery but a fresh portrayal of an old favourite, Chekhov's

The Cherry Orchard at the Aldwych, for which was assembled a cast of such talent and distinction that one could comfortably predict that no finer production would be seen for half a century (I have seen three since, and none ever began to approach it in depth of casual insight). Peggy Ashcroft, Judi Dench, John Gielgud, Dorothy Tutin, Ian Holm, Patience Collier and Paul Hardwick all carried utter conviction.

This production of *The Cherry Orchard* was supported by the big guns of the Royal Shakespeare Company which, under the direction of Peter Hall at Stratford-upon-Avon and at the Aldwych Theatre in London, was building the international reputation which endures to this day. In 1963 its rival, the National Theatre, was finally born after wearisome decades of advocacy and persuasion by those who believed in it against every discouragement, paramount among whom was Sir Laurence Olivier. Yet more years would have to elapse before the National's concrete home on the South Bank was built, and in the meantime it began, grew and flourished at the Old Vic in Waterloo. Its company of actors was as strong as the Royal Shakespeare's, with Olivier himself, Michael Redgrave, Ralph Richardson, Lynn Redgrave, Maggie Smith, Colin Blakely and Robert Stephens, and the peculiarly warm and intimate ambience of the Old Vic seemed to suit the company (for those incorrigible backward-lookers like myself) much more than the austere home it now has.

The National's inaugural production was, perhaps inevitably, *Hamlet*, directed by Olivier. It was not well served in the leading role (Peter O'Toole) and has mostly been forgotten by those who saw it, but for me it will live forever in the mind by virtue of one extraordinary performance – Rosemary Harris as Ophelia. Miss Harris was so touching and true, her ultimate insanity so pitiful and understandable (actresses usually go 'over the top' when given this plum) that I feel sorry for anyone who missed it. For what it's worth, Miss Harris was the recipient of one of only two fan letters I ever wrote – anonymous as fan letters should be, to release the actress from any obligation to reply and any suspicion that there might be motives other than abject admiration.

Hamlet was followed by *Saint Joan*, *Uncle Vanya*, and a host of sparkling comedies, of which I mostly remember *Love For Love*. The Royal Shakespeare Company countered with their own *Comedy of Errors*, starring Alec MacCowen and Ian Richardson in a double act as the two Antipholi, which has yet to be surpassed in the frequent revivals of this romp. Hardly subdued by this explosion of talent to serve the archaic, the Angry Young Men had their own representative at the Vaudeville, with Arnold Wesker's brilliant portrayal of army life in the ranks, *Chips With Everything*. (Like everything else that was new and good, it had started at the Royal Court, the theatre in Sloane Square which almost alone encouraged, nurtured and launched the new British dramatists.) There have been those happy to denigrate *Chips With Everything* as shallow, like a TV series in the afternoon (its popularity did, as it happened, spawn a number of television series devoted to a celebration of the Cockney warrior, notably *Dad's Army*). Others ventured into hyperbole and called it 'one of the noblest tributes to the English fighting man since *Henry V* and *In Which We Serve*.' The truth was that it was marvellous theatre, superbly directed by John Dexter to depict life in the barracks for raw recruits of varying types, thrown together by circumstances under the same roof as a sergeant-major with the voice of a rapturous sea-lion. This part was played by Frank Finlay. One of the most touching portrayals of a private was delivered by Ronald Lacey, who made his name in this play and promptly disappeared; a few years later he was an actors' agent. The whole was imbued with real affection and perceptive observation; it deserved its success, although it could only be called 'angry' in so far as it made the fairly obvious point that young men should not be taught how to kill other young men, especially by pompous upper-class officers who would not do it for themselves. The Angries were turning into better craftsmen of theatrical art than they were polemicists.

There is no doubt in my mind that the *annus mirabilis* of the decade was 1964, a year of such riches as have not been equalled for sheer grand theatrical effect, and a year which made it quite obvious even to the blasé cosmopolitans that London was now the best city in the world for its drama, of whatever nature and in whatever house. Both the National Theatre and the Royal Shakespeare Company produced plays of such spectacle as to make the cinema knock its knees, and the Royal Opera House had its finest operatic production as well as its finest ballet production for many years.

In February at the Aldwych, Paul Scofield gave the best performance of his career as King Lear; not only *his* best but the most mighty reading of a mighty part that anybody could recall. The production, by the erratic genius Peter Brook, and with a cast which included Alec MacCowen, Irene Worth, Michael Williams and Ian Richardson, was so successful that every performance was sold out and crowds hovered outside the theatre every evening hoping for a returned ticket. The play was performed in repertoire with an even more ambitious and on the face of it crazy undertaking called *The Wars of the Roses.* Adapted from the three parts of the rarely performed *Henry VI* together with the familiar *Richard III*, this concoction reassembled the bits into three plays narrating consecutive events, which one could either see on three evenings or, on a few choice occasions, all in one day. The first play started at 10.00 a.m., the second followed in the afternoon (after only an hour's break), and the third in the evening, so that those lucky enough to be part of this unique experience went to the theatre equipped with sandwiches and a flask of tea. It must have been as exhilarating an ordeal for the actors as it was an unnatural feast for the spectators.

There was much that made *The Wars of the Roses* unforgettable, quite apart from its grandiosity and length. It was, for example, a lesson in the art of acting to watch Dame Peggy Ashcroft as Margaret, an eighteen year old after breakfast passing through all the ages of bravado and brilliance to disillusion and bitterness until she ended a broken old harridan before our supper. David

Warner played the good and kind Henry VI, unequal to the corrupting demands of power, Roy Dotrice was Edward IV, and Ian Holm the wicked conniving Richard. The cast also included Brewster Mason, John Normington, Donald Sinden, Michael Craig and Charles Kay. Peter Hall's production made no compromise whatever with the brutal emotions and events depicted by Shakespeare, and much that was seen on stage was quite revolting, but it was never gratuitously so. The final scene, with Richard fighting for his life at Bosworth, was achieved by two figures alone among swirling fog wielding enormous clubs and chains and lances about the stage like two blinded creatures in combat; it was simply terrifying to watch. John Bury's set contributed in no small way to the candid realism of the scenes, and the audience emerged into the night chastened and proud.

Another attraction was to try spotting the scenes and the speeches which had not been written by Shakespeare but had been interpolated by John Barton in tying the Bard's four plays together into a cogent whole. Barton's mastery of the language was such that few among even Shakesperean scholars noticed the deception until they were well into the 'invented' passages.

For those interested in the curiosities of theatrical fame, there was an actress playing the part of Mrs Simpcox, with one line allotted to her, who passed virtually unnoticed. It would have been a brave man who predicted a bright future for her, and although I cannot claim to have done that, I did spot her and wondered when something more substantial might test her talent. It did not happen in the Royal Shakespeare Company, but when she left and found, by what accident I know not, the playwright who suited her as she suited him, her celebrity was assured. This was Miss Penelope Keith, and the playwright in question was Mr Alan Ayckbourn. But that is a story which does not belong to the Sixties.

The ostensible excuse for *The Wars of the Roses* was the quatercentenary of Shakespeare's birth in 1564, and it was by far the most brilliant celebration of that anniversary. Over at the Old Vic, the event was marked by a new production of *Othello* which leaves me, in retrospect as it did at the time, in an awkward spot. For Laurence Olivier played the Moor as a Notting Hill Gate Jamaican, and I found myself at the first night embarrassed by such gross misjudgement on the part of a great actor; I fully expected the Press the next day to share my misgivings, and could only conclude, by the cacophony of praise which ensued, that I was wrong and they were right. The film version was just as bad and was lauded just as extravagantly.

In August there was another sensation of quite a different order. There was a vogue for the 'Theatre of Cruelty', inspired by one Antonin Artaud and supported vigorously by Peter Brook and Charles Marowitz (of whom it was said that he required actors to audition by reciting from *Hamlet* while standing on their head). The theories of Artaud, briefly that the theatre should shock, had informed Brook's production of Lear to a certain extent. He now turned them to electrifying advantage with a production at the Aldwych of *The Persecution and Assassination of Marat as performed by the inmates of Charenton under the Direction of the Marquis de Sade*, a play by Peter Weiss. For the sake of convenience it was universally known as *The Marat/Sade*, and it gave the actors of the Royal Shakespeare Company, almost all of whom had to play lunatics, a welcome and challenging holiday from their usual endeavours. Brook's staging presented the vision of a nightmare so powerful that the audience was visibly uncomfortable, and hardly breathed. It also gave the first major part as Charlotte Corday to an unknown actress called Glenda Jackson who, as John Gross put it, 'totters along with a secretive little smile which puts to shame the kind of grimace which usually passes for madness on the stage.'

Also in 1964 we had Richard Pasco as *Henry V*, and a riotous production of *Hay Fever* with Edith Evans, Derek Jacobi, Maggie Smith and Lynn Redgrave. At the Wyndham's Theatre was revealed a totally original talent in Joe Orton, who had struggled unrecognized for years and now revealed his endearingly anarchic humour in a play called *Entertaining Mr Sloane* which was the big hit of the year in the 'commercial' theatre. Alas, his career was to be cut short, after two more plays, by brutal murder at the hands of his lover. Three more brilliant productions made London the centre of attention before the year ended. At the Royal Opera House Kenneth Macmillan created a new full-length ballet to Prokofiev's music for *Romeo and Juliet*, with choreography specially designed to suit the mercurial emotional range of Lynn Seymour and the youthful passion of Christopher Gable. During the weeks of rehearsal word travelled that this was likely to be more intense and rending a version of the ballet than any so far seen, for no choreographer was better equipped to show in dance the real cruelty of the human drama, but to everyone's surprise (and presumably for the most short-sighted of reasons – namely box-office appeal) the opening night was given not to Seymour and Gable but to Margot Fonteyn and Rudolf Nureyev.

No one would want to disparage the artistry of this extraordinary couple, probably the most accomplished (as well as least likely) partnership in the whole of twentieth-century ballet. The Sixties belonged as much to Nureyev as anyone. He had defected in 1961 and given his first performance in the West with Dame Margot in *Giselle*. From that moment his supremacy had never been questioned. Margot Fonteyn, to whom every decade belonged, was, one thought, at the end of her career, being well into her forties. But the new partnership galvanized her to such a degree that it prolonged her career by almost twenty years. They had together achieved a record, on one occasion, of over eighty curtain-calls. The fact was, however, that Nureyev was not the best casting for an Italian youth, nor Fonteyn for a shy adolescent. Though they acquitted themselves well, the real 'first night' of *Romeo and Juliet* was the performance some weeks later allotted to Seymour and Gable, at which, when in the final *pas de deux* Romeo dances with the seemingly lifeless body of Juliet whom he thinks dead, the emotions of pity and fear aroused in the audience were virtually tangible.

The second of the trio also took place at the Royal Opera House: Franco Zeffirelli's production of *Tosca*. Now, I am not one who sits comfortably in an opera audience, and cannot therefore compare this experience with the other doubtless admirable achievements of the Sixties. Only one other opera did I see, an absurdly boring thing called *Moses and Aaron*, which contained an orgy scene we were told would be shocking and which was so inept one could only conclude that singers of opera had no idea what to do with their bodies from the larynx down. There are more educated people (e.g. Bernard Levin) who can chart great evenings in this field. But as for *Tosca*, it was so apart from any ordinary idea of opera, so dramatic, so tense, so productive of acute stomach upset, that I feel sure an audience addicted to *Coronation Street* would have responded. The cast was *sans pareil*: Maria Callas as Tosca, Tito Gobbi as Scarpia, Renato Cioni as Cavaradossi. There were only six performances, and one of these, I seem to remember, was cancelled (or rather, Maria Callas' participation in it was cancelled), with the result that tickets were changing hands at outrageously black-market prices, well over £100. Allowing for inflation, that would be like spending nearly £1,200 for a ticket today. I have already told in another place how I managed to get in to see a performance without a ticket*, by buying one for something else and running round the block to lose breath before rushing in with seconds to spare and giving the doorman no time to examine the ticket.

If I were to try telling the effect of this experience, words would stumble, collide and collapse. Maria Callas, with a voice which even I could tell was strained, dominated that space to a degree one can only call magical, for there was no clear and sensible reason for it. She was acting, she was singing, but we felt she was in such danger of forgetting these basic protections that she would lose herself and actually murder Scarpia on stage in front of us. The interplay between her and Gobbi was probably (though I cannot be sure) unequalled in the history of this opera, creating such tension that the audience dare not budge. And when, having killed him, she lay candles either side of the body

---

* In *A Night at the Theatre*, edited by Ronald Harwood.

on the floor before whispering, '*E davanti a lui tremava tutta Roma*', one longed for the curtain to fall so that one could allow some breath to escape. Perhaps most extraordinary of all, Callas did not sing her arias centre-stage, arms aloft, facing the audience, but wherever the dramatic necessity placed her – into the drapes, into the armchair, into her arm-pit.

The third piece of theatrical magic came from an author who has often been dismissed as 'facile', a word I always think conceals envy. Peter Shaffer had been praised for his *Five Finger Exercise* some years before, and would delight with the farce *Black Comedy*, in which the cast were in total darkness at the beginning of the play, but did not seem to notice it, and when suddenly the lights went up, behaved as if there were a massive fuse and they were in total darkness! I saw the Queen in the audience for this, and she chuckled hugely. In the next decade, Shaffer would show with *Equus* that he could handle an audience and bring them to such a pitch of emotion at the end of the drama that they dare not applaud for about thirty seconds lest they burst into tears and disgrace themselves (precisely this happened on the first night, when, unlike now, no one knew what the play was about, our only clue to its content being that 'equus' meant horse).

Shaffer's contribution to the Sixties was nothing less than to tell the history of the conquest of Peru by the Spaniards (*The Royal Hunt of the Sun*). He reduced it ultimately to a dialogue between the conquistador, Pizzarro (Colin Blakely) and the Sun King, Atahuallpa (Robert Stephens) in which the nature of belief was explored, without at the same time losing the dramatic impact of Atahuallpa's pending death at the hands of the merciless Catholic Church. Stephens gave a magnetic performance, fittingly playing the King as superhuman, or unhuman, with a tortured liturgical voice barely recognizable to mortals. Atahuallpa was considered literally immortal by the Incas, who did not believe that Pizzarro could kill him if he wanted to, and when Atahuallpa dies, and fails to get up, the Incas in their spectacular costumes turned their huge immobile masks to the audience in silent incomprehension, and the play ended on this pitiful, tragic note. Shaffer is supremely a man of the great theatrical moment, which marks out good theatre more surely than the most pious intentions and the most convincing 'message'. For messages, one reads books; in the theatre, one expects to *feel*.

It would be too tedious to list all the theatrical moments in this glorious period, and I should be bound to offend by omitting some. Obviously, Peter Brook's circus-style production of *Midsummer Night's Dream* was historic. Equally certainly, there were plays of substance on homosexual themes for the first time, notably *Fortune and Men's Eyes*, and *Boys in the Band*. Pinter's finest play came in the Sixties – *The Homecoming*, with a haunting performance by that much underrated actor John Normington. And Osborne's fine drama, also with a homosexual theme but tangential to a deeper study of social mores under strain, *A Patriot For Me*, opened at the Royal Court. In a recent revival at Chichester, Alan Bates played the leading role created by Maximilian Schell and received an award for it; in accepting the accolade, Bates said that *Patriot* was one of the best plays of his generation.

A Patriot For Me made history in a small and in a big way. The small contribution is not generally known. An extremely talented young director at the Royal Opera House, Covent Garden, with an undisciplined sense of humour and a rare talent to sing falsetto, was Mr John Copley. Of course, he never sang in public, only at parties, his professional life being closely confined to directing. But on one recent occasion his voice had been heard by a small but enthralled audience. He had taken rehearsals of *Tosca* for the Callas–Gobbi season, and Callas had not turned up for a dress rehearsal. Undeterred, Copley said he would sing the part himself. Some Callas fans were hovering about in the foyer hoping to catch a note of their idol, and when they did hear the voice issuing forth in *'Vissi d'Arte'*, they were observed to be near swooning and muttering '*la diva, la diva*'. No one thought to disillusion them.

John Osborne knew of Mr Copley's secret talent, and persuaded him to appear on stage, for the first and only time in his career, in *A Patriot For Me*; it was a specially written part in the party scene, which required Copley to wear a large frock in singularly bad taste and to sing an aria from Mozart's *Cosi Fan Tutte*. You will not find Mr Copley's name in the programme – he is disguised there in the fiction of John Forbes.

The large way in which Osborne's play pushed history along was in the matter of censorship. The Royal household, in the office and person of the Lord Chamberlain, still maintained the sole power to approve or prohibit any theatrical production. Scripts had to be submitted to him, as they had been for two centuries, before any performance could take place. The Lord Chamberlain instructed that five whole scenes should be excised from *A Patriot For Me* before he would permit the play to be shown publicly. Not unnaturally, the playwright who had laboured over his creation refused to comply, and the Royal Court Theatre had to be made into a private club with every member of the audience being obliged to join, before the play could be seen.

The situation was manifestly absurd and scarcely credible in the latter half of the twentieth century. Even the club device could not be relied upon, as club performances had no status in law; they could be prosecuted under an Act of 1843 and the offenders fined. The Lord Chamberlain himself must have realized how daft his powers were and connived to make them look even dafter, when he found parts of Chaucer's *Miller's Tale*, written some six centuries before, unsuitable. So Osborne's obduracy helped to create the movement for reform which eventually placed the Lord Chamberlain in his lush field of retirement.

The other play to hasten his departure was Edward Bond's *Saved*, which created a mighty fuss far in excess of any intrinsic worth the play contained, by virtue of a scene in which a baby was rolled in its own excrement and then stoned to death in its pram. The text was submitted to the Lord Chamberlain in June 1965. He kept it for five weeks, then instructed that the baby-stoning scene and another scene be removed, in addition to some words here and there. Bond refused. The Royal Court Theatre became a club for the second time, and audiences flocked to see what they had already heard was a daring play. Challenged to justify the offending scene, Edward Bond had no difficulty. 'Compared to the "strategic" bombing of German towns,' he said, 'it is a negligible atrocity; compared to the cultural and emotional deprivation of most of our children, its consequences are insignificant.' In strictly logical, semantic and philosophical terms, Mr Bond was surely right, but he was suspected (unfairly) of sensational motives. Peter Watkins, the director of a film called *Privilege*, said, 'I want people to walk out of my films, and think.' Some suspected that Edward Bond wanted people to walk out of his plays and vomit, but if so, it was by now widely agreed that they should be allowed to do so and that theatres should not be restricted to suit the ethical standards of demented women or subnormal pubescents.

With the removal of the Lord Chamberlain's power to select on behalf of us all, in 1968, there were inevitably as many bad results as there were good. The most celebrated was Kenneth Tynan's concoction *Oh! Calcutta*, a collection of revue sketches which hardly at all rose above the level of miserable schoolboy smut. I recall the cast lining up at the front of the stage and showing the audience their bottoms, which was meant to be daring and was actually an aesthetic howler. The show ran for years, and at the end the audience consisted almost entirely of tourists from the Far East who thought this the ultimate manifestation of 'Swinging London'. On the other hand, there was a rollicking, exciting and energetic American musical called *Hair* which also involved a scene wherein the cast ritually stripped, in a way which was both humble and impressive. This show gave Tim Curry his first job, and a moving song for Annabel Leventon. Its appeal and impact relied at first upon its 'revolutionary' character and philosophy, very quickly dissipated by its enormous popularity with the middle classes whom it purported to shock. After the curtain call, members of the audience were invited to join the cast on stage for a celebratory bit of loose dancing, everyone free to 'do his own thing' in the jargon of the day. Among the first to jump on stage was Her Royal Highness Princess Anne, after which the whole of London seemed eager to join in the fun, and the stage was crammed with rock and rollers night after night.

As the decade drew to a close, there were other theatrical 'moments' to store in the memory. Roy Dotrice played John Aubrey in a one-man show based on Aubrey's *Brief Lives* in which disbelief was so perfectly suspended that when Aubrey died quietly in his armchair at the end, members of the audience could be seen involuntarily shifting in their seats as if they wanted to get up and help him. Judi Dench forsook her classical career briefly to play Sally Bowles in the musical *Cabaret*, and Alec McCowen at the Mermaid held audiences spellbound with his portrayal of the mad and maddening Frederick Rolfe in *Hadrian VII*; director Peter Dews contrived a magnificent scene of awe when the Pope was invited to take the throne by having all the cardinals enter the back of the theatre and walk solemnly down the two aisles towards the stage.

Robert Bolt's play *Vivat Vivat Regina* made a name for Eileen Atkins as Elizabeth I, with Sarah Miles playing Mary Queen of Scots. It is no disrespect to Bolt's consummate craftsmanship to point out that the play's success was greatly assisted by the publication the previous year of Antonia Fraser's bestselling biography of Queen Mary. At the Mayfair Theatre (transferred yet again from the Royal Court) was *The Philanthropist* by new playwright Christopher Hampton, whose first play had been produced in London while he was still a student. It again had Alec McCowen in the lead, and opened with a most unusual first scene in which a suicide pretended to spatter the wall with his brains; never was an audience's attention secured so quickly.

For me, pride of place at the end of the Sixties goes to the Royal Shakespeare Company's revival of a nineteenth-century comedy, *London Assurance* by Dion Boucicault. Its huge success seems to have taken them by surprise, for there was not room in the repertoire to give enough performances to satisfy public hunger, and it had eventually to be transferred to the Albery. *London Assurance* boasted the funniest performances ever given by Judi Dench and Michael Williams, Miss Dench turning the affliction of short-sightedness into a comic mannerism of infinite resource. It also had Donald Sinden acting, as they say, 'over the top' with such superb boldness that he dared the longest 'double-take' I have ever seen. Presented to his son (Michael Williams) whom he did not at first recognize, he actually walked off stage and remained in the wings for a full ten seconds before the light dawned and he strode back on stage to confront his offspring. The audience of course knew that he would, and wondered how long it would take him. There are few actors who could prolong a laugh so dangerously close to extinction, and it taught once more that in comedy, timing is all. This was the only occasion when I have seen grown men in the audience so helpless with laughter that they had to get up from their seats and walk up the aisle to relieve it.

Two more evenings high on my personal list were Peter Nichols' *A Day In The Death of Joe Egg* at the Criterion, which dared, for the first time, to treat in drama the painful subject of a spastic child, and moreover find humour within it, and an import from Broadway, Edward Albee's raw revelation of the torment of cohabitation, *Who's Afraid of Virginia Woolf?* The huge performances of Uta Hagen and Arthur Hill at the Piccadilly Theatre had to be seen to be believed, as night after night they skinned each other in Albee's cruel excoriating dialogue. Understandably, they were excused matinée performances.

People came to London from all over the world in the Sixties to share in the 'scene', to walk down Carnaby Street, to dine at the most fashionable restaurants and to feel the invigorating atmosphere. Those who stayed long enough to attend some of London's forty-odd theatres found, perhaps by accident, the real and solid foundation of the city's attractiveness at this time, for the theatre had never been better served, and the heights it reached have only sporadically been echoed since.

Other less obviously brilliant types of theatre thrived also, many experimental and many imported from America. A group called the Liquid Theatre performed to delighted audiences for a brief period, under the arches at Charing Cross. 'Performed' is an imprecise verb in this context, as the actors had no lines to learn and no stage to appear on. They took on the role of psychiatric therapists for an evening, and left their audiences feeling better for the experience in a much more measurable way than through mere old-fashioned catharsis.

When you arrived at Charing Cross, you were welcomed and taken to a reception area, where your shoes and coats were put in a plastic bag and you were given a token with which to retrieve them later. Then you were divided into groups of about twenty each, and sat around in a circle on the floor. Each group had its own 'actor' who made the members shake hands with each other, then initiated some basic touch games. We were meant to dispense with inhibitions and dispel the distrust we should normally feel with strangers, and relax in much the same way as toddlers are taught at kindergarten. It was all very refreshing, and a revelation to those of us without a regular analyst that to be treated like a child again, with patience, condescension, and charm, was actually quite invigorating. The other way of being treated like a child, that is with mocking disdain and disrespect, is something most people had to put up with every day, either domestically or at work, and you could see the joy on adult faces when they were spoken to in a totally kindly manner. The Liquid Theatre actors reminded us what childish hearts we carry within us all the time.

We had a distinct feeling of being looked after by our own actor and quickly developed a proprietorial attitude towards him or her. The actor then led us to the central act of our intimate drama. One by one he took us by the hand, told us to close our eyes and to keep them closed, as we were taken to the Labyrinth, a mysterious area like a semi-sagging balloon. Still with eyes closed, we walked uncertainly we knew not where until we could feel hands gently touching our neck, caressing and stroking our hair, we were hugged and we felt water on our faces. It was all very bizarre, and quite amazingly full of goodness. At the end of the Labyrinth, we were each kissed twice, by a man and a woman (though of course we did not know this until afterwards) and then opened our eyes. There followed a period to sit in quiet reflection, all drooping with unaccustomed relaxation, then a moment of taste sensation when we had first to contemplate then to eat an orange, mixed with almonds.

Finally, we were led upstairs to an area covered in a painted canvas floor, where each group invented its own slogan and shouted it in friendly competition with other groups. A single note was sounded, and we all had to sing it, building to a climax of noise at which point the band played in a kind of celebratory ritual. The actors then performed a mime, based on Genesis, and the evening finished with dancing, in which everyone participated. The sense of freedom was intoxicating.

Many people left the arches at Charing Cross with a spring in their stride and a smile on their faces. How long these delicious effects lasted was another matter, but that they should occur at all told one something about the relationship between actor/therapist and audience/patient.

It would be an exaggeration to claim that the Liquid Theatre had any lasting influence. The work of some directors in traditional theatre did for a time absorb the vogue for greater audience participation and involvement, a worthwhile aim ultimately spoilt by excess.

Even more diffuse in conception were the 'Happenings' which attracted attention in 1963 and 1964. The first was held at the Edinburgh Festival and owed its being to Charles Marowitz. The first in London was put on by the impresario Michael White, who brought from Paris, Jean-Jacques Lebel's 'International Festival of Free Exhibition' and placed it in Denison Hall, opposite Victoria Station, on 8 and 9 June 1964. Tickets for this Happening could not be obtained from theatres or agencies, but only from the renowned Chelsea bookshop of Mr John Sandoe.

What happened at Happenings, this one and others, might include:

—a man riding a tricycle across the stage and back again.
—a semi-naked woman painted in red dye.
—a footballer in a cardboard box.
—another semi-naked woman pushed around the stage in a wheelbarrow.
—the audience being told to turn 190 degrees in their seats, after which they were thanked and invited to go home.
—a third naked woman having a picture of the Pope projected on her backside.

Michael White managed to get hold of several hundred pairs of shoes that had all somehow gone wrong; shoes with two heels and no toes, shoes with the heels at the front, all making their wearers look sublimely surrealistic.

Jean-Jacques Lebel made large claims for his 'sociodramatic event,' pointing out 'important analogies with disciplines such as Buddhism, Vedanta and Samkhya Yoga, which strip away the illusory world of "form" and "name."' Mr White, more down to earth, said that the Happenings were unusual experiences, and valuable for that alone; they stimulated reactions which were new and strange and therefore an addition to one's life.

The best Happening of all was given privately by the painter Mark Boyle. He invited about thirty people to see a film at his home in Queensgate. They all sat around in the room and watched the film contentedly for about forty-five minutes, but when it came to an end the projector did not stop; it went on turning, the end of film flapping noisily around the spool. No one arrived to turn it off. Eventually, one of the thirty did get up, switch on a light and stop the projector. There was no sign of Mr Boyle. The guests began to explore, and to their initial consternation and amazement, they discovered that the entire house had been depleted of all its objects while they had been watching the film. There were no furniture, no light bulbs, no knives and forks, no pictures, no indication that the place had ever been inhabited. It was stripped of its human dimension, emptied and abandoned, the wholesale removal having taken place in under an hour. They felt, said Michael White, 'rather sheepish,' and since feeling sheepish is not a daily experience, they cherished it.

No survey of theatre in the Sixties, however personal and selective, can possibly ignore the sudden fashion in what was rather archly called 'Satire'. Starting in 1961, it was all over by 1964, but in that brief moment of glory it had become as much a feature of 'Swinging London' as Carnaby Street, the Beatles, and all the rest of the youth-worshipping culture.

One questions now whether it was satire at all. It was ever a characteristic of the British not to take themselves too seriously, to be able to poke fun at their most revered institutions and still leave them intact. J. B. Priestley said in 1961, 'We English take pride in being able to laugh at ourselves. But it is a very gentle laughter. We do not hit our follies hard, and we are extremely annoyed if one of us tries it. We are, in fact, badly in need of a huge astringent dose of self-criticism and satire, which might cut through our plummy complacency.'

It is easy to pinpoint the beginning of satire in London. The date was 10 May 1961, when a revue called *Beyond the Fringe* opened at the Fortune Theatre. Written and performed by four extremely young men just down from university, it derived its title from having been shown first as part of the 'fringe' theatre at the Edinburgh Festival. The men were neatly divided by class, two from the upper (Jonathan Miller and Peter Cook), two from the working (Dudley Moore, son of an electrician, and Alan Bennett, son of a Leeds butcher). The show consisted of a series of sketches with an iconoclastic flavour. One mocked the heroes of the war, another made idiots of black nationalists, a third treated the Royal Family with derision. Yet there was little in all this which could be considered cruel or, to use Priestley's word 'astringent'. Dudley Moore's solo item was a very clever pastiche at the piano of the styles of Benjamin Britten and Schubert. Jonathan Miller gave a soliloquy on the meaning of the instruction in railway lavatories 'Gentlemen lift the seat', musing upon whether this was a social observation or a loyal toast. The central sketch which could claim to be hard-hitting was Peter Cook's impersonation of the Prime Minister, Harold Macmillan, as a decaying old man who was losing his marbles and could cheerfully tear up a letter from an old age pensioner. It was impolite, but it was imbued with affection, and so essentially innocent that Macmillan himself went to see it and did not feel inclined to suicide as a result. The Queen was another visitor.

The best item was no more polemical than Dudley Moore's piano-playing. Alan Bennett, shock-haired and seemingly guileless, adopted a posh accent and stood in a pulpit to deliver a sermon on the sentence, 'My brother Esau is an hairy man, but I am a smooth man.' It was an hilarious parody of the kind of ramblings packed with *non sequiturs* and unintended *double entendres* that one could hear on any Sunday in any English village, and was so wickedly and accurately observed that it is no wonder Bennett has proven with time to be the most talented of the quartet. But satire? It was clear that Bennett was as fond of the preacher he mimicked as he was of his own parents, and saw him as an endearing part of the fabric of English life. (This same characteristic of affectionate but acute lampooning mingled with reverential nostalgia was the glue of Bennett's first play, *Forty Years On*, produced at the Queen's Theatre later in the decade. I suspect Mr Bennett may well prove to be the most enduring chronicler of Englishness we have.)

When Alan Brien wrote that *Beyond the Fringe* was 'rare and raw and sometimes bloody', he was guilty of forgivable exaggeration, for that is what most people thought. We were not accustomed to seeing figures of authority insulted on stage, however mildly. We believed it was deadly, because the surprise anaesthetized our critical judgment. That is not to say, of course, that there were not some in the land convinced the four young men were a menace to good order and decent life. I remember it as one of the funniest revues I had ever seen.

Things became a bit more bloody when the Establishment Club opened in Soho in the summer of 1961. Again, Macmillan was taunted and taboos challenged. Some dirty words were used.

The satirists performed on a tiny stage in a long, small room to late-night revellers eager for something daring to be said. The performers were once more astonishingly young, bringing undergraduate humour to an audience which had never experienced it, and they were much more political than the *Beyond the Fringe* team. (Peter Cook managed to appear at both places.) So popular were they that they imagined they did in fact influence events and change the destiny of the country. One of them, John Wells, wrote, 'We really began to believe that we were in some sense the underminers and detonators of politicians . . . that thanks to us Macmillan had collapsed.' To Macmillan's successor as Prime Minister, Sir Alec Douglas-Home, the Establishment satirists were merciless. Legislation had to be hurried through Parliament to enable him, as the 14th Earl of Home (pronounced 'Hume') to renounce his peerage and take a seat in the Commons. Others who benefited from this new Act were Lord Stansgate, who became Mr Anthony Wedgewood-Benn, and Lord Altrincham, who became Mr John Grigg. Lord Lambton tried to have his cake and eat it, harbouring the quaint notion that he could renounce the earldom of Durham and still call himself Lord Lambton when no such person of that name legally existed (the Earl of Durham *is* Lord Lambton). The satirists would not permit the 14th Earl to forget his antecedents or to imagine for one moment that he was intelligent enough for the job of Prime Minister; if you were a peer you must of necessity be dotty.

1961 also saw the launching of a new satirical magazine, *Private Eye*, unlike any journal we had seen in England this century. Its history has been told often enough, usually by itself, to obviate any need for repetition here. Modelled perhaps on the intelligent anarchy of the French weekly *Le Canard Enchaîné*, *Private Eye* was a curious mixture of genuine, useful exposure of humbug and corruption in high places, and gratuitous personal vilification on a schoolboy level. The mixture remains to this day, and *Private Eye* is the only survivor of the Sixties' passion for satire.

Satire reached television with the launching on 24 November

1961 of a weekly magazine programme called *That Was The Week That Was*, hosted by a twenty-two year-old unknown by the name of David Frost. This indeed was revolutionary. The BBC had never before been known to permit scurrilous attacks on authority, whereas this programme did little else, and was immediately the most successful programme on the air. Interviews were crude and contemptuous, and the nation watched in wonderment as these youngsters took on the pious, the self-important, and the crooks, before a live camera. Some of it was harmlessly amusing, as when Frost described the sinking of the Royal Yacht *Britannia*, Her Majesty, dressed in pale blue, swimming for her life. Some of it was moving, as the programme devoted to an obsequy on the assassinated President Kennedy of the United States. Most of the time it was downright disrespectful, a characteristic guaranteed to annoy politicians. In response to some public expression of distaste, the Postmaster-General, Reginald Bevins, announced that he would 'do something about it'. To his eternal credit, Harold Macmillan (who was still Prime Minister) sent a note to his desk which said simply, 'Oh no you won't.'

The Lord Chancellor, on the other hand, (Lord Dilhorne), got so fed up with the programme that he said 'those responsible for it have got to the stage of being unable to distinguish between what was humorous and what was offensive and rude. I gave up watching it some time ago. It became such a bore.' The Editor of *The Times* deplored the 'sick sniggering attitude to life', and the Director-General of the BBC, who had himself applauded and nursed the programme, was obliged on occasion to ask for some cuts before transmission.

That Was The Week That Was lasted barely a year, having quickly degenerated in content and style. But it made its mark. It also made the reputation and ultimate fortune of David Frost, who was granted an interview to the heir to the throne and sent on his way to transatlantic stardom. By the time he interviewed the most famous crook of all, former President Richard Nixon in the Seventies, he had become cautious and deferential. Had an accident of history brought these two together ten years

[158]

earlier, there might have been a confrontation to give one goose pimples.

And when it was all over, what had it meant? Did the satire fashion engender a brilliant new talent, a twentieth-century Jonathan Swift to make us reflect and ruminate? The answer, alas, must be no. It was a bubble of fun, a display of naughtiness, not a fundamental examination of values. For Christopher Booker, himself the first editor of *Private Eye*, the mood which satire reflected had a more sinister relevance. 'The satirists,' he wrote, 'were the first expression in society of a darker longing for sensation, chaos, and collapse,' and the idea of satire touched in the subconscious minds of its perpetrators 'suggestive thrills of destruction and violence which could never be made manifest.' This is a tendentious and bombastic view, which might be difficult to support (though Mr Booker has a very good, and long, stab at it). I doubt if any of the satirists were truly anarchic, any more than little boys who throw fireworks into the neighbour's garden really want the house to catch fire and burn down, or the owner to kill himself in despair.

A more potent criticism of the movement came from Alfred Sherman, who complained that the satirists were not satirists at all. 'Though satire usually assumes the guise of entertainment,' he wrote, 'its intention is quite different, being to make people feel uncomfortable, guilty, or ashamed of what they believed, did, or supported.' The Establishment Club and *That Was The Week That Was* gave the public what it wanted, whereas satire should make it hear what it is reluctant to listen to, and should do so by stealth, not by shouting.

Mr Sherman poured scorn upon the notion that the Sixties' satirists could be compared with Voltaire, Swift or de Maupassant and that they had blown away outmoded conventions and taboos. 'If sniggers at smut were attacks on taboos, then taboos would have vanished long ago. In fact this is not an attack on taboos, but their exploitation . . . Swift had no time for laughter for its own sake; for him laughter was the surgeon's knife cutting away tumours.' The angry young men currently the fashion had little experience of the dilemmas of power, and so those people who had to live with these dilemmas could not be expected to take the young men seriously. 'The pseudo-satirists approach the dilemmas of power with adolescent arrogance.'

The licensed anger of the Sixties was perhaps a useful exercise, and it certainly brightened up the theatrical scene for a moment. With hindsight it is easy to see that the 'movement' over-estimated its own importance.

▲ 17

17   Harold Wilson meets the Beatles at the
      Dorchester Hotel at the presentation of the
      Variety Club of Great Britain awards 1964

▲ 18 19 ▶

18 Crowds of hippies, beatniks and dropouts
    lounge around Piccadilly Circus 1969

19 Lord Altrincham, who published an attack
    on the Queen

◀ 20 ▲ 21

▲ 22 23 ▶

22   Earl Russell, leader of a mass
       demonstration against the H-bomb, sits
       down outside the Defence Ministry 1961

23   The atom bomb cloud over Nagasaki

24   *Overleaf left:* 'Sit-down' protest outside the
       Ministry of Defence in Whitehall

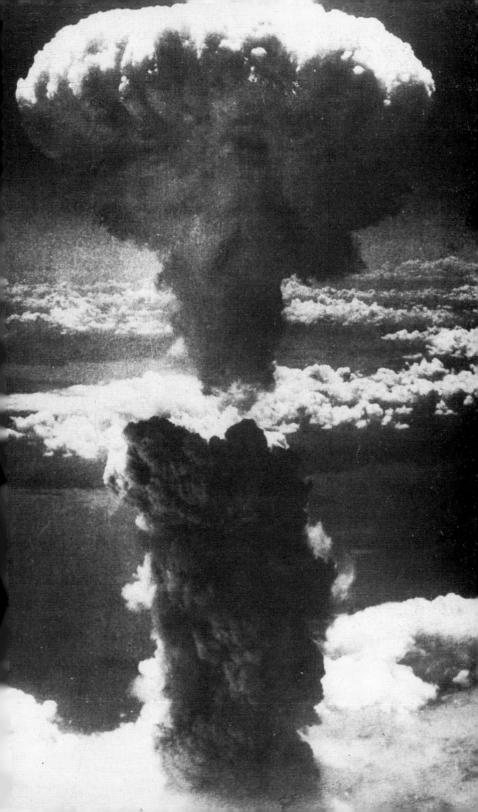

7

Pop

Plato apparently thought that popular music was a potential danger to the State, as not only did it reflect a mood but could actually create one. It would stretch hypothesis to the point of mockery to suggest that the sudden fame of four Liverpool boys singing to guitars and drums in 1963 contributed to the election of the Labour Government in 1964, but the Leader of that Government, Harold Wilson, was quick to see the connection and was not averse to claiming the Beatles as his own. They and he all owed their success (apart, obviously, from charm in the one and ability in the other) to an unprecedented bestowal of admiration by the whole country upon the young.

For the first time, people who were younger seemed to have something to teach people who were older, and the lesson combined cynical resignation with cheerful hedonism. Those born towards the end of or immediately after the Second World War had had their pleasures restricted by rationing, and their pride bludgeoned by disgrace. The Suez crisis of 1956 had had a profound effect upon the idealism one customarily expected from youth. British politicians had indulged in cheap deception on an international scale by pretending, with France, that forces were necessary to separate in a spirit of impartiality the armies of Egypt and Israel in order to protect the international waters of the Suez canal, whereas in fact Britain, France and Israel had concocted their miserable scheme together so as to invade Egypt with an 'excuse' and topple the Government of President Nasser which they did not like. The bitterest irony lay in our loss of moral probity, for virtually in the same week Russia invaded

with similar intent and greater success; to condemn
1 lamentation the iniquity of the Russians required an
y too skilful for politicians to muster. No doubt the
s which threw themselves upon public attention were
simplistic in the view of diplomatic commentators, but they held
power for the young, whose respect for age and experience took
a hard blow.

This was also the generation which was told to accept with a
shrug the permanent reality of nuclear bombs literally capable
of destroying the planet. (See Chapter Nine) A far cry from
popular music, perhaps, but it helps to explain why the young
hurled themselves into hedonism with scornful contempt for
those who told them they should embrace better values. They
acted in the Sixties as if there were no future, quite simply
because there might not be one. The present was all-important.

There was little doubt that what was felt in the Sixties was not
merely the repetition of the 'generation gap' which occurred four
or five times every century and could be identified among the
flappers of the Twenties or the macaroni of the 1780s. Social
observers all agreed on this:

It is a thoroughgoing revolt by a section of young people
against the habits, manners, standards, morals, politics, taste,
taboos, and life-style of their elders. Youthful rebellion is not
new, as trend-spotting vicars are constantly reminding us. But
no previous expression of adolescent frustration has been so
comprehensive, so self-assured, or so cynical.

(Peter Fryer)

A new spirit was unleashed – a new wind of essentially youthful
hostility to every kind of established convention and traditional
authority, a wind of moral freedom and rebellion.

(Christopher Booker)

For the first time in history a generation had appeared which

might not change its ideas or even behaviour when it got to
adult years.

(Bernard Levin)

Come fathers and mothers throughout the land
And don't criticise what you can't understand.
(Bob Dylan)

The young wanted somehow to take charge, to impose their
own values which they were no longer willing to agree must be
inferior and naive solely because they were held by youth. They
wanted exuberance, energy, noise, the exhilarating knowledge
that everything was possible and words like 'no' or 'wait' were
obsolete. They pressed this desire so far that they seemed to
proclaim that all novelty was good *per se* and all change beneficial.
Why not numb the senses with drugs? It was a new experience!
It did not matter too much if one ended up in hospital, since
tomorrow was a doubtful proposition in any case. And alcohol
appeared to be far more damaging to the personality than pot.
Even while it was going on, this blind craving for novelty alerted
some people to the awful legacy that the Sixties might bequeath.
Diana Trilling wrote, 'Our present-day assumption that the new
and dissident are good in themselves, no matter what their form,
may very well lose for us the basic and ordinary knowledge of
human decency, including the knowledge that the human mind,
even in all its weakness and error, is valuable.'

The young were joyfully celebrating sensation as an end in
itself and looking upon practical involvement with human affairs
with derision. It is this aspect of the Sixties' mood which has
been most criticized and is nowadays blamed by some politicians
as the root of all troubles from which Britain has suffered since.
In *The Times* Dr Felix Brown said that the attitude of the young
was 'the saddest and most hopeless philosophy of life which has
ever emerged.'

Nevertheless, the old were ready, nay eager, to copy the young,
a fact which alone made the Sixties revolution unique. For the

first time, they surrendered their traditional right to know better, and adopted some of the tastes and enthusiasms of their off-spring. The trend manifested itself frivolously in fashion, more seriously in political protest (especially the marches organized by the Campaign for Nuclear Disarmament), but it was nowhere more blatant than in their acceptance of popular music. The idols of ten years earlier had been treated with disdain by parents and teachers, but those who now supplanted them – Cliff Richard, Adam Faith, the Beatles, the Dave Clark Five, and so on – were resolutely clasped to the breasts of Mum and Dad. This made all the difference.

Also, it was in the world of popular music that youth could most easily assert itself and make its voice heard. There were, of course, young politicians, young artists like David Hockney, young hairdressers, young designers, young museum directors like Roy Strong, young actors, but as a general rule they had all to be in their early twenties; they were young men and women rather than children (the exception being Bernadette Devlin, elected to Parliament while still under twenty). In popular music, you could achieve fame and fortune at the age of fourteen (Helen Shapiro), and all the new heroes and heroines were adolescents.

If the pop revival can be said to have *started* somewhere, it must be a scruffy small coffee-bar in London's Soho district called The Two I's. There in the cramped smokey dimness sang unknown teenagers who within weeks would be flattered by huge public attention. One was a tall ungracious youth who called himself Marty Wilde and enjoyed enormous popularity for four years from 1958 to 1962. (His daughter, Kim Wilde, is a current favourite more than twenty years later.) Another was a cheeky Cockney seaman who jettisoned the name Tommy Hicks to become virtually an overnight success as Tommy Steele. I re-member delivering newspapers to his parents' house off the Old Kent Road in the mid-Fifties. In October 1956 he made his first record, and two months later went to the top of the Hit Parade (these days called the 'Charts') with a song called 'Singing the Blues'; he stayed at Number One for thirteen weeks. Only three weeks after the record was first issued he was topping the bill at the Café de Paris night-club, an extraordinary honour for a nineteen year-old tyro who had been totally unknown before the winter had begun, and within the year he was starring in a film of his own life story. This kind of instant admiration was to become quite normal during the Sixties. Tommy Steele heralded the future in two other ways: he had abundant energy and confidence, and he was lovable, cosy, wholly lacking in that element of threat which typified the anarchic music of a later year. Odd to think that he is now (1985) approaching fifty, and still darts about the stage like a frisky puppy. His talent was clearly not ephemeral.

The same might be said of Cliff Richard (another pseudonym), a baby-faced youth with seductive eyes who had nine records to reach the Number One position by 1968, and is still liable to attain that august height from time to time. His contemporary Adam Faith, whose gimmick was never to smile when singing, gave up after 1966 and now invests his millions in numerous successful business ventures.

Nobody needs to be told that the most famous of them all were the Beatles – Paul McCartney, John Lennon, George Harrison and Ringo Starr (Richard Starkey) – who came not from London but from the industrial north-west around the River Mersey. So much has been written about them that repetition would be tiresome and the search for fresh information fruitless. Let it simply be recorded that they began their career as the Silver Beatles in The Cavern in Liverpool and that under the inspired management of Brian Epstein they broke the American monopoly in popular music and for the first time made the British lead the world in this field.

The Beatles' first record was released at the end of 1962. Throughout 1963 they could scarcely put a foot wrong, as titles which sound dull in print but conceal an infectious sound and rhythm went to the top of the Hit Parade one after another – 'From Me to You', 'She Loves You', 'I want to Hold Your Hand', 'Can't Buy Me Love'. Still, it seemed only that they were

the most successful current singers in that particular market –
no more. Then at the end of 1963 they were listed to appear
in the Royal Command Performance, an annual variety show
attended by one or more members of the Royal Family and
notable for its old-fashioned air. For hours before the show had
begun all the streets around the Prince of Wales Theatre were
solidly blocked by thousands of screaming hysterical children
hoping for a sight of their heroes. The din would not subside in
deference to royalty, which for once took second place in the
affections of thé crowd. Suddenly it was realized that the Beatles
were more than just another pop group, and at the end of the
year a London newspaper, the *Evening Standard*, devoted a whole
special issue to 'The Year of the Beatles' which rapidly sold out
and is now a collectors' item.

The following year marked the Beatles' conquest of the United
States, which had dominated popular music throughout the
century. They held the top five places in the American charts,
and when they went to give concerts in New York the city went
berserk for days on end. Their hotel was besieged by thousands
of screaming girls round the clock, and Fifth Avenue stores
placed photographs of them in their windows. They were even
accorded the unique privilege of a concert at Carnegie Hall,
previously and repeatedly refused to Elvis Presley who in terms
of records sold was a far more important musician. They were
received at the British Embassy in Washington and unwittingly
caused yet more disruption as the party exploded into such
unruly behaviour, with guests jostling each other to have a view
of the famous four, that the Ambassadress had to apologize and
questions were asked in the House of Commons.

And so it went on. The Beatles' astonishing progress is best
understood in snippets. When they appeared on the television
programme *Sunday Night at the London Palladium*, which went
out 'live', fans broke down the stage door and police had to be
called in. In 1965 they were each awarded the MBE, causing
agonies of protest from soldiers. In 1966 John Lennon made a
casual remark which stuck with him for years and gave rise to

[166]

more protests; he said the Beatles were more popular than Jesus Christ (a pardonable exaggeration in the heat of those days). In 1969 Lennon married his second wife Yoko Ono, and the couple went to bed for seven days to celebrate, giving countless press interviews from between the sheets.

To ascribe the singular success of these four to the power of publicity is an unfair belittling of their achievement, besides which it is obviously untrue, as the publicity people were unprepared for the spontaneous scenes of adoration which took place at the London Palladium, the Prince of Wales Theatre and Carnegie Hall. Nor were the thousands of girls who appeared at London Airport whenever the Beatles were due to leave or return to England in any sense hired or persuaded to lose their heads. First on the list of possible explanations must be their acceptance by the middle class and the middle-aged; as I have said, they were not menacing or dangerous, at least to begin with. Second, it would be churlish to deny that their music was extremely good, although one need not go so far as one music critic who saw them allied to Schubert. The words of songs like 'Yesterday' and 'Eleanor Rigby' were sensitive, perceptive and poetic; for once the 'lyrics' were truly lyrical. Moreover, they really did sing them, instead of miming to their own records as is nowadays the custom, so they were true performers. Lastly, their influence, nebulous and impossible to pin down, far outclassed their considerable talents.

The actress Honor Blackman has demonstrated how difficult a task it is. 'The Beatles,' she wrote, 'did not necessarily do anything but solidify the feeling which was already there among the young all over the country. It's true that breaking out then cost people more, emotionally. That's why it was such a powerful time. Those who stuck out were individuals, worth having around. Everyone else has arrived in their wake.'

The music of the Beatles was universal. I recall hearing their records played in restaurants in Moscow, of all places, when I had been told that the Soviet Union would not permit the intrusion of decadent Western sounds. In Czechoslovakia alone there were over two-hundred pop groups established in imitation, all of them bearing English names. *The Times* opined that the influence of the Beatles:

> enabled millions more to crack the barriers that existed between classes, between London culture and that of the provinces, between souse and geordie and the accents of the BBC and Oxbridge. Their style of dress and hair and their irreverent behaviour led the youth of Britain to a new and independent identity. The Beatles were not the most outrageous or iconoclastic members of the pop scene, but their example was the most influential.

And the price they paid? Paul McCartney telephoned acquaintances he barely knew from his hotel room in 1965 because he dare not go out; he sounded desperate and trapped.

'Revolution' is possibly too portentous a word to apply to developments in the world of 'pop' music, which is generally regarded as a small and not very impressive part of the cultural life of a country. Yet the greater proportion of the population is in fact addicted to pop music on the radio, which offers all the revitalizing entertainment they require, interrupted by the barest minimum of news. Until 1964 this greater proportion was starved of nourishment. It is difficult now to conceive what it was like to switch on the wireless in the early Sixties. In the first place, the BBC had a monopoly of the airwaves, so whatever one listened to came ultimately from Broadcasting House. There was no disadvantage in this, as the variety and scope of programmes was greater then than it is now, but the system was calamitously negligent of young addicts to pop music. Only once a week, for half an hour, could you hear the latest records on the Hit Parade; singers might perform them by chance on a variety programme, in between the comedians (of whom there was a surfeit), but the notion of a station which played nothing but pop music all day long was quite surrealistic.

[168]

There was one exception to this otherwise total deprivation. Radio Luxembourg employed disc jockeys like Pete Murray and Jimmy Savile to chatter away while placing one record after another on a turntable, but reception was always bad, and children had endlessly to fiddle with the wireless if the songs were not to be obliterated by crackle. Those hours spent in the bedroom with Radio Luxembourg instilled an affectionate loyalty to the station which sounded as if it came from outer space, a loyalty which persists with some to the present day.

As the BBC showed every reluctance to cater for this taste, a young entrepreneur called Ronan O'Rahilly, manager of the *Scene* club, opened a pirate radio station operating from a ship outside the jurisdiction of English courts. The ship was called the *Caroline*, after President Kennedy's daughter, and the station was naturally known as 'Radio Caroline'. Its broadcasts caused such a rumpus that the Post Office received instructions to isolate the ship from all communication with the mainland, and the Foreign Office made formal complaint to the Government of Panama, where the *Caroline* was registered. Press and politicians alike fulminated against this dreadful invasion of the air-waves, which, it was said, merely answered a greed for profit and was not warranted by any public demand. (If the second proposition was true, then the first desire would be thwarted, but when people get worked up they rarely notice the simplest requirements of logic.)

Of course, there was an eager young public for Radio Caroline, which soon had millions of listeners. Ultimately, the BBC had to learn the lesson and run its own channel devoted to pop music all day long, and now the country is cluttered with such stations, each boasting a team of garrulous disc jockeys who sometimes talk over the music as well as before and after it. Hence one characteristic of the Sixties has become a permanent feature of national life, and yet another of the changes wrought in that turbulent decade made Britain significantly different at the end from what it had been at the beginning.

There were many groups who, like the Beatles, used charm and innocuousness to find their public (Freddie and the Dreamers is one that springs to mind). Within a very short time, however, other performers with a wild, anarchic approach to their music came to challenge the popularity of the nice young men. It was almost as if the young were embarrassed by the tolerance of their parents, and took their allegiance to other musicians whom nobody over twenty-five could *possibly* like. The very word 'musician' became obsolete when a group called the Who went on stage. Having started at a public house in Shepherd's Bush, the Who rose to enjoy a special kind of popularity. Their concerts were a sort of licensed riot, as their music grew noisier and noisier, the tunes more and more submerged beneath an ear-splitting shambles of sound, culminating in guitars being rammed into the loudspeaker, smashed by the microphone and finally hurled into the audience, who enjoyed the assault and delighted in their heroes' scornful contempt for taste. What they were singing, when you could decipher it, also writhed with proud anger; their song 'My Generation', which never reached the top of the Hit Parade but stayed for many weeks at Number Two, was adopted as a battle hymn by the frustrated young who resented condescension and positively loathed approval.

One group above all others carried offensiveness almost to the level of art. The Rolling Stones were worshipped by the rebellious young for their impudent refusal to make nice sounds or seek favour by allowing for 'taste'. Their music was loud and defiant, and if ever there appeared a danger that their performance might earn praise from the people they sought to antagonize, they made it yet more outrageous. The Rolling Stones were dominated by their lead singer, Mick Jagger, a man with undoubted 'star' attraction whom it was impossible to ignore. Through thick, sensuous, pouting lips he more or less spat out the words (it would be insulting to call them lyrics, a blatant misnomer in this case) and worked himself up into a frenzy of sweaty leaping extravagance. His performance managed to be hostile and sexy at the same time, clothing himself in tight-fitting glitter which showed that beneath the fury lay the grace of a leopard. (He was not, however, as overt as a singer called P. J. Proby, whose trousers virtually invited the audience to measure his potential.) Cecil Beaton painted a portrait of Jagger, and commented, 'I saw him on television and he inspired me. He looks like someone who has sprung out of the woods.'

John Dummer, a former member of another group, the Darts, recently reminisced on the impact of the Rolling Stones in the wake of the Beatles. They played regularly at a pub in Richmond. 'The place used to get so packed we'd all spill out onto the street and dance among the cars,' he said. 'Nobody liked the Beatles, they were regarded as kid-sister stuff; they were too well-scrubbed, too boy-next-door for us. We preferred rebels like the Stones, the Yardbirds, and the Pretty Things.'

The Rolling Stones preserved their 'image' by comporting themselves badly off-stage as well as on, and there generally seemed to be a reporter or two available to record the act. In July 1965 three of them, Jagger, Bill Wyman and Brian Jones, went to a petrol station in East London after one of their concerts and urinated against the wall. They were found guilty of 'insulting behaviour' because they had not taken steps 'to conceal this act,' and were fined £5 each.

Other offences, more serious in the eyes of the law and even more absurd in the eyes of the fans, were charged against various of the Stones two years later. On 10 May 1967, Mick Jagger and Keith Richard appeared in court at Chichester to face charges under the Dangerous Drugs Act of 1965. The charges arose from a police raid on Keith Richard's home some months earlier, and they naturally were given exaggerated publicity. Jagger and Richard were sent for trial at West Sussex Quarter Sessions, while on the same day their colleague Brian Jones was arrested for possessing cannabis and released on £250 bail. Some aspects of these cases caused serious concern.

In the first place it was rumoured that the police had been alerted by the *News of the World*, ostensibly in a spirit of moral righteousness but more likely to get a good story. Secondly, the charges were ludicrously small to be treated with such a heavy hand. Mick Jagger had four mild benzedrine tablets, bought in an ordinary shop in Italy and fully authorized by his doctor; Richard allowed his home to be used for smoking a joint. And that was that. Yet for his four legally obtained pills Jagger was sentenced to three months' imprisonment, and for his smoke among friends in his own drawing-room, Richard received a sentence of twelve months' imprisonment. Thirdly, it looked as if the 'authorities' were enjoying the spectacle of humbling pop stars, going out of their way to have Mick Jagger be photographed quite unnecessarily in handcuffs, like a dangerous murderer.

The outcry on the better side of Fleet Street was immediate and fierce. For once *The Times* did not get its morals in a twist and led the protest with a now-famous leader entitled 'Who Breaks a Butterfly on a Wheel?' The Jagger indictment, it said, was 'about as mild a drug case as can ever have been brought before the courts.' The *Sunday Times* called it 'a case of social revenge.' Lawyers were appalled that a section of the community should punish another section for habits which earned disapproval. While it was said, as it always is said on such occasions, that the law must be obeyed until it is changed, the vileness of the sentences for first offences of so tiny a nature was clearly meant to be exemplary. Demonstrations took place outside the *News of the World*, and the Who took a half page in the *Evening Standard* to assert their solidarity with the Stones in the most public manner.

Jagger and Richard did spend some time in gaol, at Wormwood Scrubs and Brixton Prisons, until they were released on bail of £7,000 each on 20 June. On appeal, both convictions were quashed. The older generation had tried to get its own back for all that awful noise, and to show the youngsters that the example set by their heroes was a bad one. If that was the unspoken intention, then it failed miserably. The Rolling Stones were now more than ever fêted, with martyrdom added to their many assets.

The clash of values between different generations was never

more vividly illustrated. The Rolling Stones would not alter their ways, and the courts would not mollify their condemnation of them. In October of the same year Brian Jones's case came up, he pleading guilty to the charge of permitting his flat to be used for smoking cannabis. He was sentenced to nine months' imprisonment by a magistrate, who said, 'The Offences to which you have pleaded guilty are very serious.' Jones was again arrested the following year when cannabis was found at his flat concealed in a ball of wool. Not even the Beatles escaped the vengeance of the law. John Lennon and Yoko Ono were fined £150 each for possession of cannabis and for obstructing the police in their execution of a search warrant.

Brian Jones's earlier sentence was amended by the Court of Appeal to a fine of £1,000 and three years' probation. Before announcing his decision, Lord Chief Justice Parker mused, 'No permitted fine could really hit this young man's pocket.' That, indeed, was the rub, for many of the pop musicians were earning fees of fairy-tale proportions. *The Observer* estimated that thirty rock performers earned more than a million pounds a year. They certainly 'earned' money rather than 'made' it, for their lives were spent in a punishing round of rehearsal, performance, recording, travelling, photo-calls and the like, occupying every daylight hour and more. As Pete Townshend of the Who remarked, 'A pop-singer's life is murder, but it's well-paid murder.'

On the other hand, many of them were so cruelly exploited that they ended up with scarcely a penny, and when they had learnt their lesson they surrendered the glamorous life for a more secure income as factory-hands. The managers of pop groups habitually took a merciless cut from their protégés' earnings, 25 per cent in the case of Brian Epstein, who managed the Beatles, sometimes with other groups as much as 40 per cent. The remainder had to be shared between four, five or six performers, apart from the army of peripheral characters (lawyers, secretaries to deal with fan mail, Public Relations men, road managers, hairdressers, and so on) not all of whom were salaried by the manager out of his percentage. Nevertheless, the most enduring of them, like Mick Jagger and Paul McCartney, are today millionaires several times over.

Some of the tasks undertaken by hangers-on were relatively easy. Messengers were sent out to buy up copies of a record in scattered shops all over the country in such numbers that they would appear on the Hit Parade as if there were a huge public demand for them; the public demand would then follow. The Public Relations man had to coerce disc jockeys to play his group's record on the radio. One of them told Jonathan Aitken in *The Young Meteors*, 'Ours is basically a very simple job because we're dealing with simple people,' a nicely understated insult. Television programmes like *Ready, Steady, Go* and, later, *Top of the Pops*, assured the success of a record merely by playing it; according to the fundamental law, youngsters could be led by the nose. Another programme called *Juke Box Jury* reached previously unfathomable depths of inanity by playing new records to a panel of four 'experts' who then pronounced upon their worth. 'Er, I think it's a hit', would denote reasoned approval, and 'No, I don't like it. A miss!', indicated a considered verdict against. As the panel was usually drawn from disc jockeys and pop musicians, their reputations were not enhanced by this weekly exposure.

It was sometimes suggested that the pop groups would be nowhere without the skilled technicians who manufactured the sounds which they purported to play. It was Mr Aitken again who prised this admission from an anonymous pop-merchant: 'It's easier to teach a group a song by singing it to them and explaining in words the sort of sound you want, rather than by writing it down in music, which 90% of them can't read anyway.' As for the technicians, 'if it wasn't for the work that is done at the mixer desk, the noise they [the groups] make would sound pretty awful.' By the end of the decade, pop groups were experimenting with such elaborate electronic gadgets (fuzzboxes, oscillators, reverberation units) that the human contribution was all but smothered. Curiously, as word spread of the basic inadequacy of pop musicians when left to their own devices, their popularity appeared to suffer in no way at all. It was irksome to the adults that pop groups should be revealed as frauds and still be venerated in an idolatrous manner. Values were as topsy-turvy as in *Alice in Wonderland.*

Of course there were exceptions, though none perhaps as notable as the American Bob Dylan (who cannot unhappily find a place in a book on England in the Sixties). Dylan's music was (and is) intelligent and genuinely creative. Professor Christopher Ricks, normally more at home when lecturing on English Literature, has been known to spend entire evenings talking about Bob Dylan and proselytizing to the more obtuse of his students.

The strain of undermining old values, of constant public attention, of great expectations, was made grimly manifest by the great toll of casualties in the world of pop music. Forgetting for a moment the American singers who succumbed to drug abuse, in England alone there were sufficient young deaths to suggest that the happy realm of light entertainment was subject to mysterious malaise. Brian Epstein, the manager of the Beatles, committed suicide at the age of thirty-two. A rich young satellite of the Swinging London set, Tara Browne, died at the wheel of his car when it crashed into a parked vehicle in Chelsea; he was twenty-one. Another member of the amorphous 'set', Robin Douglas-Home (of the same family as the Prime Minister Sir Alec Douglas-Home), took an overdose of pills at home and succeeded in putting an end to his life. The solicitor David Jacobs, overworked in representing virtually everyone in the pop music world, hanged himself in his garage. Joe Meek, manager of the Tornadoes, also committed suicide. And Brian Jones of the Rolling Stones was found dead in his swimming-pool in 1969; he had been eased out of the group owing to his persistent appearances in court which made him, ironically, unwelcome in the United States, whence derived the excessive drug culture which had ruined him. His Requiem Mass was a vast concert given by the Stones in Hyde Park, attended by half a million fans.

Many of the pop musicians and their admirers had turned to oriental mysticism in their attempt to find ideas and supportive beliefs to replace those they had unwittingly demolished in their rage to be different. Eastern 'gurus' proliferated, not all of them bogus, and their influence upon clothing, spirituality and health foods provided for a time some colour to the London scene. People wore caftans instead of shirts, dripped with multiple rows of beaded necklaces, distributed flowers and smiles to passers-by, and generally purveyed an air of wanting to 'make peace not war.' John Lennon's fine and noble song 'Give Peace a Chance' came out at this time.

The other side of the 'hippie' culture proved in the long term, alas, more powerful. As drug-taking became acceptable, even widespread at dinner-parties as well as in obscure alleys, addiction to surreality took hold. I myself once experimented with the drug LSD, to see what glorious effects it would produce, and spent the most miserably frightening eight hours of my life; I recall that what alarmed me most was the knowledge that I was impotent to put an end to the drug's hold on my mind. I was aware that thoughts were travelling down uncharted roads, and longed to return to comfortable normality, but had no power to stop them; the thoughts just went on, until I feared I might never recover. I did, of course, but there were thousands who were less willing to embrace banality and continued to seek the spurious illumination of a 'high' state. Some doctors were known to over-subscribe and thus contribute to the epidemic. As midnight approached, crowds of helpless youngsters assembled outside the all-night chemist in Piccadilly Circus to obtain their legal daily 'fix'.

It would be unfair to ascribe drug abuse (which has hardly abated in the years since 1970) to the explosion of success in the world of popular music, but it would be blind also to deny they were connected. Pride in pop music gave the young their own culture, not one handed down by generations but one they had invented for themselves. It seemed to them innocent and life-enhancing when set against the hypocritical values of a former age, values which had led to wars and which continued to encourage deceit. Part of that culture involved the use of drugs which, ideally, created the impression of a better world wherein their new values could flourish and perhaps even influence the way people treated each other on a much wider stage – the drug-takers were optimistic and ambitious, they wanted to do good. It was the responsibility of some pop musicians, and the not-so-young Chelsea 'trendies' who should have known better, to set an example which teenagers could follow without damage to themselves. They both succeeded and failed. By making British popular music paramount the world over, and contributing to the dizzy attraction of London in the Sixties, they gave young people a real sense of achievement, even of national pride. Their legacy was also the sad and sordid scenes of ruin on the faces and in the hearts of that nightly horde in Piccadilly Circus.

— 8 —

The Royal Family

Not even the Queen could escape the effects of the Sixties' mood, although, with the spontaneous carapace which her very position forms, she was one of the few to emerge from the experience without lasting damage. It was at times a bumpy ride. For the first time in her reign, Elizabeth II was subjected to criticism, even to hostility when, on one occasion, she was booed in the street, and the concept of Monarchy, or rather the way in which that concept was trivialized by hysterical adulation, was held to scrutiny. The Queen took stock and made some radical changes, and by the end of the decade she was better known by her subjects and more deeply respected than ever before.

When articles were published in 1961 discussing the role of the Monarchy and the performance of the Monarch, memories of an earlier attempt to allow comment upon the subject were still fresh, the wounds inflicted upon the delinquents still un-healed. In 1957 Lord Altrincham, Malcolm Muggeridge and Lord Londonderry had all, in different ways, expressed their disquiet about the way their Sovereign was behaving, and had all been tormented by a furiously indignant mob as a result.

It has to be remembered how the Queen was perceived in 1957. Only four years had passed since the glorious moment of her Coronation, when the awful splendour of majesty had enveloped this frail, simple girl in a white shift in Westminster Abbey, brought cruelly soon to her destiny by the premature death of George VI. Four years was time enough to 'settle in' to the job and make her personal mark on the reign. Yet still she seemed impossibly remote and aloof, so far removed from her people that a dangerous gulf was opening, to be filled with murmurs of faintly scornful derision. Press attention had been limited to the unctuous nauseating drivel put out by her former governess and other sycophants, which must surely have embarrassed her more than anyone else, and there was literally no serious debate about her role or her character. In pub conversation, Londoners were openly dismissive about what in the 1960s would be called her 'image'. Nobody knew what the Queen was like to talk to, and the only indications one had to how she sounded was in the Christmas broadcast to the nation and Commonwealth (microphones were then banned from the House of Lords at the opening of Parliament, when the Sovereign read the Speech from the Throne). That annual broadcast, delivered in a voice flat with boredom or (who was to know?) fear, was frankly unappealing.

These dissatisfactions eventually appeared in print in an issue of the *National and English Review* devoted to an examination of the modern Monarchy. One article, by the editor and proprietor, Lord Altrincham, blamed the Queen's entourage for her lamentable performance. 'The personality conveyed by the utterances which are put into her mouth is that of a priggish schoolgirl, captain of the hockey team, a prefect and a recent candidate for confirmation,' he wrote. 'Like her mother she appears unable to string even a few sentences together without a written text. When she has lost the bloom of youth, the Queen's reputation will depend, far more than it does now, upon her personality. It will not then be enough for her to go through the motions: she will have to say things which people can remember and do things on her own initiative which will make people sit up and take notice. As yet there is little sign that such a personality is emerging.'

Altrincham thought that the problem lay with Buckingham Palace, which had not moved with the times and was still run by a 'tight little enclave of English ladies and gentlemen.' The result was that the Queen did not know her people, and she was surrounded by such a second-rate bunch of unimaginative advisers that she was unlikely to get to know them.

The storm which erupted over Lord Altrincham's head was immediate and fierce. The town of Altrincham disowned him, *The Observer*, for which he wrote regular articles, sacked him, and an elderly supporter of the League of Empire Loyalists struck him in full view of television cameras after an interview with Robin Day. The magistrate who fined the assailant £1 told him he had made an unsavoury episode even more squalid.

While the *brouhaha* still raged and fellow peers were tripping over one another in their eagerness to shout 'bounder' and 'cad' at the hapless Altrincham, another nobleman innocently entered the fray.

The 9th Marquess of Londonderry was 19 years old, grandson of 'Charlie' Londonderry, Minister for Air between the wars, and his wife 'Edie', the foremost and grandest political hostess of the century. Edith, Lady Londonderry was still alive and still jealous of her formidable reputation. She had been a friend of five British Monarchs. Perhaps the young Marquess did not realize it at the time, but his illustrious name lent especial weight to the argument when he wrote a critical letter to the *New Statesman*.

Lord Londonderry wrote that Lord Altrincham's comments were 'bold and justified'. Only a moron, he said, would accept the view that the Royal Family should 'parade benignly and sedately, flashing toothpaste smiles, displaying their latest hair-do's, and exhibiting their deplorable taste in clothes.' Londonderry now concedes that his strictures may have been naive, but his only intention was to initiate a debate in the correspondence columns. For what did happen he was totally unprepared.

The *Daily Mirror* columnist Cassandra wrote, 'the voice of the pipsqueak is heard throughout the land.' The pavement outside Londonderry's house in Park Street was daubed in yellow paint, with the slogan ATTACKS ON OUR MONARCHY MUST CEASE. Threatening letters arrived daily, challenging him to a fight or a boxing-match, and nasty telephone calls could not be stopped. Lord Londonderry was indeed frightened by the volume of abuse he encountered and the degree of hatred he aroused; he felt he dare not show his face.

He was still a minor (majority was not reached in those days until the age of 21) and had therefore to face his family as well as an indignant public. His guardian Simon Combe, his late mother's brother, sent him for chastisement to the Outward Bound school in Eskdale for a month, where the errant Marquess had to endure half-naked mountain-climbing in freezing conditions in an attempt to teach him a lesson; it left him fitter than he had ever been. Meanwhile, the Dowager Lady Londonderry issued a statement humiliating in its condescension. Her grandson, she said, was 'young for his age'. His letter had 'no literary merit', it was 'not only vulgar but silly and childish'. His extreme youth precluded his having had any opportunity yet to meet men in public life and to have exchanged views with them. As for Lord Altrincham, he must be suffering from an inferiority complex.

Lord Londonderry himself issued an apology through the Press Association. It was long and abject:

Public reaction to my letter has made it abundantly manifest that a personal attack on the Royal Family is much resented, especially if the attack should come from someone both insignificant and unqualified. Criticism of the monarchy must always be on a general level and any attempt to make the Royal Family a target for personal criticism merely degrades the attacker in everyone's eyes and sets him up as an object of contempt. I have been guilty of the latter crime and for that I am truly contrite. I fully comprehend and appreciate the resentment of those who accuse me of cowardice in pointlessly attacking someone who cannot retaliate. For any personal attack on the Royal Family I am sincerely sorry and humbly apologise for my bad manners.

It is astonishing that such an apology should have been thought necessary in quite those terms. Talk of 'guilt' and 'contempt' and 'cowardice' was entirely misplaced, as Londonderry had not

[181]

suggested the Queen was in any way a 'bad' woman, only that her public appearances did her little credit. In this he was voicing an opinion held widely in the country.

The Press was hopelessly incompetent in judging the popular mood, and assumed that the Empire Loyalist lunatics were representative. Talk of collusion and rebellion was quite absurd, as the Lords Altrincham and Londonderry had never met, but this did not prevent journalists from beseeching comment from Lord Altrincham on this latest development. 'I am not Lord Londonderry's keeper,' he said. 'I was not responsible for his original letter and I am not responsible for his recantation. It is nothing to do with me.' Privately, he wrote to Londonderry thanking him for his support, adding that he did not share the younger man's opinion of the Royal Family's sartorial taste; their clothes, he thought, were perfectly adequate.

Scarcely had the fuss time to blow itself out, than another article appeared, this time in an American newspaper, the *Saturday Evening Post*, by the very distinguished English journalist Malcolm Muggeridge, who had shown his colours on other occasions. 'There are probably quite a lot of people – more than might be supposed – who, like myself, feel that another newspaper photograph of the Royal Family will be more than they can bear. Even Princess Anne, a doubtless estimable child, becomes abhorrent by repetition.' That had been in the *New Statesman*. The article in the *Saturday Evening Post* was cogently argued, serious, and in many ways complimentary to the Queen, but the British Press was in no mood to dilute their scandal. In various British newspapers, Muggeridge was misquoted disgracefully, to such an extent that he consulted a lawyer on the possibility of taking action for libel. To his consternation and alarm, he was advised that he would be unlikely to encounter any jury which would not be prejudiced against him.

The abuse which was then hurled at Muggeridge was shameful in the extreme. A flood of angry letters descended upon him, one correspondent expressing delight that his youngest son had recently been killed in a skiing accident. The BBC banned him from appearing on the television screen, on the direct instructions of the Director-General, and the *Sunday Dispatch* summarily cancelled his contract to work for them. When Muggeridge appealed to the Press Council, his complaints were not upheld. Only one moment of humour helped relieve the quite oppressive vilification from all quarters; the chief executive of an American television network which was about to transmit an interview with Muggeridge warned that 'this Queen is the only bulwark against Communism.'

After these experiences, it was quite clear at the beginning of the Sixties that to initiate a dialogue on the role of the Monarchy and on the competence of the Court of Elizabeth II to fulfil that role was tantamount to professional suicide. To a certain extent this ferocious protection was born of gallantry, in so far as most people felt the Queen had a difficult task and tackled it to the best of her ability, given that she was still learning. She would not always, one hoped, be surrounded by antique advisers. That the situation had changed so drastically by the end of the decade was due in part to the gradual demise of these advisers, and to a greater degree by the Queen's own instincts. Her antennae grew more acute, and the influence of her husband, the Duke of Edinburgh, became more visible.

By 1961 it was possible to discuss these matters at last without being found guilty of treason by 'public opinion'. Malcolm Muggeridge returned to the subject with an article in *Encounter* entitled 'The Queen and I' in which he registered his astonishment that interest in the Monarchy appeared to grow in inverse proportion to the Monarch's constitutional ability to shape events. 'Ladies drop creaking curtsies to an image of authority which history has rendered ineffectual and irrelevant,' he wrote. One would have logically expected the status of royalty to decline, instead of which it had undergone 'a quite contrary development, becoming, as it shed its power, even more popular, and the subject of an even more rapacious curiosity.' His own experience, four years earlier, when he had interfered 'with the propagation of the legend of popular monarchy', had taught him that very few people genuinely believe the legend with 'authentic passion', while the rest are 'swept along on a tidal-wave of subliminal, stereoscopic emotion.'

The explanation which Muggeridge gave for this strange state of affairs was the very same that we have discerned underlying the prosecution of *Lady Chatterley's Lover*, the resistance to homosexual law reform, and the savage destruction of John Profumo – 'the intensification of snobbishness which has accompanied the transformation of England into a Welfare State. Never have class divisions been so acute and anguished as since they were, theoretically, abolished.' There existed in all levels a desperate need to feel socially superior, to talk like a BBC announcer (they were all literate and articulate in those days), to dress better, to know better people. 'The social mountaineers, setting forth with their nailed boots and climbing equipment, doggedly essaying now this peak, now that, see in the distant mists an ultimate summit – the Monarchy.'

According to this argument, people were enraged by what they perceived as throwing mud at their idol, for if the idol was not sacrosanct, their ambitions to get close to it appeared rather silly. Muggeridge and Altrincham had unwittingly taken on the vanity and snobbery of a nation, and been made to pay the price reserved for the subversive – they had been thrown overboard.

Three months later, Henry Fairlie replied to Muggeridge in the same journal. In the first place, he said, it was quite wrong to assume, as Mr Muggeridge appeared to, that the Sovereign was without any power at all. She retained the constitutional right to be consulted, to advise, and to warn, and as the years passed and she grew in experience, she would exercise this right with increasing effectiveness. (In this prediction Mr Fairlie has been proven right; it is now a very foolhardy Prime Minister who will attend the weekly meeting with his Monarch without doing his homework, and a stupid one who will not heed the accumulated wisdom of thirty years.) Furthermore, the Queen's most powerful quality, which she shared with many of her forbears, was a simple, almost naive conception of her duty to her subjects. 'It is equally apparent,' he wrote, 'from the available evidence, that the very simplicity of this conception of duty has normally had, and cannot fail normally to have, a softening and civilising influence on those engaged in the embittering struggle for power.'

As far as snobbery was concerned, Mr Fairlie agreed that it was endemic in British society, as it was in most others, but he was far happier that deference and obsequiousness should be focused on the Monarch than on a politician or a newspaper proprietor. It was important that the vanities of ordinary men should find their outlet in harmless sycophancy directed at a person who could not advance them, and not at a man corrupted by power and wealth. The Queen was aware of this, and had contrived since coming to the throne to divorce herself from all the unwelcome claptrap that was written about her. It was a real achievement (Fairlie implied) that the Queen managed to retain her personal as well as her royal dignity, while her worshippers and her critics alike jettisoned theirs.

Turning on Lord Altrincham, Mr Fairlie asked why his lordship should be so keen on having the Queen say something important and well-phrased, when we had carefully evolved over the centuries a system which prevented her from doing anything of the sort? 'Did we not execute one king, and boot out another, just to ensure that their successors would confine themselves to clichés in public?'

Fairlie concluded by suggesting that Muggeridge's obsession with royalty was dangerous, for it deflected attention from the real faults in British society, its materialism and not its snobbery, its lack of national purpose and not its class-consciousness.

Mr Fairlie was perhaps right to chastise Muggeridge for selecting the wrong target, but the signs are that Buckingham Palace thought otherwise. Events during the 1960s, some loud and obvious, others subtle and scarcely perceptible, indicated that the Royal Family took seriously its need to adjust to changing patterns of behaviour, and above all to come closer to the rest of the people. If snobbery could not be eradicated, it could be flattered and tamed, its satisfaction made available to all.

It was a slow process. The Queen was insistent that her privacy when 'off duty' be respected, and that her children should be allowed to go to school without being molested by photographers. How to reconcile this natural desire for occasional anonymity, without which any normal person (and one of the Queen's great strengths was her endearing normality) would go rapidly insane, with the equally natural desire of the public to know more about her, was a real problem. It was not realized at the Palace until much later that this curiosity was less directed at details of the Queen's breakfast menu than at how her working day was constructed, nor that such curiosity could be fairly satisfied without compromising in any way the 'mystique' of the Monarchy. On the contrary, it would be enhanced. The British public was more intelligent than either the purveyors of magazine gush or the critics acknowledged.

Relations between Buckingham Palace and the world's Press were abysmal. The Press Secretary, Commander Sir Richard Colville, had been in royal service since 1947, and did not pretend to enjoy his contacts with newspapermen. He succeeded, on the contrary, in giving the impression that he disdained their vulgarity. On one occasion he told a Canadian reporter that he was not 'what you North Americans would call a public relations officer.' Most questions went unanswered. It was therefore for want of any real information that journalists had to invent nonsense.

At least a PR man might have had some success in dealing with the perennial indignation over the Civil List and how much the Queen should 'cost'. In fact, the Monarchy costs nothing, but you would hunt the newspapers in vain for any hint of this truth. Under the terms of a bargain struck with George III in 1760, the Crown lands were surrendered to the nation in return for an allowance. To this day, the Exchequer still makes a net profit on the arrangement, receiving more from the Monarch than it returns in the Civil List. Criticism to the purpose that the taxpayer supported the Queen in her way of life was founded on historical ignorance.

The first steps towards gentle reform of her relations with her subjects were undertaken by Elizabeth II with the advent of the Sixties. She dispensed with the annual presentations at Court, when hundreds of young ladies were paraded before her to no clear purpose, a ceremony which had caught her uncle Edward VIII looking pathetically bored in 1937. She undertook to deliver her annual Christmas broadcast before television cameras instead of by radio. As broadcasts were then 'live' and teleprompters did not yet exist, the Queen had to learn her speech by heart and give it before an audience of millions immediately after her Christmas lunch. As Robert Lacey has written, 'Her smile of relief to her husband when she did not realise that the cameras were still focused on her at the end was worth a thousand articles on "The Monarchy."' And in 1964 she announced that she would no longer use the special Royal Train, eight coaches including a children's coach built in 1955 for Prince Charles and Princess Anne; henceforth the royal party would travel in special coaches attached to an ordinary train on scheduled service. The distance between Monarch and people was in these various ways at least symbolically diminished.

By a Royal Proclamation of 1960, the Queen declared her 'Will and Pleasure' that her family name should thenceforth be Mountbatten-Windsor. They had since 1952 been the family of Windsor, while in strict genealogical truth they were the family of Schleswig-Holstein-Sönderborg-Glücksburg, this being the Duke of Edinburgh's surname. The new surname served to emphasize the invincible Englishness of the Queen, and the solid influence of her husband.

In 1960 the Queen's sister, Princess Margaret, married Antony Armstrong-Jones, a commoner with aristocratic connections. His name was less significant to the British public than his status. He was a photographer who earned his living on commissions for the *Sunday Times*, and though he was soon created Earl of Snowdon, he continued to work and be paid for it. Lord Snowdon had colleagues and friends in the arts, in the media, and among the young 'trendies' who were beginning to inherit the earth. Being friendly and approachable, his wide acquaintance introduced into royal circles a much more varied section of the public than had hitherto been allowed anywhere near a royal presence. Princess Margaret, too, while not abandoning the country-based upper-class friends she had known all her life, spread her acquaintance more widely, and felt at ease with people who would, a decade earlier, have been strictly excluded – film-stars like Peter Sellers, newsreaders like Derek Hart. The young couple could be seen attending rehearsals of a play or a ballet, mingling unceremoniously with the cast and stage-hands. They dined frequently in inexpensive restaurants like San Lorenzo in Beauchamp Place, where no one pointed or jostled or stared, but left them in peace.

Of course it was never expected that the Queen herself would have dinner in San Lorenzo, her position being uniquely circumscribed, but there is every likelihood that the rest of the family noticed with what mature respect the British public treated Princess Margaret and her husband when they ventured forth. It is not in the nature of the British to make a fuss or embarrass public figures. Dean Rusk, the Secretary of State in President Kennedy's administration, was astonished when it was suggested he might leave his hotel and go for a walk; he did, and returned in one piece.

The Queen's own Thursday lunches, inaugurated to afford Her Majesty rather more opportunity to meet so-called 'ordinary' people, became progressively more adventurous. The guest-list included not only prominent industrialists and masters of hounds, but successful actors, designers, writers. The Queen went often to the theatre in an informal capacity, simply to see something she fancied. With no royal box and no bouquets to be presented, she saw Lionel Bart's musical *Oliver*, plays at the Aldwych given by the Royal Shakespeare Company, and on one occasion when the present author was in the audience, she went privately to see a double-bill of Strindberg's *Miss Julie* and Peter Shaffer's hilarious *Black Comedy* at the Old Vic. People in the auditorium, or some of them, were aware of the presence of their

Sovereign among them, but they recognized the occasion as private, and made no attempt to draw attention to it. I also remember, about 1965, seeing the Queen and Princess Margaret sitting together in the stalls at the Royal Opera House for a routine performance by the Royal Ballet, and the Queen and her Prime Minister in the stalls at the Aldwych Theatre. Presumably, some security men were disguised as usherettes, but one would never have known, and the Head of State and Head of Government were in the centre of a row in a theatre filled to capacity. It became clear in the Sixties that the public would stare at the Queen when she was being Queen (and no one can be more used to being stared at than she), and protect her privacy, without inducement, when she had a night off. This was a real advance in the relationship.

Perhaps the Queen's most revealing *sortie* to the theatre was to see *Beyond the Fringe*. The four Cambridge undergraduates who returned satire to the London stage (Peter Cook, Dudley Moore, Jonathan Miller, Alan Bennett) included among the targets of their irreverent lampoons the Prime Minister Harold Macmillan, the military establishment, the Church, and the Royal Family itself. There in the audience one evening was Queen Elizabeth II, laughing heartily.

Prince Charles and Princess Anne passed their adolescence in the Sixties. This, too, was a factor which contributed to the increasing accessibility of the Monarch. Both Prince and Princess attended schools, in contrast with earlier generations which had been educated privately, and they naturally formed friendships with other youngsters. Just after Christmas in 1964 they gave a huge party at Windsor for one hundred teenagers, dancing to Beatles and other pop music, which the Queen and the Duke of Edinburgh looked into for half an hour, presumably to make sure nothing got out of hand. Such an innocuous gesture would have been unimaginable before 1960.

Yet another indication of fresh thinking was the opening of the Queen's Gallery at Buckingham Palace, where members of the public could view pictures from the royal collection, pre-

viously only visible to servants and ambassadors. Quite apart
from the rare pleasure of seeing such masterpieces, there was
the perhaps illogical feeling that the Monarch had somehow
opened her home to us, was ready to share some of her 'things'
with us. It is significant that when the Queen shows a personal
visitor around the Palace, it is she herself, and not a curator,
who unlocks the drawers, selects an item, and discourses upon
its history and acquisition. The Queen's knowledge of what
hangs on her walls is apparently comprehensive and fascinating.

The effect of these accumulated glimpses behind the curtain
was entirely beneficial: their paradoxical product was a healthy
diminution of public obsession with Monarchy. (This was not
matched on the continent of Europe, however, where glossy
magazines invented pregnancies and squabbles and scandals
almost every week.) When a new magazine devoted entirely to
the Royal Family was launched under the title of 'Majesty', it
had to fold after a few issues for lack of interest and paucity of
advertising. The Sixties therefore represented an interlude of
sanity, at least in this regard, between the saturation of the
Fifties, and the even worse proliferation of froth and prattle
which obtains now (1985). In the 1960s the Queen's subjects
grew up.

On deeper and more important levels, the Queen displayed
her own maturity. In 1965 she paid a visit to her aunt-by-
marriage, the Duchess of Windsor. To appreciate just how
historic was this meeting, one has to remember the dramatic
events which preceded it by thirty years. As Mrs Wallis Simpson,
the Duchess had 'stolen' England's King, Edward VIII, and
been forced into exile with him, causing deep bitterness on both
sides.

Even a Christmas Carol reflected the crisis when children in
1936 were heard to chant, 'Hark the Herald Angels Sing, Mrs
Simpson's pinched our King.'

The Windsors never forgave what they regarded as shabby
treatment by the family in keeping them out of the way and
banishing them to the status of 'non-persons'. The Queen

Mother, for her part, nursed an abiding distrust of the 'usurper' and would not countenance any kind of reconciliation. Now the former King was an old and saddened man. He was admitted to the London Clinic for a series of eye operations, and the Duchess made the journey to London with him. The Queen's gesture of visiting the clinic and consoling the worried Duchess may well have followed long family discussion as well as consultations with her ministers, but it was perceived by the public as generous and sensible. The feeling in the country was that old wounds should be allowed to heal, and it cannot have been accidental that the Queen gave visible interpretation to this mood. It was the first time she had seen her uncle since 1936, when she was ten years old.

Three years later, in 1967, recognition of the Windsors was given almost formally. The Duke and Duchess were met by Lord Mountbatten at Southampton and driven to his home in Hampshire – Broadlands. Two days later, the Duchess of Windsor stood next to the Queen outside Marlborough House when the Royal Family were present at the unveiling of a plaque to commemorate Queen Mary, who had fought hard to prevent her son marrying Mrs Simpson. The point made was quiet but impressive: the Duchess of Windsor took her place as, at last, a member of the Royal Family.

One may argue that none of this mattered very much, but it was symptomatic of more responsible attitudes on all sides. The days of mere toothpaste smiles and the 'hockey-stick' Queen were past. Furthermore, at the same ceremony in the Mall was present the Queen's cousin, the Earl of Harewood, who had recently been divorced after fathering a child in an adulterous liaison (he later married the mother). Nobody seemed to mind any more.

The Aberfan disaster of 1966 offered further evidence that the Queen was a woman with her people, no longer a puppet aloof from them. A mountain of refuse from a coal-mine had slid and engulfed the Aberfan primary school in South Wales, tragically burying alive scores of children. When the news broke, the Earl of Snowdon immediately drove down, without waiting for official sanction, and spent hours comforting the bereaved amongst the debris. He was not there as royalty, surrounded by photographers and security men, but as a man who suffered. The Duke of Edinburgh went to Aberfan shortly afterwards. The Queen wanted to go as well, but Robert Lacey tells us she knew well enough that she could not appear without attracting an army of newsmen, nor could she dispense with the inevitable protocol, and her presence might impede rescue work. So she waited a few days. When she did arrive upon the pitiful scene of devastation, her face gaunt and miserable, Elizabeth II was vividly the servant of her people. One saw quite clearly that had she been allowed to, she would have scratched away the rubble herself.

With the advent of the Labour Government in 1964, the Queen was faced with her first Socialist Prime Minister, Harold Wilson, and the first man with whom she had to deal who was not of the same social class as herself. How on earth could their necessary co-operation be achieved when they appeared, on the face of it, to be fired by quite separate purposes? Those who worried, seriously misconstrued the Queen's interpretation of duty. She does not have to be reminded that she is above politics; she is more keenly conscious of this than any Bagehotian commentator. The people may choose by whom they wish to be represented, *her* only consideration is the state of the nation. With this in mind, it should be no surprise that Elizabeth II and Prime Minister Wilson came to operate, as Mr Lacey once more indicates, almost as a team. He respected her knowledge (and later advised future Prime Ministers not to enter the Palace unprepared, as the Queen reads all her boxes and expects direct answers to searching questions), and she responded to his trust. To the consternation of Tories ever since, it became generally known that the Labour leader was the Queen's favourite Prime Minister so far. They became friends, and Wilson valued the Queen's supportive role as one of the most precious assets of his premiership. The Garter he received on his retirement was a personal gift from her, not a politically recommended honour. It has been suspected ever since that if the Queen ever did allow her private feelings to be expressed, she would perhaps prefer to deal with a Labour rather than a Conservative administration. It is worth taking vitamins in order to live long enough to read the entries in Elizabeth II's private diary (it is known she keeps one) when her authorized biography is eventually published. For the moment, the Monarch's understanding with her Socialist First Minister must be seen as one of the potent influences of the Sixties, intuited throughout the country and recognized even on the international scene.

All roads led ultimately to the decision to allow the BBC to make a full-length documentary film on the Queen and her family both at work and at leisure. Apparently, it was Prince Philip who persuaded his initially reluctant wife to co-operate in this project, which she did on condition that she should not know where microphones were placed, nor when they would be turned on. To judge by the result, the Queen did not even seem to know when the cameras were focused upon her. Richard Cawston's film took a whole year to make, and was shown in 1969. It contrived to combine an awesome impression of the Queen's work-load, and her dignified execution of dozens of duties from Privy Council to industrial visits to ambassadorial receptions, with an intimate portrait of a family. One heard for the first time the Queen speaking without, as it were, an organized audience, making jokes, telling her husband to hurry up as they prepared to make entry to a glittering reception, chatting over dinner about the things that can go wrong, shopping in a village store near Balmoral, and cooking a barbecue. The marriage between Sovereign and people was now complete, brought about by a serious examination of her role and not a grovelling list of her childhood fancies revealed by former royal servants. It is a pity that this interesting experiment in documentary has never been repeated, but perhaps a second film could only be second-best.

The booing of Elizabeth II which had occurred as a protest

against the state visit of Greek royalty to London in 1963 was now not even a dim memory. It could not occur again, nor could the complaints of Altrincham and Muggeridge. The Queen had come a long way in this decade of upheaval, yet, magically, she had harnessed all that was best in the new mood of the Sixties and ignored all that was fatuous and ephemeral. 'When the bubble burst in the early 1970s she was seen to have stood all along for values closer to those of her average subjects – who, in the last resort, were happiest with a Sovereign who preferred the commonplace to the craze, the conventional to the eccentric, a day at the races to an evening of atonal music.' (Robert Lacey.) She had done this not by closing the door upon all that the Sixties had to offer, but by judging the mood and selecting which innovations and advances it demanded.

CND

The first atomic bomb was detonated in New Mexico on 17 July 1945, with a blast-power two thousand times that of the largest bomb previously known. The effect upon the imaginations of those who witnessed this historic explosion left them awe-struck with foreboding. Mankind had never been so powerful; we had come so far along the evolutionary path that we were now in control of existence, for all other species as well as for ourselves, on a final scale. God could propose, but henceforth mankind would dispose.

Mankind wasted little time. On 8 August 1945, a similar device was exploded over the Japanese city of Hiroshima, immolating thousands of people and causing devastation of hitherto inconceivable horror. Before the aeroplane carrying the bomb from the United States took off on its miserable journey, it was publicly blessed by an American chaplain. Amazingly, a second bomb was later dropped on Nagasaki, with similar (and by now predictable) results.

The effects were predictable, of course, only by those who knew. American censorship in occupied Japan was severe enough to prevent the truth from being disseminated. It was not immediately clear how the world, the rest of the human race, would respond to the news of its sudden ability to obliterate. As it happened, the realization was gradual, and the response inarticulate. Meanwhile, the MacMahon Act of 1946 in the United States prevented the Government of Great Britain from being privy to atomic secrets, which one might have thought a blessing, both economic and moral. Post-war recovery would certainly have been encouraged if Governments had not wasted untold millions of our earned income in developing the British bomb. But politicians are by nature irrational people. The Labour Government under Prime Minister Attlee started atomic research more or less from scratch and the very first official communiqué from 10 Downing Street in the reign of the new Monarch, Elizabeth II, was to announce the intention of exploding a British bomb; this was duly performed in October 1952.

Only a month later, the Americans tested their first hydrogen bomb, thousands of times more destructive even than the atomic bomb, at Bikini Atoll in the Pacific. A few months after that, the Soviet Union began its own series of hydrogen bomb blasts. The first British hydrogen bomb was built and exploded under the Conservatives in 1957, at Christmas Island. Less than one year later, the Campaign for Nuclear Disarmament (CND) was born.

It was by no means the first time men had viewed with alarm the development of a new weapon and banded together to protest against it. When the cross-bow was invented, enabling people for the first time to kill each other at a great distance without seeing the eyes of their victims, the Second Lateran Council in 1159 declared that it should not be used against Christians 'under penalty of anathema', which prompts the untidy reflection that the Church had changed its colours in the interim if the atomic bomb could now be blessed by one of its ministers. Yet it was another minister of the Church, Canon John Collins, who initiated the Campaign for Nuclear Disarmament in England.

Parallel with the sense of terror in contemplating nuclear potential was a growing awareness of the largely intuitive science of ethology, which sought to explain man's condition in terms of his behavioural inheritance from the smaller-brained animals who preceded him on the evolutionary ladder. According to this, animals were much more successful in deflecting aggression, or turning it to beneficial use, than was man, whose cleverness had proceeded at such a fast rate that he was now capable of blowing himself to bits. To say that a man behaved 'like an animal' was to pay him the highest compliment, for it was tantamount to

[196]

praising his actions as responsible, selfless, and conducive to the continued development and survival of the species. It was beginning to look possible that, with nuclear bombs in their hands, men who behaved more like men than animals were deeply dangerous.

It is perhaps not coincidental that an understanding of ethological principles and the wide and passionate support for nuclear disarmament both reached their apogee in the early Sixties and affected the mood of the new generation.

The best-known apostle of ethological perception was Konrad Lorenz. In a lucid and eloquent introduction to Chapter XIII of his *On Aggression* (which appeared in Germany in 1963 and in England in 1966), he wrote:

Let us imagine that an absolutely unbiased observer on another planet, perhaps on Mars, is examining human behaviour on earth, with the aid of a telescope whose magnification is too small to enable him to discern individuals and follow their separate behaviour, but large enough for him to observe occurrences such as migration of peoples, wars and similar great historical events. He would never gain the impression that human behaviour was dictated by intelligence, still less by responsible morality. If we suppose our extraneous observer to be a being of pure reason, devoid of instincts himself and unaware of the way in which all instincts in general and aggression in particular can miscarry, he would be at a complete loss how to explain history at all. The ever-recurrent phenomena of history do not have reasonable causes. It is a mere commonplace to say that they are caused by what common parlance so aptly terms 'human nature.'

Unreasoning and unreasonable human nature causes two nations to compete, though no economic necessity compels them to do so; it induces two political parties or religions with amazingly similar programmes of salvation to fight each other bitterly and it impels an Alexander or a Napoleon to sacrifice millions of lives in his attempt to unite the world under his sceptre. We have been taught to regard some of the persons who have committed these and similar absurdities with respect, even as 'great' men, we are wont to yield to the political wisdom of those in charge, and we are all so accustomed to these phenomena that most of us fail to realise how abjectly stupid and undesirable the historical mass behaviour of humanity actually is.

Others had attempted to draw attention to this stupidity and the ultimate threat it now posed, but had been largely ignored. Ten years before, Earl Russell (the philosopher Bertrand Russell) called upon Heads of State to convene an international conference of scientists to discuss the implications of nuclear power in warfare. The American millionaire Cyrus Eaton placed his estate at Pugwash, Nova Scotia, at the disposal of the congress, which eventually took place there in 1957. The Pugwash Conference was attended by scientists from East and West, including three from Soviet Russia, but the communiqué which emerged from it was not reported by a single American newspaper, and was given derisory coverage in England.

It was not erudite discussion which sparked public interest, but a naked appeal to emotion, disguised as simple common sense, by the eminent novelist and essayist J. B. Priestley in the London weekly, the *New Statesman*. His article 'Britain and the Nuclear Bombs' was published in November 1957. It said that the British were fed up with having their petty self-interest flattered and desperately needed something great and noble to make them feel good again. 'And this might well be a declaration to the world that after a certain date one power able to engage in nuclear warfare will reject the evil thing forever.' This was the first call to what became known, with inelegant polysyllables, as 'unilateral nuclear disarmament'.

The impact of Priestley's article was astonishing. For months afterwards the editor, Kingsley Martin, was bombarded with letters of assent clearly indicating that a nerve of real alarm had been touched. Bertrand Russell contributed an Open Letter to

Nikita Krushchev, Premier of the USSR, to which the Russian leader replied four weeks later. I well remember the eagerness with which one awaited next Friday's edition, and the amazement one felt at the very fact that Krushchev could be induced to write an article in a British journal. One had been told so often that the Russians were inscrutable and obstructive, and here was one ready to exchange ideas with an eminent British philosopher, over the heads of obtuse politicians. That at least was the impression. It seemed to indicate that concern was apolitical, unshackled by ideology, and ultimately a sign of brotherhood in the face of a common danger. The feeling was enhanced when John Foster Dulles, the US Secretary of State, himself contributed an article to the debate. J. B. Priestley had set in motion a simple thought which, like a chain-letter, would culminate in a mass movement of the Sixties.

Apart from Martin, Russell and Priestley, others who helped create the Campaign for Nuclear Disarmament (which supplanted a much less publicized group pressing for the cessation of nuclear tests) were Professor Blackett, George Kennan (former US Ambassador in Moscow), Sir Julian Huxley, Rose Macaulay, Denis Healey, James Cameron, Ritchie Calder and Michael Foot. These and many others assembled in the flat of Canon Collins at Amen Court to plan their strategy. Within a very short time, they had sponsors and supporters from all disciplines and professions (except the military) boasting an impressive array of eminence. Playwrights John Osborne, Robert Bolt, Arnold Wesker and Shelagh Delaney were among them; actresses Dame Peggy Ashcroft, Flora Robson, and Dame Edith Evans; novelist E. M. Forster; publisher Victor Gollancz; sculptors Barbara Hepworth and Henry Moore; composers Benjamin Britten and Michael Tippett; Sir Compton Mackenzie; and others who would fill a page or more. The influence of this galaxy of talent was not to suggest dilettantism but to show the public that the matter which united them must indeed be of crucial seriousness in order to persuade so many men and women to drop everything, as it were, and give their time and energy.

Moreover, the list was remarkably intelligent and level-headed.

The aims of CND were, from the outset, bold and clear, viz: to seek to persuade the British people that Britain should 'renounce unconditionally the use or production of nuclear weapons and refuse to allow their use by others in her defence.' Such an aim had the incomparable attractions of simplicity and moral excellence. There were subsidiary purposes, involving the persuasion of other nations to join in, the prohibition of American aeroplanes carrying nuclear weapons over British soil, the refusal to supply nuclear weapons to other states; but at no time was CND interested in discussing the subtleties of military probability or the theory of deterrence. The CND Executive announced that it had no intention of forming a political party, or even of being a permanent organization. It wanted only to have its views aired and ultimately adopted by Parliament. There was to be no membership.

In one way, the purpose of CND was fairly modest, namely to bring realities of nuclear engagement to public attention. In this it was wholly successful. The Government, whose defence policy blithely and quite openly included the threat to bomb Russian cities out of existence in retaliation for an attack by *conventional* non-nuclear forces, and even went so far as to admit that a catastrophe might occur by accident, was not at all keen that people should know what that catastrophe might involve. By the time CND had been established for three years, there was hardly a literate man in the country who did not know exactly what was involved. CND effectively informed public opinion, helped to shape it, and finally brought its weight to bear upon successive Governments who never again dared to publish such a callous and thoughtless defence policy.

The ultimate object of the campaign, however, to throw all the bombs away, was never achieved.

From the very beginning it was obvious that CND fulfilled a profound need in the country. Their first public meeting, on 17 February 1958, in Central Hall, Westminster, surpassed even the most exaggerated estimate of numbers that might be expected. Five thousand people crammed into the hall and milled around the surrounding streets; it was the kind of crowd one might anticipate at a pop concert, not at a sequence of speeches totally devoid of amusement or entertainment.

They were also attracted, to be honest, by the collection of speakers, which included Bertrand Russell, J. B. Priestley, Michael Foot, Canon John Collins, Sir Stephen King-Hall (one of the few men who, before CND, had thought about the nuclear threat and been horrified by the conclusions to which he was drawn, and moreover had written about them with cool precision), and the historian A. J. P. Taylor. Russell and Taylor both impressed the audience as men of wisdom who spoke with passion. Lord Russell stated firmly that it was only an even bet that there would be any human beings in existence within forty years, and Mr Taylor spelt out in ghastly detail what the effects of a nuclear blast would be for miles around, such details as were carefully hidden by Governments. It is difficult now to realize that the people were profoundly ignorant of such matters. The men on the platform at Central Hall thought they should not be kept in ignorance, and thought also that there was something to be said, after thousands of years, for human worth.

So successful was the meeting that about a thousand of the audience, against the advice of the speakers, walked to 10 Downing Street afterwards and shouted 'Ban the Bomb.' Thus the very first 'march' was not a manufactured and organized demonstration, but a spontaneous act, a sudden expression of frustration.

In the first year, 270 public meetings were held all over the country, and a measure of the level of public concern may be judged by the fact that sixty-five letters on the subject were published by *The Times* in one month.

A smaller group called the Direct Action Committee believed that speeches were not enough to make the Government behave responsibly and that some demonstration of popular anxiety in visible form might have more effect. One line of a campaign song of the time said 'the way to shift a donkey is to wallop its behind.' How to wallop the behind of 10 Downing Street?

Hugh Brock, editor of *Peace News*, suggested that the unexpected walk to Downing Street after the Central Hall meeting might be expanded. Some years before, a pacifist friend of his whose hobby was map-reading had noticed a road which led from Reading to somewhere called 'Aere'. Following the road, he found it ended at the Atomic Energy Research Establishment just beyond the village of Aldermaston. Brock proposed that a march from Trafalgar Square to Aldermaston be organized for the Easter weekend of 1958. The idea was greeted with enthusiasm, though no one imagined that a crowd of more than about three hundred could be mustered.

As it turned out, the Easter weekend was the wettest since 1900, and Good Friday the coldest for forty-one years. In spite of this, about 4,000 people assembled in Trafalgar Square and set out for the three-day walk. They slept on the floor in church halls or schools, numbers diminishing and rising as some left and others joined the march. There were never less than 500 and for the last mile towards the atomic weapons plant between 5,000 and 10,000 people walked in total silence. It was an intensely moving occasion, so unusual and ordinary at the same time, and so eloquent, that Alex Comfort may be forgiven his hyperbole in saying it was 'the greatest movement in this island since the days of the Chartist.'

There could be no question that the Aldermaston march, which became an annual feature of the Sixties, was unprecedented in its scale and feeling. Who were all these people, walking hand in hand or side by side in the rain, not shouting or waving but quietly showing that they minded? Alan Brien, writing in the *Daily Mail*, voiced the general perplexity:

The marchers were mainly middle-class and professional people. They were the sort of people who would normally spend Easter listening to a Beethoven concert on the Home Service [the original Radio Four], pouring dry sherry from a decanter for the neighbours, painting Piccasso designs on

[202]

hardboiled eggs, attempting the literary competitions in the weekly papers, or going to church with the children. Instead they were walking through the streets in their old clothes. They were behaving entirely against the normal tradition of their class, their neighbourhood, and their upbringing.

To borrow a slogan from a later age, they were, perhaps, the 'silent majority'.

There has been some disagreement with this observation, especially from those who did not approve of the march. Christopher Booker described them as 'a somewhat aimless crowd of five thousand-odd assorted pacifists, Young Communists, venerable liberals, bearded anarchists and duffle-coated students,' forbearing to point out that he was one of them. Communist involvement was, in fact, virtually nil at that stage. There was certainly a high proportion of teachers as well as students (and teachers were then respected rather than denigrated as they habitually are now), professional writers and, surprisingly, journalists.

In subsequent years, they were joined by daughters of aristocratic families and Eton schoolboys, and the numbers grew inexorably, especially when the direction of the march was wisely reversed, to finish up in London rather than on a damp Berkshire marsh. In 1960, the walkers formed a column four miles long, containing anything between 30,000 and 100,000 people, and they consumed 80,000 cups of tea and 30 tons of food on the way. People not on the march came out of their houses with sandwiches and drinks to thrust into strangers' hands.

Another striking characteristic of the marchers was the large number of young people among them, boys and girls between fifteen and twenty-one, who a few years before would have scoffed at the idea of wasting their time on a trudge of the sort. It was hardly possible to claim that they went along 'for the fun', as there was nothing especially amusing about blisters on the feet, and at least in the early years there was not the attraction of easy access to drugs. They went simply because they were bewildered and worried, and they contributed to the vision we now have of the Sixties as a time when the young gave a lead to the older. Christopher Driver, in his book *The Disarmers* makes the observation that 'a number of strikes by schoolchildren were a reminder of the profound, yet often neglected, impact of the Bomb in the minds of adolescents. Even in the sedate atmosphere of a famous public school, where I happened myself to be spending part of the crucial weekend, a housemaster told me that never in his experience had any external event so darkened the mood of his house.' E. P. Thompson, also quoted by Mr Driver, put it more dramatically but with no less truth. The new generation was, he wrote, 'the first in the history of mankind to experience adolescence within a culture where the possibility of human annihilation has become an after-dinner platitude.'

It would be wrong to give the impression that everyone applauded the march. There was always a handful of spectators to jeer and mock, though not enough to satisfy the right-wing gutter press on the look-out for a scandal or two to rob the marchers of their noble air. One newspaper sent a young girl reporter on the march, disguised as a shabbily dressed student, in the hope that she might be raped or at least corrupted. It was, I suppose, to the editor's credit that when she came to no harm a sensational story was not invented, as it would be nowadays.

The involvement of the Church was another cause for argument. Before CND was formed, it had been almost entirely in ecclesiastical circles that the moral questions raised by the Bomb had been aired, much to the dismay of those who still thought the proper function of bishops was to sing hymns with ladies wearing hats, and not dabble in matters they did not understand. The Bishop of Exeter said that 'the hydrogen bomb is destructive of God's natural creation. It can have no conceivable moral warrant.' There were about a dozen bishops in Britain who publicly supported the Aldermaston marchers, and it could not be ignored that one of the instigators of the movement was Canon Collins (called by the *Daily Telegraph* 'this turbulent priest,' a handy quote which hacks have brought out regularly;

the latest to be described thus is the Bishop of Durham in 1985). On the other hand, some bishops openly stated that it would be better to destroy humanity than live under the Soviet system. That such a view was held to be Christian should not surprise us. It was, after all, a Christian order which chose Nagasaki to be the victim of the second atomic bomb; Nagasaki was the foremost bastion of Christianity in Japan.

While the Aldermaston marches were undoubtedly impressive as an expression of mood, there was no hope of translating that mood into policy without a political base. With this realization, the campaigners became more ambitious, and set their sights on persuading the Labour Party to their cause. The Labour Party had been as adamant as the Conservatives on the absolute desirability of Britain remaining within the NATO Alliance and at the same time maintaining its own nuclear deterrent force. The success of CND in its first two years made it seem possible that the Labour Party, traditionally representing the people, could be swung round to the unilateralist view, and, once in government, could ultimately pass legislation to chuck the nuclear bombs away. It was indeed an exhilarating prospect.

The campaigners were helped by events not of their making. First, a typically intemperate pronouncement by Field-Marshal Lord Montgomery, in which he said that if he were in charge he would use the bomb first and tell the politicians afterwards, caused some jitters and served to illustrate just how dangerous it was merely to possess the bomb. Second, the Government's sudden cancellation of the Blue Streak missile (which was to carry the bomb), having spent millions on developing it, showed the nuclear deterrent to be wastefully expensive. And third, the abject failure of the Summit Conference demonstrated that owning the bomb was also diplomatically useless.

As the Labour Party's annual conference approached, to be held in 1960 at Scarborough, the likelihood of a unilateralist resolution being passed looked very strong. Three large unions, controlling huge block votes at the conference, had already indicated at their own separate meetings that they would oppose any defence policy which included the potential use of nuclear weapons. The politicians, on the other hand, were determined to keep the bomb, if only because its abandonment would cause more international tensions than it would relieve. The Scarborough conference promised to be one of the most turbulent and important in Labour's history.

And so it was. CND was very much in evidence, lobbying those who had union votes in their pockets, and everyone was aware the debate on the motion demanding the renunciation of nuclear testing, manufacture, stockpiling and harbouring, put forward by the Engineers' Union, would be the most crucial. Nobody knew this better than Labour's leader, Hugh Gaitskell, who delivered the most impassioned speech of his career, imploring delegates not to be seduced by alarmist claptrap and pledging that he would always fight to save the Labour Party which he loved. The motion was carried amid jubilant scenes, but they were not enduring. The politicians discovered a loop-hole in the rule-book which saved them from having to adopt what they saw as a suicidal measure as part of official party policy.

The campaigners were desolate, not only at being beaten by cynical pragmatic political manoeuvring, but at the slur cast upon their motives. It was suggested that in seeking to denude Britain of its defences, they were unpatriotic, whereas the whole of the CND movement was fuelled by intense pride in Britain and a profound wish to see the country earn the respect of the world by being the first power to take a positive step away from the precipice. Their mood now turned to frustration, and that enabled some elements within the movement to recommend a more militant strategy.

Lord Russell, now under the malign influence of a young American called Ralph Schoenmann, announced that he would lead a new movement away from CND dedicated to a campaign of civil disobedience. The successor of the Direct Action Committee, it would be called the Committee of 100. Most of the founders of CND, including Canon Collins, declined to follow the Earl into what they suspected would be a plan of action detrimental to their peaceful image and would lose them much support, but among those who did follow were John Osborne, Lindsay Anderson, John Braine and Vanessa Redgrave. Russell pointed out that they were bound to act more defiantly in order to claim attention from the Press, which had steadfastly ignored peaceful and responsible demonstrations. (This was in itself a curious notion in view of all the publicity over the last two or three years.) 'Until the press pursues a wiser policy,' he said, 'it is only by such methods that public opinion can be made aware of the fact that our population is being led blindfold towards mass extinction.'

Thus began the famous 'sit-downs' of the 1960s. The first took place at a rocket-launching site in East Anglia, when forty-five people were arrested for sitting in front of lorries which sought access to the base. Most of them refused bail, and as Christopher Driver vividly put it, 'with the first pictures of puffing policemen hauling away limp bodies the British public now took in the fact that 37 otherwise respectable citizens were spending Christmas in gaol for being too enthusiastic about peace on earth.'

Russell must have been gratified by the outrage voiced by many sections of the Press, and by the knowledge that the Committee of 100 was succeeding in driving the Government into panicky, ill-considered moves. The arrests had been made under an Act which dated from 1361 and had been intended to control vagabonds. Members of Parliament pressed the Home Secretary to release the offenders on the grounds that no crime had been committed and that the arrests, called 'preventive', were intended to prohibit the free expression of opinion. He refused, and more arrests were made for similar reasons in Harrington and Southend.

The most quiet and ruminative sit-down took place on the afternoon of 18 February 1961, when thousands of people (some estimates said as many as 6,000, walked in silence from Trafalgar Square down Whitehall to the Ministry of Defence, then sat down in a solid mass in the road for two and a half hours, Lord

Russell at the front. The police said it was the most orderly and impressive mass demonstration ever to be held in London. It certainly gave pause for thought, as pictures of the venerable old philosopher, nearly ninety and internationally regarded as one of the most intelligent Englishmen of the twentieth century, were published showing him sitting impassively, teeth clenched and mouth firm, in support of what he clearly thought was the most important issue of his life.

Lord Russell was not interested in mere gimmickry. He stuck to the door of the Ministry a declaration itemizing his purpose; that the Government should reject all policies and alliances which depended upon nuclear weapons, that scientists should refuse to work on nuclear research, that the workforce should withhold their labour if it was connected with the manufacture of nuclear bombs. 'We hereby serve notice on our Government,' it concluded, 'that we can no longer stand aside while they prepare to destroy mankind.'

The next demonstration, in April, marched on the same route and terminated in Parliament Square. This time there were 2,000 people, and this time the police drafted extra men to London to meet them. When the demonstrators encountered a phalanx in their path, they simply sat down and awaited arrest. Eight hundred and twenty-six of them were carried off, unresisting, into black marias, an operation which took a few hours and looked supremely silly. The demonstrators, once again, contrived to be more dignified than those who would prohibit them.

Within one week of each other in early September, both the Russian and American administrations resumed the testing of nuclear weapons which they had previously interrupted. Immediately over a hundred people sat down outside the Russian Embassy to protest, but by this time it was becoming apparent that no amount of moving gestures would deflect those who control our destinies from their folly. Governments were indifferent to sit-downs, and the closeness in date of the two resumptions of nuclear testing indicated that the Russians and Americans each knew what the other was about to do, and might well have colluded. (It would not be possible after all, to set up the complex machinery for a nuclear test within six days.) Some campaigners lost heart and resigned themselves to failure. One who did not, and who at his great age would have every excuse for giving up, was Lord Russell himself. I spent a day with him at his home in North Wales and well remember the passionate idealism with which he spoke, his wisdom and his worry; he retained all the nerve and fight of a twenty year old, and though still sceptical in philosophy, had managed to avoid the cynicism which habitually comes with descent into adulthood and age. It was a remarkable day and he a remarkable inspiration; one felt almost ashamed to feel oneself caring less than he did.

. Insanely, it was the demonstration in front of the Russian Embassy, seat of the postulated enemy, which most embarrassed the Government and impelled them to their most desperate act. The large sit-down planned for Battle of Britain Sunday, on 17 September, threatened to attract yet more attention and prove yet more awkward to deal with. If the demonstrators persistently refused to cause trouble, it was the police who were made to look ridiculous. The Government arranged for thirty-six prominent members of the Committee of 100 to be summoned to Bow Street Magistrates' Court and asked to be bound over, under the 1361 Act, to be of good behaviour for one year. Almost all them declined, as everyone engaged in the charade knew they would, thus obliging the magistrate to send them to prison for two months. Lord and Lady Russell were among their number, but the magistrate reduced their sentence to a week in view of his age and health. It did not matter. One day's martyrdom would have done more for the Committee of 100 than any ministerial reprimand. The old man was driven off in a police van with BAN THE BOMB scrawled on the side the Government of Great Britain had rarely looked so foolish or scared. When he came out of Brixton Prison a week later, Lord Russell said that he had had a much needed holiday and had read detective novels in his cell.

The arrest of Lord Russell and friends did not, of course

prevent the demonstration of 17 September from taking place. One wonders if the Cabinet had really been so naive as to expect that it would. On the contrary, their action ensured that the sit-down in Trafalgar Square would be the largest of all. Some 12,000 people took part, watched by 4,000 police. It took seven hours for the police to arrest 1,314 people, and at one o'clock in the morning they were still sitting. As fast as some were removed, others took their place. Now it was the turn of the police, who throughout these months had the Government's absurd orders to follow and were constantly looking embarrassed (as well as tired), to get frustrated, with unpleasant results. One observer, more readily believed because he held no brief for CND and was antagonistic to their aims, called police behaviour after midnight 'vicious'. Suddenly, people were being kicked, punched, thrown into fountains, knocked to the ground. 'Middle-aged women were slammed down and dragged by one leg through puddles, face down against the concrete pavement. Several people, alarmed by the thug-like brutality erupting in the Square, tried to flee. They were hauled down from behind and kicked and beaten where they lay.' At the police station, many people had high-pressure hoses trained upon them. And by no means all of these were involved in the sit-down; some had been passers-by. Put simply, the patience of hard-pressed policemen understandably snapped. No apology from the Government was forthcoming for having placed good men in the intolerable position of having to perform the largest mass-arrest in English history for no good reason.

Politicians of all parties were fond of telling the marchers that they should go and shout their slogans or wave their banners in front of the Kremlin (they still are); the point rather crudely made was that the British were free to make their protest, the Russians were not, and the bomb was necessary to maintain the freedom which only the West protected. It was, then, rather alarming, that people who carried banners in Trafalgar Square were carted off in their hundreds, while those who went to make their point in Moscow were left unmolested.

[210]

To be honest, the Russian authorities were so taken by surprise that they had no time to consider their reactions. The occasion was the World Council of Peace Congress in Moscow, attended by delegates from all over the world. It was of course a propaganda exercise, financed and controlled from the Kremlin. Britain sent 145 delegates, some from CND, others from the Committee of 100, others independent of both organizations, some churchmen, journalists and politicians. Lord Russell told *Pravda*, the Russian newspaper, quite openly that the struggle which he encouraged had to be widened in scope and that he intended to make his views known to the Russian people. 'Fat chance,' murmured the sceptics.

The Congress was boring in the extreme, as such gatherings usually are. There were long speeches with predictable political bias and yawn-inducing irrelevancy. Mr Krushchev spoke, as did both Earl Russell and Canon Collins, from England. The interesting aspect of the affair was, however, the distribution of leaflets in the Russian language setting out all the views of British CND for the information of Russian workers. This was precisely what one had been told would never be permitted in the Moscow Streets. CND handed out to passers-by 5,000 such leaflets without a squeak of complaint from the Russian authorities. More remarkable still was the leaflet distributed by the Committee of 100, which spoke directly to the ordinary unsophisticated Russian and invited him to pose dangerous questions.

'What has happened to your revolution that your rulers should threaten the workers of other lands with these weapons?' was one of the awkward thoughts contained in the leaflet; which also questioned whether the revolution had actually achieved the abolition of class structures, suggesting that there was still a heavy division in Russia between rulers and ruled. Did the working Russian decide to manufacture these weapons of mass destruction, or was the decision made for him on high? This was blatant and candid criticism of the Soviet dream. Two thousand of these leaflets were handed out by English men and women to Russian men and women in Gorki Street, Kalinin Street and the suburbs of Moscow. Victor Zorza, the respected Kremlin expert on *The Guardian*, wrote that this indicated 'the most direct challenge of official Soviet politics and ideas to have been presented to the Soviet man in the street since freedom of speech died under Stalin.'

Belatedly, the Kremlin authorities got the wind up. They invited the British not to distribute any more leaflets (which were, from their point of view, propaganda), but made no attempt to interfere with the march planned to end in Red Square. That Americans and British (as well as many other nationalities) took part in this display of banners was quite remarkable. It did not last long, but the point had been made very forcibly that the nuclear disarmament movement was international and untrammelled, that it represented the deepest yearning of inarticulate man to get rid of the most monstrous device of his creation. It was a high point in the history of CND.

The Cuban missile crisis, when Russia began building launching sites in Cuba directed against targets in the United States and the future of the world seemed to depend upon the exchange of telegrams between Mr Krushchev and President Kennedy, contributed to the standing of CND, though the aftermath hastened its temporary decline. Put crudely, the Americans told the Russians they must turn back their ships bound for Cuba, or else. Lord Russell took upon himself the role of mediator, sending telegrams to both leaders, imploring them to desist. Historians will one day assess how far Russell's intervention helped defuse the crisis, but to the world at large his voice appeared to counsel sanity and to express the fears of mankind in general.

Two things compromised Lord Russell's effort. In the first place, his impartiality was placed in question by the contrast in tone he adopted when addressing the two leaders. He sent a message to Kennedy which suggested the American President was a madman in need of control, and another to Krushchev calling upon the Russian's statesmanship and good sense. The text of the published telegrams was as follows:

To President Kennedy: YOUR ACTION DESPERATE. THREAT TO HUMAN SURVIVAL. NO CONCEIVABLE JUSTIFICATION. CIVILIZED MAN CONDEMNS IT. WE WILL NOT HAVE MASS MURDER. ULTIMATUM MEANS WAR. I DO NOT SPEAK FOR POWER BUT PLEAD FOR CIVILIZED MAN. END THIS MADNESS.

To Prime Minister Krushchev: MAY I HUMBLY APPEAL FOR YOUR FURTHER HELP IN LOWERING THE TEMPERATURE DESPITE THE WORSENING SITUATION. YOUR CONTINUED FORBEARANCE IS OUR GREAT HOPE. WITH MY HIGH REGARDS AND SINCERE THANKS.

Russell's appeal was also compromised by the memory of his astonishing attack on both leaders and other political men only a year before. 'We used to call Hitler wicked for killing off the Jews, but Kennedy and Macmillan are much more wicked than Hitler,' he had said. 'We cannot obey the murderers. They are wicked, they are abominable. They are the wickedest people in the story of man and it is our duty to do what we can against them.' Only slightly less hysterical was the statement he had issued from prison, claiming that 'Kennedy and Krushchev, Adenauer and de Gaulle, Macmillan and Gaitskell are pursuing a common aim, the ending of human rights. You, your families, your friends and your countries, are to be exterminated by the common decision of a few brutal but powerful men.'

Charitably, it had to be supposed that senility had caught up with the admirable Earl, as for the first time in his long career the cool use of logic and empirical analysis had deserted him. The comparison with Hitler, especially, was offensive and absurd, and Lord Russell's credibility suffered a blow from these extraordinary remarks from which he was not to recover.

More seriously, Russell's attitude hurt the reputation of the movement itself, for it seemed to prove correct the charges which had been made by Conservative politicians for years, that CND and particularly the Committee of 100 were in the control of and served the purpose of the Communist Party. Certainly, had the Kremlin drafted Lord Russell's telegrams for him, they could not have done a better job. In fact, the Communist Party in England had never enjoyed any influence within the CND. When the movement first surfaced, in 1957, communist votes at the annual Labour conference were actually cast *against* the motion for unilateral nuclear disarmament. In subsequent years, the communists were bewildered by the extraordinary cross-section of the British public which supported CND, from grandmothers to stockbrokers, and did not evolve a strategy for infiltrating it, because they did not know how to. CND demonstrations were frequently directed against Soviet as well as American embassies. The Young Communists, who also marched with CND, held no influence over policy. None of this prevented government spokesmen from accusing the campaigners of being Soviet stooges or agents, and when one sympathizer, who was employed as newsreader by the BBC, wore his distinctive CND badge on television, this confirmed for some of the most frenzied Conservatives that the BBC was really a Communist front organization. This must be a deep-seated Tory suspicion, for it crops up regularly even now, and in spite of the manifest truth that the BBC is the most reliable and impartial source of news information in the world. Nevertheless, Lord Russell's unbalanced response to the Cuban missile crisis lent weight to the conspiracy theory, and CND support noticeably diminished.

And so it remained until very recent times, when again the debate explored the same questions as in the Sixties – the moral issue, the deterrent value, the chilly contemplation of imminent doom. Again, ecclesiastical figures are involved, again the charges of Communist infiltration persist, again the Labour Party is constantly hedging over whether or not it will in government throw all the bombs away. (Quite where they should be thrown is not a matter which has exercised anyone's judgment, though it is tacitly recognized that the things cannot be de-invented.) CND did not succeed in getting rid of a single hydrogen bomb, nor in reducing the frantic rate at which stockpiles in the East and the West increased. There are now tens of thousands of them, capable of destroying the planet several times over. At least the campaigners brought debate into the open, and we are all now better informed about what would (will?) happen when the next bomb falls. But CND could never take cognizance of the point of deterrence, that the world is theoretically safer as long as no one can be sure whether the bomb will be used or not. As General André Beaufre succinctly put it, 'In the final analysis it is uncertainty which forms the essential factor of deterrence.'

Which brings us back to the lessons of ethology. When geese are about to enter into combat, they hiss and arch their necks and make threatening gestures, but rarely come to grief, because they 'know' that the survival of their kind depends upon their behaving themselves. They indulge in a kind of dance which enables their antagonism to be ritually expressed. Bird song is likewise a shout of defiance in defence of territory. Rattlesnakes can kill one another with a single bite, so what do they do? They never bite in a quarrel, but push each other with the head until one emerges the stronger, and lets the other slink away. If they did not, there would soon be no more rattlesnakes. Could it be that the absurd noises of threat and antagonism which the Russians and the Americans habitually hurl at each other year after year are a ritual expression of a fight which will never take place? Each manufactures more and more bombs to demonstrate that its bite is still effective, and the other knows that as long as it remains effective it will not be used. If this be true, then evolution has found a mighty method of making mankind grow up and emulate the sensible protections long ago adopted by the lower animals.

Louis J. Halle expressed this idea in 1968. The parallel between behaviour of vertebrates and behaviour of nations was not merely metaphorical, he wrote:

Precisely the same logic as applies to the one applies to the other. It has, by genetic evolution, endowed rattlesnakes with certain behaviour inhibitions conducive to their survival as a species; for they would quickly become extinct if they did not have these inhibitions. In the case of nations, the governing logic, directly appreciated, inspires behavioural inhibitions conducive to the survival of the human species. But it is the same logic that has imposed itself upon the instincts of rattlesnakes and on the reasoning powers of men, to the same end, and so far with the same result in each case.

These are the kind of perceptions which gradually emerged from specialist into general knowledge during the 1960s. When politicians said that nuclear bombs kept the peace, they were right, but they did not know why they were right. When CND sought to extract a promise that the bombs would never be used in any circumstances, they were wrong, but they did not know why they were wrong. It does not help that they should remain in ignorance, for a great deal of money could be saved, talent harnessed, and hardship alleviated if the balance of the rattlesnake bite could be kept at a certain level and advanced no further.

— 10 —

Conclusions

At the root of the Sixties' spirit, of its achievements and mistakes alike, is the search for pride. It is important to remember that this was essentially a post-war period, albeit slightly delayed, and that it is at such times that a country takes stock of itself, alters its perspectives, amends its ambitions. Moreover, the war in question had been fought on a global scale on a frankly moral issue (to resist the spread of Fascism), and Britain had emerged the victor. Yet she has mysteriously been deprived of the rewards of victory. The generation which grew up immediately after the war and reached maturity in the 1960s nursed an inarticulate but profound resentment because they felt their country had been cheated.

Britain had every cause to feel great national pride in its extraordinary wartime resilience and courage. The young were constantly being told (and still are so told) that when pushed into a corner the British can discover reserves of strength and honour which astonish the rest of the world and unite them in one powerful endeavour. The war had been Britain's 'finest hour'. While it was true that the Russians had suffered more, and that the Russian army had contributed more than the British to the final Allied victory; also that the involvement of the United States had crucially altered the course of events; nevertheless Britain had been the only nation to fight without cease from September 1939 until August 1945, and the entire world owed her an enormous debt for her brave stand alone against Hitler in 1940. If Britain had not been able to resist Hitler then, the shape of subsequent history would have been radically different.

The whole of Europe would have been subjected to German dictation, with its vile inhuman philosophy, or it would have been 'liberated' by Soviet armies and shared the fate of Hungary and Czechoslovakia. Praise was lavished upon the British. We felt we had done well.

But the irony of our pathetic condition in 1945 caused bitterness to fester. Had a hermit been dragged from the Amazon and taken on tour of Europe in the years 1945–50, then asked which country he thought had lost the war which had devastated large areas of the continent, and had still not recovered from defeat, he would certainly have guessed it was Britain. The war had cost the country a quarter of her entire net wealth – $30 billion. $320 million alone had been spent in 1946 on feeding the Germans, $330 million on keeping the peace in Palestine. London was still pock-marked with rubble – as children we found the greatest adventure playgrounds were what we called 'bomb sites', of which there were several on every street. Food was scarce and of poor quality, clothing rudimentary. What, we asked, had been the point of winning the war at all? Keynes had demonstrated that the country was bankrupt, and could not survive without American support.

It appeared that the lion had roared, then had all its teeth pulled out. Germany, too, was laid in ruins, yet was busily building a bright future. France had suffered the humiliation of occupation by enemy forces and had had to be rescued by countries she secretly despised (Britain and the United States), yet she was gradually finding her voice again and bending her energies towards construction. We were slovenly, inert, indifferent, because we did not feel we should be required to make superhuman efforts; we had already done that and were awaiting our just deserts. The fact that they did not come made young people rebellious against a system of values and priorities which seemed lunatic in its results. The upheaval of the Sixties, when these people reached adulthood, stems largely from this insult to national pride. It did not rest, of course, upon careful analysis or any understanding of economic truths, but arose from a feeling of injury.

[218]

The headlong disappearance of the British Empire intensified this feeling. The prose of Paul Johnson accurately conveys the pained wonderment that such a thing could happen in less than half a lifetime. He writes:

> In 1945 British power was stretched over nearly a third of the globe. In addition to legitimate possessions, Britain administered the Italian Empire in North and East Africa, many former French colonies and many liberated territories in Europe and Asia, including the glittering Empires of Indo-China and the Dutch East Indies. No nation had ever carried such wide-ranged responsibilities. Twenty-five years later, everything had gone. History had never before witnessed a transformation of such extent and rapidity.

Once again, praise was happily given for the orderly and sane manner in which transference of power had been effected (and was still being effected in the 1960s). But no apparent reward. Other overseas territories were relinquished by other European countries who then proceeded metaphorically to shrug their shoulders and not look back. The British have still not ceased to look with nostalgia on their glorious past and compare it with their bereft and inadequate present. The loss of Empire caused damage to the spirit of Britain because it was not obviously accompanied by concomitant advantages. There was little to induce pride except unproductive nostalgia.

The politicians' solution to this profound dissatisfaction was to expand the Commonwealth from the former association of old Dominions (Australia, New Zealand, South Africa, Canada) into a wider, more polyglot family which included nations in Africa and Asia. The Left was pleased because Britain appeared to be doing the 'right thing', the Right equally so, because imperialist traditions were somehow to be given new life in a different form. But the people did not care too much either way. They perceived well enough that the Commonwealth was a unique collection of people bonded by shared traditions and many personal cross-influences, but they did not think it mattered nearly half so much as politicians liked to pretend. As John Mander wrote, 'To the outsider it is obvious that the British are constructing a surrogate, a fantasy empire to console for the loss of the real one. In no European country are the ex-colonialists so obsessed with their colonial past. Italians, Frenchmen, Dutchmen do not continually boast of their colonial achievements.'

The young, alas, did not see that there was anything to boast of. They looked to Europe and noticed that the reality of cultivating one's own garden was more beneficial and sensible than continually trying to show other people how to dig theirs. Europe was going forward, Britain was stagnating. As Konrad Adenauer, the German Chancellor, cruelly put it, 'England is like a rich man who has lost all his property but does not realise it.' Britain was lamentably slow to recognize the promise of the European Economic Community (soon to be known as the Common Market), and when the British application to join the club was vetoed by the arrogant General de Gaulle, who of all people should have been grateful to us, pride suffered another blow. The De Gaulle veto hit the headlines on 14 January 1963, and one might comfortably date the final push into Sixties frivolity from that day.

Baldly put, the British were tired of seeking approbation when they ought to have been dispensing favours. They were tired of waiting for the glories of their wartime record to be translated into a better life. They were tired of their pride being bludgeoned.

Young people were particularly restive and resentful. Surveys taken at the beginning of the 1960s indicated that between 40 per cent and 60 per cent of people under twenty-five would have been happy to emigrate if the opportunity arose. I well remember how widespread was that urge to 'get out', to turn one's back upon the country. That it should affect roughly half the population under twenty-five is a measure of the scale of the problem. The trouble was, Britain was firmly and unrepentantly a gerontocracy, sustained as well as atrophied by nostalgia. In the rest of Europe a social revolution had taken place immediately after the war which had propelled young men into positions of power and influence in England, they were still waiting in the wings. In the famous *Suicide of a Nation* edited by Arthur Koestler in 1963, reference was made by one contributor to a learned study by anthropologist Mary Douglas on the Lele tribe in the Congo. The Lele, apparently, though cultivated and intelligent, were prone to stagnation. Mrs Douglas wondered why. She discovered they had a potent tribal custom which dictated they should avoid the humiliation of old men losing power and becoming dependent on their juniors, to prevent which they had built up an elaborate system of controls to keep the young men in prolonged idleness and lack of purpose in order not to infringe upon the prerogatives of the elders. 'In this way a delicate equilibrium has been achieved, but at an enormous price in efficiency, since the most vigorous section of the community is prevented from playing any effective part in it.' There was a real danger that Britain might slip into a status as the Lele of Western Europe. The young despised this idea, and would shortly show their contempt in a blazingly colourful kidnapping of Britain's reputation in the world. It is significant that the Labour Government, with all its hope and promise, came to power only one year after these gloomy comparisons with the stagnant Lele were published.

The young were determined to invent their own reasons for pride, to make Britain noticeable again, but the old were unlikely to thank them for it. The old could not see anything robust in the new Sixties spirit. 'The hard-headed . . . mill-owners and steel-masters of the North have bred . . . the little flirts of Chelsea and Kensington', wrote Michael Shanks. 'It is gay, it is madly amusing, and it carries with it the smell of death.' There were many who were prepared to see decadence where others found joy, decline where there was renewal, trivia where there was invention. They are still around today, glumly tracing Britain's failure to the King's Road, still morbidly blind to the explosion of achievement and self-respect which occurred after 1963.

Of course there was frivolity, and how refreshing it was, too. Of course there was complacency; after years of feeling we were finished as a nation, it was beguiling to realize that we were nothing of the sort. Of course we were chippy, and hopeless servants. We no longer made good bus conductors or waiters, because, frankly, having saved the world fifteen years before, we did not think we ought to be servile. It may seem an unattractive character trait, but I believe it to be the truth. The spirit of the Sixties threw out the servility, the apologies, the guilt, and celebrated with loud fanfares the qualities of affability, of tact and of tolerance, which were more valuable in Britain than anywhere else. They had been taken for granted, but the mood of resurgence determined to assert them. Britain was, after all, a kindly, civilized place. We no longer wanted to be as efficient as the Americans or as harsh as the Germans. We wanted merely to be ourselves, and found that was nothing to be ashamed of.

If pride was the leitmotif of the Sixties, then one can see how all the achievements of that period grew out of the affirmation of what was best in the British character. Tolerance was our forte; well, then we should demonstrate its civilizing power, not meekly acknowledge its presence, and earn the world's admiration. Hence the anachronistic and slightly dotty powers of the Lord Chamberlain with regard to the theatre were quietly buried: no longer would an artist's vision of life have to be submitted to St James's Palace before it could be imparted to the rest of us. Hence also literature was freed from the shackles of archaic prejudice and one no longer had to smuggle books past Customs and Excise officials. Tolerance extended to all kinds of private emotional or lustful activity, and homosexuals finally ceased to be criminals. Even the noise of popular music, far louder than it had ever been before, was tolerated along with outrageous dress. Dissident political views, especially concerning the control of nuclear weapons, were freely entertained and widely discussed. (This may seem fatuously obvious, in the light of the British tradition of free debate, but one only had to listen to the amazed response of some Americans when they heard such debate taking place at Speakers' Corner in Hyde Park, for example, to be reminded that such a tradition was to be cherished and never held cheap; it was yet another source of pride).

The partisans of intolerance were not suddenly silenced, but by the end of the decade they were made to feel distinctly archaic. Their ritual martyrdom of Mr Profumo, surely a disgraceful monument to hypocrisy and snobbery, was virtually their final triumph. Similar scandals have occurred since them, but good sense has prevented their development into florid hysteria.

As for the theatre, actors, writers, directors and designers all contributed to the rather surprised realization that British talent in this field was second to none, and that the genius nurtured for three centuries, since the Restoration, was still vibrant. The Royal Family, too, represented a tradition of imponderable value which was unique in the world, and by the end of the decade the powerful influence of Elizabeth II's work and life upon national pride could not be questioned.

It is significant that this sounds and reads like a congratulatory hymn rather than a conclusion. That is because it has become the fashion to denigrate the advances made in the Sixties and deplore their consequences. Those who want more muscle, dynamism, greatness, are usually hostile to the gentler virtues which flourished at that time, and which must continue to be applauded if the essential British character is to endure.

Sources

Chapter One: SWINGING LONDON?

Time magazine, 16 April 1966
The *Daily Mail*, 30 March 1982
The Times, 10 December 1980
TV Times, 5 March 1981
Encounter, March 1962, August 1962, October 1964, August
  1965

Chapter Two: THE NEW MORALITY

Time magazine, 1963
Jean Stein, *Edie* (1982)
The *Guardian*, 20 March 1982
The *Daily Mail*, 30 March 1982
Encounter, May 1959, October 1963, October 1965, February
  1966, March 1966, December 1967, March 1968
C. H. Whiteley and Winifred M. Whiteley, *The Permissive Morality* (Methuen, 1964)

Chapter Three: RETREAT OF THE CENSOR

H. Montgomery Hyde, *A History of Pornography* (Heinemann,
  1964)
John Sutherland, *Offensive Literature* (1982)

C. H. Rolph, *The Trial of Lady Chatterley*
Antony Grey, *Pornography and Free Speech*
The Times Literary Supplement
Encounter, February and March 1962
The Obscenity Laws (André Deutsch, 1969)

Chapter Four: PROFUMO

Hansard, 17 June 1963
The Times, 6, 7, 8, 10, 12 and 18 June 1963
Lord Denning's Report, Cmnd 2152 (Her Majesty's Stationery Office, 1963)

Chapter Five: HOMOSEXUAL LAW REFORM

Antony Grey, 'Homosexual Law Reform', in *The Tactics of Pressure*
H. Montgomery Hyde, *The Other Love* (Heinemann, 1970)
Peter Wildeblood, *Against the Law* (1955)
Rupert Croft-Cooke, *The Verdict of You All* (1955)
Leo Abse, *Private Member* (Macdonald, 1973)
Brian Magee, *One in Twenty* (Secker & Warburg, 1966)
Antony Grey, 'Homosexual Rights and Wrongs', in *New Humanist*, November 1978
Ray Gosling, 'Homosexuals Now', in *New Society*, 29 August 1968
The Rt Rev. John Robinson, 'The Place of Law in the Field of Sex' (Beckly Lecture, 1972)
Hansard, House of Commons Debates, Vols. 596, 625, 655, 699, 713, 724, 731, 738, 749.
House of Lords Debates, Vols. 206, 266, 269, 274, 284.

Chapter Six: THE THEATRE

Who's Who in the Theatre
Encounter, June 1963
Theatre programmes
Information from Michael White and Stuart Cox

Chapter Seven: POP

Tim Rice, Paul Gambaccini, Mike Read, *The Guinness Book of British Hit Singles*
The Times, 10 December 1980
Daily Express, 18 February 1983
Encounter, October 1967
TV Times, 5 March 1981
The *Daily Star*, 19 February 1981

Chapter Eight: THE ROYAL FAMILY

Robert Lacey, *Majesty* (1977)
L. G. Pine, *Ramshackledom* (1962)
New Statesman, 21 August 1957
The Times, 26 August 1967
The National and English Review, August 1957
Malcolm Muggeridge, 'The Queen and I', in *Encounter*, July 1961
Henry Fairlie, 'Muggeridge's Monarch', in *Encounter*, October 1961

Chapter Nine: CND

Christopher Driver, *The Disarmers* (Hodder & Stoughton, 1964)
Konrad Lorenz, *On Aggression* (Methuen, 1966)

SOURCES

Stephen King-Hall, *Defence in the Nuclear Age* (Gollancz, 1958)
Bertrand Russell, *Common Sense and Nuclear Warfare* (Allen & Unwin, 1959)
Bertrand Russell, *Unarmed Victory* (Penguin, 1963)
New Statesman, November and December 1957
Anthony Hartley, 'The Bomb', in *Encounter*, May 1964
Louis J. Halle, 'Lessons of the Nuclear Age', in *Encounter*, March 1968

Index

Blakely, Colin, 139, 146
Blond, Anthony, 58
Bloom, John, 20
Blundell, Sir Robert, 70–1, 72, 76
Bolt, Robert, 136, 150, 199
Bond, Edward, 60, 148–9
Booker, Christopher, 14, 25, 35, 131, 159, 162, 203
Boothby, Robert, 119, 120
Boucicault, Dion, 150–1
Boyle, Mark, 154
Boyson, Dr Rhodes, 45–6
Brabazon of Tara, Lord, 119
Brady, Ian, 50–1, 52
Braine, John, 133, 207
Brien, Alan, 156, 202–3
Brock, Hugh, 202
Brook, Sir Norman, 83
Brook, Peter, 141, 143, 147
Brooke, Henry, 87, 88, 94
Brown, Dr Felix, 163
Browne, Tara, 175
Burgess, Anthony, 76
Burgess and Maclean, 113
Burnett, Alan, 189
Burroughs, William, *The Naked Lunch*, 50 & n, 57, 73–5
Burton, Richard, 40–1, 99
Butler, R. A., 118, 121

Cabaret, 150
Caine, Michael, 16, 135
Calder and Boyars, *Last Exit to Brooklyn* published by, 75–7
Callas, Maria, 145–6, 147
Camus, Albert, 133–4
The Caretaker (Pinter), 136–7
Carnaby Street, 22, 151
Carstairs, Professor, 37
Casserole restaurant, 16
Castle, Barbara, 87
Cawston, Richard, 193
censorship, 15, 33, 51, 53–78; literary, 55–9, 60–78; theatrical, 14, 39, 60, 148–9
Chancellor, A. C. B., 93

Charles, Prince, 189
The Cherry Orchard (Chekhov), 138–9
children, and the new morality, 45–6
Chips With Everything (Wesker), 140
Christmas Island, 1st British H-bomb exploded on (1957), 196
Church of England: and nuclear weapons, 204–5; *The Problem of Homosexuality* (pamphlet), 115
Churchill, Winston, 81; death of, 29, 30
class system, 26–8, 184
Cleland, John, *Fanny Hill*, 69–73
Clermont Club, 16, 17
Cliveden estate, 81, 82
CND (Campaign for Nuclear Disarmament), 33, 164, 196–216; Aldermaston March, 202–5; and Church's attitude, 204–5; Committee of 100: 206–10; and Communist Party, 213–14; creation of (1958), 198–201; Cuban missile crisis, 212–13; Direct Action Committee, 201, 206; and Labour Party, 205–6, 214; World Council of Peace Congress, Moscow, 211–12
Collins, Canon John, 196, 199, 201, 204, 206, 211
Colville, Sir Richard, 186
A Comedy of Errors (Shakespeare), 140
Comfort, Alex, 202
Committee of 100: 206–10, 211–12, 213–14
Commonwealth, 219–20
Communist Party, British, 213–14
Connaught Hotel, David Frost's TV breakfast at (1966), 25
Conran, Terence, 20
Cook, Peter, 155–6, 157, 189
Copley, John, 147–8
Corbett, Ronnie, 17
Cordle, John, 94
cost of living, 19–20
Courtenay, Tom, 135, 138

INDEX